A CENTURY
OF VIOLENCE
IN A RED CITY

A CENTURY OF VIOLENCE IN A
RED
CITY

Popular Struggle,
Counterinsurgency,
and Human Rights
in Colombia

LESLEY GILL

■ ■ ■

DUKE UNIVERSITY PRESS

Durham and London 2016

Designed by Amy Ruth Buchanan
Typeset in Chaparral Pro and Franklin Gothic
by Tseng Information Systems, Inc.

Library of Congress Cataloging-in-Publication Data
Gill, Lesley, author.
A century of violence in a red city : popular
struggle, counterinsurgency, and human rights in
Colombia / Lesley Gill.
pages cm
Includes bibliographical references and index.
ISBN 978-0-8223-6029-2 (hardcover) ISBN 978-0-
8223-6060-5 (pbk.)
ISBN 978-0-8223-7470-1 (e-book)
1. Human rights—Colombia—History—20th century. 2. Working class—Colombia—History—20th
century. 3. Labor disputes—Colombia—Barrancabermeja—History—20th century. I. Title.
JC599.C7G55 2016
986.1′25—dc23
2015026279
Cover design: Jenni Ohnstad

IN MEMORY OF MY
MOTHER, JOAN GILL
(1927–2012)

CONTENTS

ACEDEGAM	Asociación Campesina de Ganaderos y Agricultores del Magdalena Medio (Association of Middle Magdalena Ranchers and Farmers)
ANAPO	Alianza Nacional Popular (National Popular Alliance)
ANUC	Asociación Nacional de Usuarios Campesinos (National Association of Peasant Landholders)
AUC	Autodefensas Unidas de Colombia (United Self-Defense Forces of Colombia)
BACRIM	*bandas criminales* (criminal gangs)
BCB	Bloque Central Bolívar (Central Bolívar Bloc)
CINEP	Centro de Investigación y Educación Popular (Center for Research and Popular Education)
CODHES	Consultoría para los Derechos Humanos y Desplazamiento (Consultancy for Human Rights and Displacement)
CONVIVIRs	Cooperativas de Vigilancia y Seguridad Privada (Cooperatives for Vigilance and Private Security)
CREDHOS	Corporación Regional para la Defensa de los Derechos Humanos (Regional Corporation for the Defense of Human Rights)
CSTC	Confederación Sindical de Trabajadores Colombianos (Union Confederation of Colombian Workers)

CTC	Confederación de Trabajadores Colombianos (Confederation of Colombian Workers)
CUT	Central Unitaria de Trabajadores (Unitary Workers Central)
DAS	Departamento Administrativo de Seguridad (Department of Administrative Security)
ECOPETROL	Empresa Colombiana de Petróleos (Colombian Oil Company)
ELN	Ejército Nacional de Liberación (National Liberation Army)
EPL	Ejército Popular de Liberación (Popular Liberation Army)
FARC	Fuerzas Armadas Revolucionarias de Colombia (Revolutionary Armed Forces of Colombia)
FEDENAL	Federación Nacional del Transporte Marítimo, Fluvial, Portuario y Aéreo (National Federation of Maritime Transport, River, Port and Air)
FEMSA	company name
FILA	Frente de Izquierda Liberal Auténtica (Front of the Authentic Liberal Left)
JACS	*juntas de acción comunal* (neighborhood action committee)
LGBT	lesbian, gay, bisexual, and transgender
MORENA	Movimiento de Reconstrucción Nacional (Movement of National Reconstruction)
MRL	Movimiento Revolucionario Liberal (Liberal Revolutionary Movement)
NGO	nongovernmental organization
OFP	Organización Femenina Popular (Popular Feminine Organization)
PANAMCO	company name
PCC	Partido Comunista de Colombia (Colombian Communist Party)
POSTOBON	a Pepsi bottling company
PSR	Partido Socialista Revolucionario (Revolutionary Socialist Party)
SINALTRAINAL	Sindicato Nacional de Trabajadores de la Industria de Alimentos (National Union of Food and Beverage Workers)

SINTRAINDRASCOL	an older union
TROCO	Tropical Oil Company
UNIR	Unión Izquierda Revolucionaria (Revolutionary Left Union)
UP	Unión Patriótica (Patriotic Union)
USO	Unión Sindical Obrera (Syndicated Worker Union)

ACKNOWLEDGMENTS

Acknowledgments are expressions of solidarity: they give one the opportunity to connect the people whose support, patience, insight, and affection intertwine in the production of a book. Because the research and writing of *A Century of Violence in a Red City* took ten years, I owe an enormous debt of gratitude to a number of individuals and organizations.

In Colombia, the project would have been impossible without the sustained support of SINALTRAINAL, the indomitable Colombian trade union that never succumbed to intimidation and terror, even in the darkest days of the dirty war, and that continues to fight for equality, peace, and justice. Javier Correa, Juan Carlos Galvis, Luis Eduardo García, Efraín Guerrero, Armando Jurado, William Mendoza, Edgar Páez, Alfredo Porras, Gonzalo Quijano, Efraín Zurmay, and many more answered my endless questions, introduced me to others, pointed me in new directions, and, on occasion, put me up in their homes. Their generosity, humor, and political insights meant a lot to me, and their resilient struggles are a source of continuing inspiration.

In addition to SINALTRAINAL, a number of people and organizations educated me about daily life in the working-class barrios of Barrancabermeja, after right-wing paramilitaries tied to the military occupied these neighborhoods and made life a living hell for a great many residents. Enrique explained the specific problems faced by sexual minorities. Eduardo illuminated the workings of the neighborhood action committees. Discussions with Pedro Lozada about rural life in the Middle Magdalena made me understand anodyne concepts, such as "displacement," in more visceral, emotion-laden ways and to appreciate the challenges faced by displaced people in the city. Salvador described the frustrations and dilemmas of the young, and Jaime Peña demonstrated what it takes to demand justice. The women of the Popular Feminine Organization (OFP) introduced me to residents in different neighborhoods and explained the history of female popular struggle in Barrancabermeja. I am particularly grateful to Yolanda Becerra and Jackeline Rojas for their time and patience. The Christian Peacemaker Teams generously accommodated me for a period of time and helped me understand the nature of human rights activism in the city. Special thanks to Susana Collerd for her insights about life in northeast Barrancabermeja and to Amanda Martin of Witness for Peace for housing me in Bogotá and letting me tag along during a trip to Barrancabermeja.

In the United States, I have benefited from years of ongoing discussions with Aviva Chomsky, Forrest Hylton, Sharryn Kasmir, Steve Striffler, and Winifred Tate, who read all or portions of the manuscript. The book is immensely better because of their insights and observations. Chris Krupa and David Nugent stimulated my thinking about the state during a conference they organized in Quito, Ecuador. Camilo Romero was a great friend, and Camilo Garcia listened to my arguments over the course of several years and helped me grasp life in the Middle Magdalena through his stories of working as a journalist there. I feel exceptionally fortunate to have all these individuals as friends and colleagues. I have also had the pleasure to work with Emma Banks and Gloria Pérez, graduate students at Vanderbilt University, whose own research in Colombia has enriched my thinking. Teresa Franco provided editorial assistance.

I was fortunate to have institutional backing at various stages of research and writing. American University, Vanderbilt University, and the National Science Foundation provided crucial financial support for the project. Gisela Fosado of Duke University Press was a supportive editor, and the Duke University Press staff was always helpful.

As he has in the past, Art Walters made it easier to navigate the dead ends and deal with the frustrations that typically arise in the course of writing a book. He was always willing to listen to me talk about issues and concepts that I had still not gotten my mind around. More important, his love and support made it possible to keep life in perspective.

INTRODUCTION

. . .

The fraudulent alienation of the state domains, the robbery of the common lands, the usurpation of feudal and clan property, and its transformation into modern private property under circumstances of reckless terrorism, were just so many idyllic methods of primitive accumulation. — **Karl Marx**, *Capital*

When I traveled to Colombia in 2004, at the invitation of Coca-Cola workers from the Sindicato Nacional de Trabajadores de la Industria de Alimentos (National Union of Food and Beverage Workers, SINAL-TRAINAL), it was the most dangerous country in the world to be a trade unionist. For several years, labor leaders had alleged that clandestine paramilitary groups were murdering and terrorizing them and union members with the collusion of Coca-Cola Company management. A lawsuit filed by SINALTRAINAL in U.S. federal court had charged Coca-Cola with gross human rights violations, and the union, feeling its back to the wall, was desperately trying to build international support for a campaign against Coca-Cola that would pressure the corporation and the Colombian government to stop the repression that was rapidly eroding the ranks of union membership. Coming on the heels of the 1999 protests against the World Trade Organization in Seattle — the so-called Battle of Seattle — the efforts of SINALTRAINAL to focus international attention on the crimes taking place in Colombia, amid a vicious, decades-long civil war, struck me as a compelling aspect of what was still referred to as the "global social justice movement."

The leaders of SINALTRAINAL sent me off on a five-city tour in which

I talked with workers from various industries and walks of life about the violence that was tearing their lives apart. The oil-refining center of Barrancabermeja, located on the torrid plains of the Middle Magdalena River valley, was my first stop. Juan Carlos Galvis, a member of the SINALTRAINAL local directorate and a longtime Coca-Cola worker, met me at the airport. As I stepped off the small, propeller-driven plane, it took some searching before I spied Galvis among the cluster of people waiting in the passenger arrival area; he was a head shorter than most of the other men. Yet Galvis stood out in his own way. Dressed in a T-shirt emblazoned with the image of Ernesto "Che" Guevara on the front and stamped with the slogan "Hasta la victoria siempre" across the back, Galvis was making a political point at a moment when Barrancabermeja was coming out of a long strike decreed by the oil workers' union, the Unión Sindical Obrera (Syndicated Worker Union, USO), Colombia's most militant and powerful trade union. For Galvis, Che was much more than an ageless icon of youthful rebellion. The murdered guerrilla leader represented a utopian vision of socialism and commitment to ideals that had inspired Galvis for years.

As we left the terminal, two men emerged from the shuffle of departing travelers and hovered around us. Galvis introduced them as his bodyguards. They followed us to the parking lot, where a large SUV with darkened windows baked in the sun. Galvis got into the right-side backseat, a place designated by his security protocol; I sat behind the driver. With one bodyguard at the wheel and the other riding shotgun, the four of us headed into town along a winding road. We passed pipelines and birdlike oil pumps that monotonously dipped up and down as if drinking from the earth. Pastures covered in low trees and shrubs and crisscrossed by cow paths interspersed the oil fields that pockmarked the countryside. Enervated cattle chewing their cuds and brushing away flies clustered under the occasional tree large enough to cast a circle of shade. Galvis talked about the tensions that the oil strike had generated in the city.

The USO had called the strike on April 15 to halt government plans to privatize the state oil company, the Empresa Colombiana de Petróleos (Colombian Oil Company, ECOPETROL) and further open the door to multinational corporations to exploit Colombia's mineral reserves. The work stoppage lasted more than thirty days, and ECOPETROL fired 248 workers. Operations had still not resumed in the oil fields, and rumors were circulating that a special team of paramilitaries from Cali had come to town to assassinate strike organizers. As Galvis filled me in, his cell phone rang repeatedly, interrupting his account and forcing him to circle back to previous points after each hurried conversation. When we reached the outer ring of neighborhoods that rimmed Barrancabermeja, the bodyguards detoured past the refinery, which was bristling with concertina wire and surrounded by soldiers, before heading down Calle 52 to a large, two-story cement building that housed the USO headquarters, where a meeting was under way. Galvis and I joined USO leaders and representatives of several popular organizations who were planning a march through the city to protest the detention of dozens of strike leaders. Although I did not appreciate it at the time, I was witnessing the last gasp of a once-powerful working class.

Over the next couple of years, I returned to Barrancabermeja, or Barranca, as locals referred to it, and visited other Colombian cities, interviewing scores of Coca-Cola workers and their family members and accumulating information about Coca-Cola's worldwide operations. Yet I gradually spent more and more time in Barrancabermeja, where Galvis and SINALTRAINAL president William Mendoza went out of their way to facilitate my research. Both men insisted that I talk with other trade unionists, human rights defenders, neighborhood activists, and peasant leaders because they understood that there was a deeper story to tell than the one about Coca-Cola.

Galvis and Mendoza opened the world of left political activism to me, or at least what remained of it, and the opportunity to talk with so many social movement leaders and grassroots activists was thrilling. But it was also overwhelming. My research subjects quickly cast me in the role of human rights defender because of my willingness to hang around with them and do whatever it was that they were doing. What I understood as participant observation—a basic anthropological research method—they defined as *acompañamiento* (accompaniment), which, when done by a foreigner, especially one from North America or Europe, was widely believed to make people safer from paramilitary attack.[1] There were, in fact, several human rights organizations in Barrancabermeja that specialized in this kind of practice.

Being identified as a human rights advocate overestimated my capacity to do anything about what was happening.[2] People expected me to speak out against the violence that was shredding the social fabric because doing so would demonstrate that they were part of international networks that were capable of mobilizing a rapid response in case of emergency. I was happy to oblige, but I could not always verify the stories that I heard, nor did I have the international connections that some imagined. In addition, the horrifying accounts that people told me initially did not go beyond tales of individual victimization. The traumatic narratives, and the urgency and presentism of human rights accompaniment-cum-participant-observation, complicated any exploration of the political projects and organizations in which people were involved or the passions that motivated working people, especially at a time when discussing one's involvement, past or present, with the legal or illegal left was dangerous. All of this made it easy to overlook a story that went beyond Coca-Cola and the individual stories of brutalization.

The deeper story was about the violent destruction of a working class and about how violence was neither a peripheral nor an accidental part of the disorganization of labor. As the Colombian economy became one of the most liberalized in the Americas during the 1990s, harsh new laws had made it easier for firms to hire temporary laborers, while escalating paramilitary violence suppressed opposition to the new policies with threats, massacres, and targeted assassinations. Between 1977 and 2004, 114 members of the USO were murdered; 89 of them lived in Barrancabermeja (Valencia and Celis 2012: 125). Between 2000 and 2003, the number of permanent workers affiliated with the USO dropped by 50 percent, while the number of temporary workers rose. At the same time, the government outsourced much of ECO-PETROL's maintenance and support operations to thousands of private contractors, some of whom were tied to illegal paramilitary groups that placed their own people in jobs once held by USO members and weakened the union from within. Under such conditions, the USO's ability to maintain a prolonged strike in 2004 and the popular support that it received were remarkable. But the effort was not enough. The 2004 strike was never repeated, and the privatization of ECOPETROL and the restructuring of its labor force continued. Violence was a central part of capitalist development and the dismantling of a once vibrant, politically militant working class, and the experiences of the USO and SINAL-TRAINAL were being repeated over and over again.

Although international human rights organizations documented the deaths and relentless violence in Barrancabermeja and across Colombia, their reports did not explain what people were fighting for or the intense emotions that drove them into conflict. In an era when wealth and power were being redistributed upward, the accounts of the dead, the disappeared, and the massacred provided few clues to understanding the setbacks of organized labor. This was because the class dynamics tearing Colombian society apart were largely ignored. They were replaced by a moral argument against abusive state power that became a consolation prize for working people struggling to expand the parameters of democracy and to protect their jobs, organizations, and social arrangements from the neoliberal capitalist order envisioned by state policy makers, Colombian elites, and corporate managers.

Political violence and capitalist development were ruthless engines of social fragmentation, but even though the late twentieth-century terror that engulfed Barrancabermeja was extreme, the dispossession and disorganization of its working class were not unique. From the cold tin mines of Llallagua in the Bolivian mountains to the sprawling automobile factories of Detroit in the American Midwest, working classes and centers of working-class power were fracturing under the combined pressures of capitalist restructuring, free-trade policies, austerity programs, and political oppression. The production of precariousness in the lives of ordinary people stood in stark contrast to the emergence of enclaves of wealth, where newly minted global billionaires withdrew from the turmoil affecting the rest of the world. As working-class lives were uprooted and people thrown into the breach, the chaos forced people to reimagine and re-create their ties to each other, even as the dispossessed and disenfranchised were incorporated into new relationships of domination and exploitation to which they had never agreed.

A Century of Violence in a Red City documents the making and unmaking of a working class amid the violent conflicts that shaped the Middle Magdalena region of northwest Colombia, particularly the oil town of Barrancabermeja. Beginning in the early twentieth century, a heterogeneous group of peasants, oil workers, small-scale merchants, and prostitutes transformed the sleepy Magdalena River port of Barrancabermeja into a center of working-class power. They did so as the advent of petroleum extraction drew impoverished people from the far corners of Colombia to the middle stretch of the Magdalena River valley and forever changed a tropical frontier region in one of Latin America's most conservative countries. Hoping for a better life, these intrepid souls fought the humidity, diseases, torrential rains, petroleum contamination, and the oil company—a subsidiary of the Standard Oil Company of New Jersey—to forge a confrontational class culture leavened with anti-imperialist nationalism. Until the early 1980s, diverse working people forged relationships of solidarity and fought to enact a vision of popular democracy that went beyond the official state's promises of modernity and national progress. They also challenged the presumptions of foreign oil corporations and regional elites to dictate the terms of social life. Their democratic vision embraced national sovereignty, agrarian reform, labor rights, public services, the rights of liberal citizenship (e.g., legal equality, constitutional protections, and individual freedom) and socialist-inspired notions of the common good, and it opposed the disruptive forces of capitalism that roiled Barrancabermeja and the Middle Magdalena region.

By the early twenty-first century, this vision had dimmed. Barranca's dense infrastructure of popular solidarity—unions, neighborhood associations, church groups, student organizations, left political parties, and, for a time, guerrilla militias—lay in ruins. Counterinsurgent violence that escalated in the 1980s and spun out of control in the 1990s and the first decade of the new millennium led to the deaths, forcible displacement, or disappearance of thousands of people. Many people suffered the trauma of losing family members, friends, neighbors, and workmates. Years of dirty war and neoliberal economic policies had sparked a boom in extractive minerals and biofuel production on the graves of those who had imagined a different future. Worker rights and protections won in past struggles either no longer existed or lingered in degraded form, and anyone who questioned the status quo was warned against their challenge with death threats. As dispossessed peasants, downsized workers, and impoverished urbanites negotiated a path through a more unequal and authoritarian city, they found themselves much more alone than in the past, severed from the social networks and institutions that once sustained them and exposed to forces beyond their control. The specter of Barrancabermeja's defeated working class and divided memories about the dirty war hung over the lives of the victims and survivors like a hungry ghost, haunting their efforts to rebuild livelihoods and bedeviling the reimagination of a shared future.

This book is less concerned with documenting the existence of a class and its subsequent dissolution than with analyzing the violent political struggles that undergirded the composition and decomposition of working-class power, organization, and culture. It places uprooted peasants, wage laborers, and unwaged and wage-insecure urban immigrants within a single analytic framework and explores how their struggles over labor rights, public services, and human rights brought them together and pulled them apart over nearly a century. These struggles were central to the formation and dissolution of class. The book contributes to the development of a new anthropology of labor that dispenses with static typologies—waged and unwaged, rural and urban, and formal and informal—and revives the notion of class as a fluid analytic category that captures the centrality of conflict to the formation of social relations. In this way, it attends to E. P. Thompson's (1963) insistence on a processual and relational approach to the study of labor, one that focuses on the always open-ended making of class. This perspective helps us explore the common understandings and alliances, as well as the social ruptures and ideological divisions, that propel changes in how working people understand their experiences, their ties to each other, and their relationships to more powerful groups and institutions.[3]

A Century of Violence in a Red City also examines how processes of class formation and capital accumulation generated fierce battles over territory in which, at different times, transnational oil companies, guerrilla insurgencies, and paramilitary organizations operated alongside, with, or against official state representatives and institutions and attempted to regulate the lives of people under their control. I argue that "the state" never operated alone but in overt or covert alliances with other powerful actors to promote particular projects of rule that sought to produce, normalize, and legitimate different forms of political and economic inequality. Such complex geographies of power were dynamic, unstable, and violent. They arose from the contradictions generated by capitalist accumulation practices and forms of popular mobilization, or demobilization, in particular historical moments. They also conditioned the ability of working people to sustain themselves, their organizations, and their visions of the future and to connect their struggles to wider political movements. Building on the work of previous scholars who have examined the tensions between popular political struggles and processes of state formation (e.g., Joseph and Nugent 1994; Mallon 2005; Nugent 1997), this book places working people at the center of concern. It shows that shifting configurations of power and processes of state formation turned on the control of resources, changing forms of labor exploitation, and the making and unmaking of class in which the demands, visions, and struggles of a heterogeneous group of working people played a central part. State and class formation were thus imbricated with each other and shaped changing forms of social regulation over time.

State formation, as well as the making, unmaking, and remaking of class, is rooted in violence. Yet violence often passes unobserved in abstract, economistic accounts of capitalist processes in which the market's "invisible hand," capital, the state, and globalization have a deceptive coherence and rationality. To the extent that violence appears at all, it does so as an episodic, regrettable, and temporary side effect of the disruptions that accompany the reforms demanded by ruling classes and state officials for economic expansion to take place. The experience of working people in Barrancabermeja, however, suggests a more critical perspective in which violence is one of the major tools that forges the development of capitalist relations, propels the formation of competing projects of rule within and across space, and drives the pace of social change. The story of working-class Barrancabermeja offers insights into how violence becomes enmeshed within the interrelated processes of capital accumulation, state formation, and working-class disorganization and dispossession.

The Politics of Labor and Class

With notable exceptions, anthropologists have not focused on "class" as an important social relationship or analytic category.[4] As August Carbonella and Sharryn Kasmir (2014) note, scholars have often interpreted the decline of Fordist production systems in the United States and Europe as the end of class itself, rather than the passing of a historically specific class formation and its accompanying social welfare state. Meanwhile, the collapse of Soviet and Eastern European communism, China's "capitalist turn," and new labor relations and forms of inequality generated by the post–cold war expansion of neoliberalism have incorporated millions of new workers into capitalist processes, while the so-called Great Recession that began in 2008 has deepened social suffering and amplified previously unheard critiques of the unfettered "market" as the source of freedom and well-being. The outsourcing of production from traditional manufacturing centers to low-wage regions has dispersed working-class power away from former union strongholds, while the opening of new extractive frontiers in oil, natural gas, precious gems, minerals, and drugs, secured by paramilitaries, mafias, and private security firms, has created new spaces of marginalization and exploitation (e.g., Ferguson 2005; Richani 2007). Yet despite the proliferation of new and remade ways of working, as well as wide-ranging evidence of stark disparities in wealth and social well-being, discussions of class have only recently reentered mainstream political debate, after a wave of social protests, from Occupy Wall Street to revolts in Europe and Latin America, pried open the public agenda and energized new research.

What David Harvey (2003) calls "accumulation by dispossession" — the recurrent dispossession of working people under capitalism — has made or reconfigured working classes over and over again, creating new divisions and labor relations, and forcing people to assess what they can, and cannot, do with each other. Updating Marx's notion of "primitive accumulation," a one-off process that entailed the enclosure of common property, the expulsion of peasants, and the commodification of their labor at the dawn of capitalism, Harvey argues that what Marx described as the "reckless terror" of plunder and enslavement is actually a feature of capitalism that happens, and has happened, repeatedly in the long history of capitalist development. It consists of a variety of processes that include usury, violent physical displacement, debt, and the privatization of public assets, such as land and natural resources, as well as the social wage (pensions, health care, welfare, etc.) won through years of struggle (Harvey 2003: 137–82). In the past three decades, accumulation by dispossession and the violence associated with it have intensified poverty, marginalization, and social fragmentation among a larger swath of the world's population through the monetization of social relationships and the upward redistribution of wealth. It has obliged more people to become dependent on cash incomes and migrate to find work. In the context of so much upheaval, how to categorize the people whose lives have been uprooted and torn apart, and who counts as a worker, is not always clear.

Hernando de Soto (1989), for example, is well known for claiming that the ruined peasants and part-time laborers in the impoverished fringes of Latin American, African, and Asian cities are less workers than "microentrepreneurs," eager for property titles and microcredit to propel their capitalist ventures forward. Yet the notion of microentrepreneur and older categories, such as "penny capitalist" (Tax 1963), fail to draw a distinction between small-scale accumulation and bare survival, and they imply that the rights of property, rather than rights and protections for labor, are the central issue faced by impoverished urban residents today. In contrast, Jan Breman (1994) characterizes the denizens of India's peri-urban settlements as "wage hunters and gatherers," and Michael Denning (2010) emphasizes the centrality of wagelessness among the poor, marginalized inhabitants of burgeoning urban peripheries, arguing that the imperative to earn a living, not the wage contract, constitutes the analytic starting point for understanding contemporary labor processes. Breman and Denning remind us that being without a wage is a widely shared experience of contemporary capitalism and, as Carbonella and Kasmir note, "solidarity, as well as difference, is always a possibility" (2014: 9). Similarly, Charles Bergquist argues that issues of control lie at the core of labor studies and that by addressing the multiple ways that diverse people struggle to control their work, the products of their labor, and their living conditions, social scientists can "see the informal sector less as a school for petty capitalists than as an extension of the working class" (1996: 193). Addressing these issues, Bergquist insists, enables scholars to move beyond conceptualizing labor as "the study of free but not coerced workers, urban but not rural workers, industrial but not agricultural workers" (184–85).

Carbonella and Kasmir suggest that who gets labeled as a "worker" and what sorts of labor arrangements (e.g., formal/informal, waged/unwaged, rural/industrial) figure as valued economic activities are political questions whose answers have not always provided analytic clarity. They argue that labor is best understood as "*a political entity*, whose social protests and quietude, formal and informal organizations and political cultures reflect its multiple engagements with capital and the state, as well as the relationships with other workers, locally, regionally, and globally" (Carbonella and Kasmir 2014: 7). This understanding of labor embraces numerous ways of working and is not limited to the proletariat, and it makes room for exploring how working people come together (or not) within shifting fields of power. Various combinations of waged and unwaged labor have always been present—and simultaneously produced—throughout the long history of capitalism.

Multiple forms of dispossession, such as land loss, forced displacement, the privatization of public utilities and resources, job loss, and cuts to pensions and health care, have given rise to a new mix of labor relations in places like Colombia, where political violence and neoliberalism are intertwined. Peasant production systems are in decline; temporary or part-time, nonunionized workers are replacing a relatively small group of people who once had stable union jobs; and unwaged, wage-insecure, and criminalized labor are intensifying on the impoverished urban peripheries, where the victims of dispossession have settled. These transformations open the door for exploring the fluidity of class relations over time. They enable us to focus our attention on the numerous, changing ways of working, as well as the connections and divisions that arise among working people within shifting contexts of violence and inequality, as states, corporations, guerrilla insurgencies, and paramilitary armies contend with the organizational forms (e.g., unions, neighborhood associations, political parties) that express and channel popular concerns. We can also begin to grasp how memories of the violent past take shape in particular political contexts and inform how diverse people understand the present and imagine the future.

Studies of the "precariat" (Standing 2011), or "informal proletariat" (Davis 2006) in the global South, where its expansion is most pronounced, reveal the importance of wage-insecure and wageless labor to the production of wealth within local, national, and international circuits of capital flows. Judith Whitehead (2012), for example, documents the extreme fragmentation of labor markets and labor in a Mumbai shantytown, where most of the laboring population works as street venders, home workers, petty commodity producers, contract workers in larger firms, construction workers, and so forth. She explores how specific livelihood practices are repeatedly connected, disconnected, and reconnected to global and national capital flows in a context where capital is hypermobile and labor is relatively fixed in place. Her work offers insights into the ways that neoliberal capitalism sucks surplus value out of poor neighborhoods by creating a range of new, spatially configured labor relations that localize working people while simultaneously incorporating them into volatile national and international networks of capital accumulation that are constantly fragmented and recomposed. This process creates vulnerability and constant uncertainty among those who must continually scramble to get by.

In Barrancabermeja, the discovery of oil propelled the growth of a heterogeneous workforce and the accumulation of laborers through recurrent rounds of dispossession, disorganization, and displacement that generated powerful forms of solidarity and deep divisions over the twentieth century. Beginning in the 1920s, migrants from the tropical northern plains and the mountainous Andean highlands fled poverty, landlord violence, and property enclosure for the prospect of jobs in the nascent oil industry. Barrancabermeja quickly acquired the largest concentration of wage laborers of any Colombian city, and the organization of a powerful oil workers' union proved decisive in decades-long popular struggles against the transnational oil corporation and, subsequently, the state-owned oil company. Yet despite their organizational power and importance to a key industry, the oil workers rarely acted alone. Semiproletarianized peasants, petty merchants, and impoverished urbanites backed their demands for better conditions in the oil fields and the labor camps, and the oil workers, in turn, supported struggles for land, access to markets, social services, and national sovereignty. Diverse working people forged a remarkable degree of self-organization and mutual support that was nurtured by various political currents—liberalism, anarchism, socialism, communism, and Christian humanism. The dismantling of this tightly knit class culture did not happen all at once. It was an uneven, discontinuous process that erupted during the mid-twentieth-century period of national bloodletting known simply as "La Violencia" and then spiraled into a deadly vortex at the end of the century, when an emergent far-right alliance of drug traffickers, cattle ranchers, politicians, and neoliberal entrepreneurs unleashed a dirty war in the countryside and the city that remapped power and swept in neoliberalism on a river of blood.

The history of Barrancabermeja demonstrates that the struggles of oil workers—the classic proletariat of Marxist theory—had a broad base that extended beyond the oil fields and the refinery, and for the better part of the twentieth century, diverse working people forged connections that spanned the country and the city and claimed identities within a simmering stew of diverse labor relations. Barrancabermeja's complex labor history further demonstrates that neither the fragmentation and dispossession affecting the lives of contemporary working people in the city nor the emergence of new and remade labor relations and cultural differences elsewhere are unprecedented. Rather, it suggests a need to reexamine how labor and conventional labor conflicts are understood.[5]

A focus on class politics highlights the unfolding ways that working people understand their experiences, organize livelihood strategies to get by, and conceptualize and create relationships as they engage with each other and contend with more powerful groups. We can grasp how, at times, they may build relationships that connect people across racial, ethnic, national, and gender divisions to press claims on the powerful. We can also understand how dispossession, social ruptures, and fear sever social ties, expose working people to new kinds of discipline, and aggravate old and create new forms of inequality (e.g., Carbonella 2014; Kasmir 2014; Narotzky and Smith 2006). Class as an analytic category captures the conflicts, accommodations, and alliances that shape and reshape power-laden relationships. This book seeks to understand how a century of capitalist development and popular mobilization continually remade class relations through the periodic dispossession, displacement, and disorganization of working people and their institutions. Central to this process were intense political struggles over the spaces of labor exploitation, capital accumulation, and power.

Geographies of Power

By 1930, the growth of the oil export enclave had transformed the sleepy river settlement of Barrancabermeja into a thriving outpost of working-class culture and society. After oil workers received their pay on what became known as "big Saturdays," an exodus from the rudimentary encampments in "El Centro," where the oil fields were located, to the bustling river port began. Gonzalo Buenahora, a physician who worked in Barrancabermeja for forty years, recalled that "Barranca only had 16,000 inhabitants, and the workers who arrived [from the oil fields] were like three thousand." They came on a train owned by the oil company, "dressed impeccably in white from the feet to the bow tie and with pockets full of money. . . . And they all came, nobody remained [behind]" (qtd. in Archila 1978: 98). The men spent their money in bars, restaurants, and bordellos, where regional accents from the north coast and the Antioquian valleys mixed with the foreign-accented Spanish of merchants from as far afield as Lebanon, contract laborers from the British West Indies, supervisors and engineers from North America, and prostitutes from across Colombia and abroad.

Although it is tempting to view the continual accumulation of diverse workers in Barrancabermeja—from the early migrations that gave birth to the enclave to the recent displacements of the dirty war—as a "local" phenomenon, the temptation should be resisted. The enclave, and subsequently the city and the region, took shape amid violent struggles over the rights of labor and the rights of citizenship in the places where people worked and lived. While working people sought to produce and control space through the extension of their institutions and alliances, the oil company drew on its ties to the United States and mobilized the institutional state, the police, and the military to create and regulate space in the interest of global capitalism. The dispossession, localization, and isolation of diverse people molded the initial formation of the enclave, while disrupting and dislocating more or less settled social and political arrangements was key to subsequent projects of rule in Barrancabermeja and the Middle Magdalena. These processes underscored the ways that class and state formation were constitutive of each other. How different, power-laden geographies emerged from conflicting political and economic agendas and how working people organized within and against them to advance their concerns are important questions.

This book addresses them by examining the tense dialectic that shaped class formation and the production of fragmented and differently organized forms of territorial control in which, at different times, a transnational oil company, guerrilla insurgencies, and right-wing paramilitaries regulated social life in the areas under their control and alongside, within, and against the institutional state in diverse ways. It argues that the "state" always acted through overt and covert alliances with other actors who wielded varying degrees of power and who attempted to consolidate, extend, and naturalize what were, in fact, self-interested and particular claims about the organization of social life in the name of the common good.[6] Yet these political configurations have always been unstable, and they are a central feature of the perpetual crisis of hegemony in the Middle Magdalena. The book considers three distinct periods in which shifting regimes of capital accumulation, the coercive capacities of different actors, and the organization and claims making of working people gave rise to changing geographies of power.

First, it explores the development of Barrancabermeja as a foreign-controlled export enclave from the 1920s to 1960, when the Tropical Oil Company (TROCO)—a subsidiary of the Standard Oil Company of New Jersey—acquired the subsoil rights to a vast extension of tropical forest. The TROCO recruited legions of impoverished migrants to cut access roads, construct buildings, and eventually drill for oil. The process of sinking wells in the tropical soil and creating an infrastructure to support them required that the company physically control territory and manage a labor force that was still unschooled in the practices of industrial work discipline. The creation of the enclave brought together the managers of a global corporation, state officials, and diverse working people in far-flung relationships of domination and exploitation that were strengthened by the threat of U.S. military intervention; in addition, it placed the TROCO in competition with the Texas Petroleum Company and Royal Dutch Shell, which also won permission to drill for oil in concessions along the river. The development of the oil industry in the Middle Magdalena mirrored contests between expanding global corporations and nascent working classes in the Mexican Huasteca and Venezuela's Maracaibo Basin, where Royal Dutch Shell, British Petroleum, and the Standard Oil Company operated, as well as in the emergent banana zones of the circum-Caribbean and Ecuador (Santiago 2006; Striffler 2002; Striffler and Moberg 2003; Tinker Salas 2009; Vega 2002).

Historian Paul Kramer suggests that export enclaves constitute "strategic hamlets" of empire that concentrate extraordinary power through the control of space and power; they are, he argues, "spatial exceptions" (2011: 1356) in which corporations produce commodities and accumulate capital by enclosing and isolating populations, severing territory from local jurisdiction, and arrogating the right to control social life within the enclaves.[7] Yet because corporations in early twentieth-century Latin America controlled capital more easily than workers, their bid for sovereign power ran up against the contradictions that had produced export enclaves from their inception: the generation of economic differentiation and cultural differences simultaneously and the ensuing tensions that arose from them. The sharp cultural and economic divisions that separated foreign managers from Colombian, Ecuadoran, Venezuelan, and Mexican workers stoked nationalist resentment, fueled anti-imperialism, and magnified political repression. Colombian oil workers fought for a more democratic, sovereign state, one that would regulate conflicts with the TROCO, better control access to natural resources, and extend the guarantees and protections of liberal citizenship, such as the right to unionize, freedom of assembly and speech, and collective bargaining. As historian Charles Bergquist (1986) notes, working classes in export enclaves formed the bedrock of radical labor movements in early twentieth-century Latin America, and their influence was felt well beyond geographically isolated zones of commodity production. They periodically mobilized national sentiment in their support, and they sometimes even shook the foundations of liberal capitalism, obliging corporations to deal with more far-reaching demands than what the firms encountered from workers in the United States.

The contests between labor and capital that gave birth to the enclave in the 1920s contributed to its demise in the middle decades of the twentieth century, the second period in which labor relations and capital accumulation were remapped in Barrancabermeja (1960–90). By the late 1950s, the foreign-owned enclave was in decline almost everywhere, including Barrancabermeja, where growing nationalism, intensified union activity, and a government search for more export revenue persuaded the TROCO to allow its concession to expire and to subsequently relinquish control of the oil industry to the Colombian state.[8] The midcentury creation of the state-owned ECOPETROL inaugurated an era of direct state control of the Colombian oil industry that coincided with the modernization of the economy.

A more interventionist central state embarked on an agenda of capitalist modernization. It assumed a greater role in the stewardship of economic development, promoting import-substitution policies and spurring agro-industrial development though the extension of subsidized credit and machinery to large landowners (Safford and Palacios 2002). It also oversaw the expansion of the public sector between 1950 and 1980, which transformed oil workers into employees of the state and generated an increase in the number of other public sector employees, including teachers, civil servants, and health care and telecommunications workers, who joined unions and expanded the labor movement in Barrancabermeja. Yet even though *barranqueños* no longer suffered under the arbitrary power of the TROCO, they were not incorporated into the modernizing state as fully entitled citizens. The relationship between working people and the institutional state ran aground over the provision of public services, labor rights, and the repressive hand of state security forces. A new wave of uprooted peasants was washing over the city, pushed out of the countryside by landlord violence and the expansion of large-scale commercial agriculture, but unlike in the past, the newcomers did not find jobs in the oil industry; they erected shantytowns on the edge of town and became part of a floating population of wageless or wage-insecure workers. Popular demands for public services, backed by the oil workers' union, were criminalized and repressed, as rising cold war tensions and the exclusive nature of the National Front (1958–74) narrowed the parameters of political participation.

Although Colombia became the showcase for the Kennedy administration's Alliance for Progress, an economic and military assistance program launched in 1961 that sought to stave off demands for radical social changes, the state-led process of capitalist modernization sidestepped the deep inequalities and political exclusions that characterized Colombian society, especially the lopsided landholding structure. Successive National Front governments, in which the Liberal and Conservative Parties alternated in power, marginalized reformist initiatives and repressed revolutionary demands for more far-reaching political, economic, and social transformations. Political exclusion, an unresponsive state bureaucracy, and the equation of protest with communist subversion spurred the organization of guerrilla insurgencies that put down deep roots in the Middle Magdalena. The insurgencies advocated the overthrow and transformation of the state, and, as the Fuerzas Armadas Revolucionarias de Colombia (Revolutionary Armed Forces of Colombia, FARC) and the Ejército Nacional de Liberación (National Liberation Army, ELN)—Colombia's largest and most enduring guerrilla organizations—grew more powerful and laid claim to territory in the Middle Magdalena, they created a political crisis for the state that aggravated the fragmentation of sovereignty.

As Barrancabermeja shed its identity as an oil enclave and took on the appearance of a thriving urban center in the 1960s and 1970s, the juxtaposition of a profitable oil industry with its well-paid workforce and destitute immigrant neighborhoods, formed by uprooted peasants expelled from the countryside by the expansion of commercial agriculture, laid bare the ways that capitalism produced spaces of poverty and wealth concurrently. It also undergirded the role of the state in this process. Diverse working people found common cause in the demand that the central government live up to its promises of development and modernization. The oil workers' union, neighborhood organizations, unions, left political parties and movements, and civic organizations claimed a "right to the city" (Harvey 2010), that is, a right to the reinvestment of the surpluses some of them had created into public services. A series of civic strikes rocked Barrancabermeja in the 1960s and 1970s and zeroed in on the dearth of public services, especially water. As they had in the past, working people met in the streets to demand that the state take care of its citizens. Guerrilla insurgencies, especially the ELN, built on this discontentment and constructed long-term relationships with sectors of the urban working class. Yet unlike in other cities, such as Vienna in the 1920s (Gruber 1991) or El Alto, Bolivia, today (Hylton and Thomson 2007; Lazar 2008), where working-class self-organization and municipal control defined the contours of urban life, Barrancabermeja's working people never controlled state and municipal offices. Their power resided in unions, Christian base communities, student organizations, neighborhood associations, left political parties, and ties to the insurgencies. The strength of their reformist and revolutionary challenges prefigured the intensity of the terror directed against working people between 1980 and the early twenty-first century. The rise of the illegal cocaine economy and an intensifying, counterinsurgent dirty war reterritorialized power, reshaped labor relations, and transformed the ways that people advanced claims on the state from a focus on national sovereignty, labor protections, and public services to human rights.

The emergence of violent paramilitary mafias, the counterinsurgent war, and the advent of neoliberalism fired a violent new phase of territorial struggle, working-class decomposition, and state formation from the 1980s to the present, the primary focus of this book. Political violence intensified in Colombia even as the conclusion of the cold war led to the cessation of hostilities in Central America, where the signing of peace accords in the 1990s brought an end to decades of civil war. Insurgencies that were militarily strong but politically weak controlled huge swaths of the country's richest land. In addition, the decline of the traditional coffee economy and the increasing importance of other legal and illegal export commodities — oil, gold, African palm, bananas, emeralds, and especially cocaine — bolstered the configuration of regionally based, reactionary power blocs. These new configurations of regional power drew their strength from powerful paramilitary armies and formed alliances with state officials and security forces to push the insurgencies out of resource-rich areas of the country and destroy any organization deemed sympathetic to them (Hylton 2014). Although the counterinsurgent war was supposed to extend the power of the central state, it deepened the fragmentation of power by abetting the formation of regional sovereignties, or parastates, that ruled within, alongside, and sometimes against the official state and that adopted extreme forms of labor repression (Richani 2007). This process was facilitated by political and economic state decentralization, which enabled violent mercenaries and their supporters to capture municipal, provincial, and national elected office and to reconfigure state territory on deeply undemocratic terms (López 2010; see also Ballvé 2012). The counterinsurgent war was financed by the growing fortunes of major drug lords who made sophisticated weaponry, vehicles, airplanes, and communication equipment available, first, to hit men and emergent death squads to protect their extensive operations from the guerrillas and, then, to standing armies that conquered and controlled territory. It was also supported by U.S. intervention in the form of Plan Colombia, a multibillion-dollar counterinsurgency program initiated by President Bill Clinton in 2000 that provided helicopters, training, and intelligence equipment to the police and military, who were key allies of the paramilitaries, and through a CIA program, financed by a multibillion-dollar black budget authorized by President George W. Bush and continued by President Barack Obama, that provided intelligence and "smart bombs" to decimate insurgent forces.[9]

In Barrancabermeja, right-wing paramilitaries tied to state security forces and regional elites crushed working-class power, expelled the guerrillas, and took over the city and most of the Middle Magdalena region by 2003. The mayhem was fueled by impunity, an aspect of power that allowed perpetrators to get away with murder again and again, and that made it nearly impossible for working people to do anything about what was happening. The crisis reconfigured urban space and created a sense of pervasive fear and insecurity, which paved the way for the incorporation of working people into more authoritarian forms of labor discipline, rent extraction, and political subjugation. These new and remade relationships provided the grounding for a particularly pernicious form of armed neoliberalism. The "peace" that reigned in Barrancabermeja after 2003 was a chimera; it rested on a deep reservoir of fear, coerced collaboration, insecurity, and grudging acceptance that regulated the lives of residents and made it difficult to repair ruptured social relationships and stitch together fragmented memories so that urban residents could explain and understand, in shared ways, what happened and continued to happen to them.

The configuration and reconfiguration of Barrancabermeja as a center of capital accumulation and popular struggle raises questions about how power operates through uneven connections to imperial structures and distant national institutions, and how these connections transform societies and condense power in key points on a broader global tapestry. It prompts us to ask how distinctions between foreign/ domestic and state/nonstate are constructed and how rights are defined and distributed to different kinds of people. How, too, do working people envision the state and formulate claims against it? Such questions open the conceptual possibility of exploring how the kinds of social relations, understandings, and forms of political participation that become institutionalized as "the state" are themselves the outcome of contending projects of rule, which operate in different scalar dimensions (e.g., Nugent 1997). Indeed, as Christopher Krupa and David Nugent (2015) argue, national-territorial models of the state mask how conflicting claims to legitimate rule are embedded in the fabric of social life. These models and the formal fiction of nation-state sovereignty and national control that they preserve shroud the often considerable power of subnational groups to command and control territory and regulate social life within it. They also mask the imperial power of the United States by maintaining its invisibility, even as its corporations, security forces, diplomats, and aid programs intrude into the ability of client states to control economic activity, regulate social life, and command territory (Kramer 2011; Tate 2015). Outdated conceptual models have prompted analysts to address new questions about what the state is, where it is located, and how political life should be organized (Krupa and Nugent 2015).

A number of scholars note that the capacity of states to claim effective control over a territory in the name of the nation and its citizens has always been limited because subnational populations play an important part in how state institutions, ideologies, and practices become established in any given locality. Power may be wielded by different "illegal armed groups" (Ávila 2010), warlords (Duncan 2006), and paramilitaries or self-defense forces (Romero 2003) and organized among various kinds of fragmented "informal sovereignties" (Hansen and Stepputat 2006), "state proxies" (Krupa 2010), "proto-states" (Bejarano and Pizarro 2004), "shadow powers" (Gledhill 1999; Nordstrom 2000), "parastates" (Gill 2009), and forms of "subnational authoritarianism" (Bonilla 2007) that enjoy varying degrees of legitimacy. Moreover, frontier regions, such as Colombia's Putumayo province, that have long been perceived as lawless, violent, and "uncivilized" disrupt the territorial uniformity often ascribed to the state (Ramírez 2011).

What emerged in Barrancabermeja and other Colombian regions at the dawn of the twenty-first century was less the hegemony of a particular group than the domination of regionally based alliances of right-wing politicians, landlords, drug traffickers, and sectors of the security forces organized into various narco-paramilitary blocs (Ávila 2010). Based in provincial cities and small towns, these powerful coalitions dominated municipal and provincial offices, controlled much of the legal and illegal economy, and pushed the fulcrum of political power to the right (Hylton 2014; Richani 2007). They were more successful than the insurgencies in what Philip Abrams identified as the central activity of state formation: "legitimating of the illegitimate" (1988: 76). Through the creation and financial backing of new political movements that reflected the concerns of their most violent elements, they gained national power through the election of candidates to high political office, as they sought to legalize ill-gotten lands and wealth, avoid prosecution, and gain political legitimacy. *A Century of Violence in a Red City* demonstrates how processes of state formation generated various territorially based forms of power in the Middle Magdalena region that generated conflicting claims to rule. These shifting geographies of power regulated social life to different degrees and operated in complex relationship to government officials and institutions. They were deeply intertwined with the making and unmaking of class and the changing scale of working-class power.

Political Violence and Class Politics

As is apparent by now, violence has been constitutive of state formation, the organization and command of space, and labor processes in the Middle Magdalena. Colombia has long been regarded as one of Latin America's most violent countries, and the Middle Magdalena region is one of the most violent places in Colombia. Yet government officials like to insist that their country is Latin America's oldest democracy. With the exception of a brief period in the 1950s, Colombia has not experienced the brutal military dictatorships that ruled over most of mid-twentieth-century Latin America, and it has held regular elections for decades. But the numbers of murdered and disappeared people in Colombia are among the largest in twentieth-century Latin American history. According to the Grupo de Memoria Histórica (2013), an official body charged with clarifying more than fifty years of armed conflict, at least 220,000 people died between 1958 and 2012 as a result of the war. Between the 1980s and the early twenty-first century, more trade unionists have died than in any other country in the world (Solidarity Center 2006), and the forcible displacement of more than seven million people has generated the largest internally displaced population in the world, after Sudan.[10]

Even though violence—that is, brute force that aims to crush, eliminate, or mentally destroy an individual or group—is a recurrent feature in the periodic dispossession and reconfiguration of working classes, its centrality to capitalism is frequently overlooked in social science analyses and human rights reporting. Greg Grandin (2010) notes that scholars have substituted analytic categories, such as exploitation, for humanistic ones, such as suffering, and have chosen violence as a primary topic of research rather than trying to explain how it emerges as a by-product from conflicts with deep historical roots. A spate of social science theorizing has sought to extend the concept beyond instrumentalized force to better understand how it pervades the fabric of social life. Notions such as "structural violence" (Farmer 1997) and "continuum of violence" (Scheper-Hughes and Bourgois 2004) promise deeper insights into the social, cultural, and economic dimensions of violence. Yet despite the utility of these formations in certain contexts, they risk diluting the concept by finding it everywhere and reifying it. Although violence is, indeed, an experiential reality that has important meaningful and symbolic consequences, it cannot be dissociated from broader analyses of power, such as "the transformation of economic relations and the state, and the evolution of competing ideologies vying for common-sense status" (Grandin 2010: 7).

The entanglements of violence and capitalist processes are also left unexplored in much human rights reporting on the Middle Magdalena region. Reports enumerate the details of massacres, disappearances, and extrajudicial executions, illuminate the operations of clandestine security forces, and document incidents of torture, but they leave unexamined the social, political, and economic relationships that drive victims and perpetrators into conflict (e.g., Human Rights Watch 2001, 2010). This kind of reporting strives for high levels of factual accuracy and political neutrality, but the move to depoliticize human rights accounts and to place them above and outside politics is itself "political."[11] It removes targeted groups and individuals from the history of social, economic, and political struggle that generated violence in the first place and treats them as passive victims, obscuring how they lived and often died. Despite the crucial importance of documenting human rights violations, the language of human rights does not offer an adequate framework for analyzing political violence because

it separates repression from complex, competing political agendas and distances itself from any association with politics (Striffler 2015). A more dynamic, relational approach that goes beyond the description and enumeration of atrocities is necessary, one in which violence—massacres, extrajudicial executions, torture, and so forth—is less the object of analysis than the outcome of social conflicts and examined within the broader social and political field from which it arises. How force and counterforce operate at the intersection of working people's changing relationships to each other and more powerful groups, on the one hand, and their feelings about these transformations, on the other hand, is a key question that needs to be addressed.

Although Barrancabermeja represents an extreme case of political violence and neoliberal restructuring, it cannot be disconnected from the upheavals, polarization, and ideological hardening that buttressed Latin America's cold war, which was less a battle between superpower proxies than a campaign by the United States, beginning in the early twentieth century, to suppress insurgent challenges to various forms of social, political, and economic exclusion and inequality (Grandin and Joseph 2010). Grandin (2004) argues persuasively that U.S.-backed counterinsurgent violence in Latin America dismantled capacious forms of democracy that prevailed in the 1940s and replaced them with narrower, restricted democracies defined in terms of personal freedom, rather than social security. Several scholars have explored how cold war terror paved the way for neoliberalism through the repression of demands for change, the dismantling of organizations that channeled popular calls for justice, and the replacement of collective movements for social change with individual survival strategies.

A number of analysts, for example, demonstrate how General Augusto Pinochet's assault on Chilean labor unions and shantytown activists disarticulated resistance to his dictatorship and terrorized working people into passivity, enabling the regime to enact neoliberal labor policies detrimental to worker interests (C. Schneider 1995; Winn 2004). In Guatemala, Deborah Levenson-Estrada (1994) examines how the clash between Coca-Cola workers, who wanted to form a union, and the intransigence of management and the Guatemalan state generated brutal military repression. She also documents how Guatemala's genocidal war and its aftermath transformed relatively benign youth gangs into violence-obsessed groups focused on drug consumption and killing each other (Levenson 2013). Elsewhere in Colombia, Forrest Hylton

(2010) analyzes the "refeudalization" of social relations in the city of Medellín as the outgrowth of economic liberalization and the paramilitary repression, and Aviva Chomsky (2008) describes how political violence suppressed labor protests in the Urabá banana zone and enabled banana growers to force former peasants, previously displaced from their lands, to labor under appalling conditions on the plantations. Although the intensity of the violence that accompanied neoliberal restructuring across Latin America varied, repression was particularly severe in those places where the organized opposition of peasants, workers, indigenous, and students resisted the rollback of hard-won rights and opposed the handover of fertile, mineral-rich lands to foreign corporations and domestic elites.

David Harvey (2005) suggests that neoliberalism is a political project, one designed to re-create the conditions for capital accumulation and to sustain or restore the wealth and power of elites. This project has been a particularly sanguinary affair in Barrancabermeja. Nowadays, there is no common memory of the past that can help working people better understand the present and get their arms around the future. A durable disorder has settled over the city. Threats against labor activists, human rights defenders, and leaders of community organizations persist; state prosecutors pursue critics of the status quo on trumped-up charges; and selective assassinations remain a chilling reminder of the consequences of questioning the established order. The violent unraveling of Barrancabermeja's militant working class has diminished a vision of the state as responsible for the welfare—social, economic, and political—of all working people, and the language of class as a form of claims making has been stifled. A limited conception of individual "human rights" has replaced more ambitious dreams of social transformation. More generally, political terror has led to the atrophy of working-class consciousness and solidarity, while individual rights and actions have become the new, narrower political horizon for working people in Barrancabermeja. This reconceptualization of self and solidarity is what Grandin (2010) identifies as the key victory of cold war, counterinsurgent terror, and the basic requirement for the neoliberal regimes that followed in its wake.

Human rights appealed to a moral vision of a global community that was not hemmed in by any political system or repressive dictator. It represented a form of internationalism that replaced older internationalist utopias, such as anticolonialism and communism, which em-

phasized collective self-determination and national sovereignty over individual freedom, and which underscored the importance of the state, rather than the supremacy of international law (Moyn 2010). The liberal concept of human rights, with its emphasis on the individual, was not central to leftist traditions in Barrancabermeja, and many activists once criticized it for failing to address the main reasons of social conflict. By the time of my fieldwork, human rights acompañamiento had become *the* form of international solidarity, one that strove less to connect popular struggles than to provide a modicum of cover for activists targeted by the state whom the left could not protect. The violent destruction of the left, beginning in the 1980s, moved persecuted people to understand human rights as both an immediate concern and a strategy to generate international support to force the Colombian state to respect its own citizens. Rights-based opposition, however, offered less a vision of a better world than a critique of what was wrong with the present, and the nongovernmental organizations (NGOs) and state-sponsored offices that manifested the institutional configuration of human rights activism could not address the economic marginalization and social fragmentation that deepened under neoliberalism. Because of the overwhelming pressure of the paramilitaries and the state security forces, the practice of human rights never developed beyond a defense of the right to life to rearticulate a collective political project, which was crucial at a time when new, far-right coalitions were making a bid for power.

Human rights claims represented a defensive strategy that emerged when civilian massacres happened with greater frequency and when working-class solidarity in Barrancabermeja was being snuffed out. Although the endless repetition of massacres and the documentation of them could hardly have been more disempowering of working people, human rights activism was the last resort for people desperate to stem the violence raining down from all sides. Human rights became the central concept around which some working people made demands on the official state for justice and accountability (Tate 2007) and struggled to rebuild old and craft new forms of alliance. Human rights discourse emerged as the "language of contention"—that is, a "common language or way of talking about social relationships that sets out the central terms around which and in terms of which contestation and struggle can occur" (Roseberry 1994: 361)—as left political movements and organizations were crushed in Barrancabermeja, and as the insur-

gencies' participation in kidnapping, drug trafficking, and extortion discredited "socialism" as a viable political project. Yet whose rights mattered, and what rights counted? What kind of a political project did the struggle for human rights represent? *A Century of Violence in a Red City* takes up these questions.

The book is organized in the following manner: chapter 1 examines the creation of Barrancabermeja as a foreign-dominated, oil export enclave over the first half of the twentieth century. It analyzes how contests over the command of space, the control of labor, and the accumulation of capital shaped relationships between a foreign oil company, the Colombian state, and the rural migrants who sought work in the oil fields. It asks how the creation of a foreign-dominated export enclave concentrated power in the allegedly sovereign territory of the nation-state and made the extreme exploitation, domination, and subordination of working people possible. It also asks how the accumulation of working people fueled radical popular struggles that led to the formation of the USO, Colombia's most militant trade union, and that eventually contributed to the demise of the enclave and the nationalization of the oil industry.

Chapter 2 considers how, in the wake of the nationalization of the oil industry and amid the hardening divisions of the cold war, processes of state formation and popular struggle entered a new phase. The institutional state, rather than a foreign corporation, became the target of discontent, and new social movements in alliance with the oil workers' union demanded the provision of public services, as the capitalist modernization of the countryside propelled the accumulation of waged and wage-insecure workers in the city and the emergence of shantytowns on the urban periphery. The "civic strikes" that rocked Barrancabermeja in the 1970s had much in common with earlier labor strikes in which demands for unions, an eight-hour workday, higher wages, and so forth, predominated: both forms of popular protest brought together diverse working people who overcame their differences, built alliances, and rattled the chains of power. Taken together, chapters 1 and 2 lay out the alliances and connections that made and remade class relationships in Barrancabermeja over the early and middle decades of the twentieth century, and they preview what was lost in subsequent years.

Chapters 3 and 4 discuss how counterinsurgent, paramilitary terror unmade Barrancabermeja's working class by rupturing the fabric

of popular solidarity and dispossessing and displacing working people from the late twentieth century to the present. Political violence provided both the preconditions and the bedrock for the expansion of neoliberalism. Chapter 3 considers how the paramilitary takeover of the city created a crisis for working people, one that tore them from their social and institutional moorings and exposed them to political and economic forces beyond their control. It focuses on how impunity, fear, and betrayal shaped working-class disorganization and defeat. Chapter 4 then demonstrates, through the example of the Coca-Cola workers, how political violence and accumulation by dispossession unraveled a relatively privileged and well-organized sector of Barrancabermeja's working class and facilitated the growth of insecure and temporary employment.

Chapter 5 takes up the emergence of a violent new configuration of power in Barrancabermeja, between 2000 and 2006, in which paramilitaries forged a realm of de facto sovereignty that was grounded in the violent repression of labor, the suppression of democratic processes, and the control of illegal activities, especially the cocaine traffic. The paramilitary victory shuttered a vision of the state as the guardian of the public interest and raised questions about where the state was located and who had the legitimate right to rule. The chapter explores how barranqueños were incorporated into new or reconfigured forms of exploitative labor discipline, rent extraction, and political subjugation that characterized the militarized neoliberalism that the paramilitary takeover solidified. It also considers how ordinary people understood "the state" in a context in which the boundaries between paramilitaries and the institutional state and between illegality and legality became blurred.

Chapter 6 analyzes the rise of human rights activism within the context of political terror, working-class setback, and ascendant neoliberalism. It traces the emergence of human rights advocacy from earlier forms of activism and considers how it arose as a new way of making claims on the institutional state. It argues that while human rights activism opened some room for a new politics of rights to develop in a repressive political environment, it was unable to withstand the power aligned against it and remained a defensive strategy that never moved beyond the condemnation of individual acts of terror. This was, in part, because of what the violence had already destroyed: a way of understanding and acting on the world rooted in class identities and orga-

nizations. This chapter argues that what got lost in human rights discourse and activism was this sense of class consciousness and collective action at a time when a resurgent ruling class was tightening its grip on power.

Finally, chapter 7 focuses on the aftermath of counterinsurgency in Barrancabermeja, an unstable moment in which the war continues but by other means. It considers how the dirty war produced an unstable social "order" that rested on a foundation of disorder in which radical uncertainty and continuing violence undermined working people's ability to establish control over their lives. The chapter explores how, in the absence of common memories about the past and disagreement about the causes of persistent violence in the present, working people struggle anew on a fragmented social terrain to rebuild relationships to each other. How, it asks, can men and women create a peaceful coexistence when they are forced to compete with each other for daily survival, and when they hold different memories about the past? By addressing such questions, the chapter draws attention to the multitude of contemporary claims and concerns that shape the ongoing making and unmaking of class.

ONE

BLACK GOLD,

MILITANT LABOR

. . .

Nowadays, in Colombia, when the topic of Barrancabermeja arises in conversation, people often raise their eyebrows and inhale deeply, or they purse their lips and shake their heads. While their expressions reflect a range of emotions—horror, dismay, disgust, and sometimes approval—about the dirty war that scarred the city, Barranca has always provoked strong passions among Colombians. Some have viewed it as a symbol of working-class resistance to foreign imperialism; others have insisted that it is a hotbed of communism, moral decay, and unruliness, a place where "the dangerous classes" run amok. The roots of these contradictory images lie in Barranca's birth as a foreign-dominated oil export enclave and the organization of a powerful working class that was not averse to rattling the chains of power.

In this chapter, I reconstruct a history of the Barrancabermeja labor movement in the early twentieth century based on secondary sources and the recollections of residents I interviewed at the time of fieldwork. My analysis begins to lay out the importance of class as an analytic category that captures the violence that gives form to social relations under capitalism. It highlights the fluid, highly contingent "making" of class, a process in which diverse working people built alliances across different categories of work (industrial, agricultural, commerce), established institutions to voice their concerns, and attempted to create scale-spanning solidarities, and in which a foreign oil company and the Colombian state tried to disrupt and marginalize these nascent connections and organizational forms. My perspective runs counter to prevailing views of the working class as a static category associated with industrial proletarians. It does so by placing politics at the center of analysis and focusing on the tendency of power-laden social relationships to cohere around the pursuit of capital accumulation on the one hand and making a living on the other hand. It also emphasizes the violence, disruptions, and contests over the control of space associated with class formation. In this way, we can better grasp the level of solidarity and the organizational strength achieved by working people in early twentieth-century Barrancabermeja and appreciate the scale of their defeat at the end of the century, when the intensification of paramilitary violence and the rise of neoliberalism "unmade" class and obliged people to find new ways to reestablish what had been lost.

In the early twentieth century, after the invention of the internal combustion engine and the airplane, oil permanently transformed the way humankind lived; the mass production of gasoline-powered automobiles alone redesigned the physical geography of cities. Although most of the oil came from the United States and Europe, a number of powerful corporations began to scour the planet for the newly precious commodity, and the Middle East and several Latin American countries, including Mexico, Venezuela, and Colombia, attracted their attention. In Latin America, the oil firms leveraged states for territory, often in sparsely settled, weakly regulated frontier regions with vulnerable populations. They mobilized enormous political resources and economic clout to concentrate capital, technology, management, and labor within spaces carved from the national territories of sovereign states, where they created new imperial connections that linked "foreign" enclaves to corporate headquarters in North America and Europe. They then set about disciplining emergent working classes, in part by localizing class relations within the confines of export-oriented zones of commodity production over which they strove to exercise complete control. The importance of the oil giants lay less in the total number of people they employed than in the strategic position they occupied in the global economy and in their ability to produce space, control labor, and command power.

In Colombia, with the exception of the United Fruit–dominated banana enclave on the Caribbean coast, immortalized in Gabriel García Márquez's *One Hundred Years of Solitude*, Barrancabermeja was the country's most important export enclave. It was forged at the nexus of uneven relationships of social, political, and economic power between the most powerful corporation of the time—the Rockefeller-owned Standard Oil Company of New Jersey and its subsidiary, the TROCO—Colombian state officials, regional elites based in Bucaramanga, the provincial capital, and diverse working people who migrated to Barrancabermeja and the Middle Magdalena region. To the extent that the Middle Magdalena registered at all on the compasses of early twentieth-century corporate managers and urban Colombians, it was as a "wild," "uncivilized" place where the institutions of the central state barely reached. Corporate and national elites viewed indigenous peoples and mestizo peasants who inhabited the riverbanks as obstacles to the advancement of "civilization" and did not consider their various livelihood strategies "work," which they understood as the production of commodities for profit by human laborers under their control (Larson 2004). The Middle Magdalena never lost its stigma as a turbulent, ungovernable region with an ambiguous relationship to the institutions of the central state. This infamy, in turn, marked labor struggles, which expanded at times into battles over membership in the nation and the meaning of national sovereignty.

Nowadays, the region is generally understood to encompass parts of five provinces—Santander, Antioquia, Boyacá, Bolívar, and César—that border the Magdalena River. Stretching along the riverbank for 340 kilometers, from Puerto Nare in the south to Rio Viejo in the north, the Middle Magdalena region sits in a torrid valley between two spectacular mountain ranges. Barrancabermeja today is its most important commercial center, with a population of some 350,000 people. Small boats called *chalupas* and motorized canoes carry passengers and goods between Barrancabermeja and other river ports, and a recently modernized airport accommodates travelers from much farther afield. Still visited by foreign oil engineers and supervisors, the city is home to Colombia's largest refinery, which is now owned by the Colombian state and processes approximately 70 percent of Colombian crude oil. A two-hundred-foot flare burns above the refinery, and a wire statue of Jesus Christ—*el Cristo petrolero*—commissioned by the state-owned oil company and inaugurated in 1995, rises with outstretched arms from a contaminated lagoon. On certain days, a thick, sulfurous odor spreads across the commercial district and hangs in the air like a noxious belch, while at night, the grunts and bangs emitted from the refinery's tangled intestines of metal pipes float across the city.

Barrancabermeja's emergence as a corporate-controlled oil export zone raises questions about how power operates in and through long

MAP 1.1 Map of Colombia.

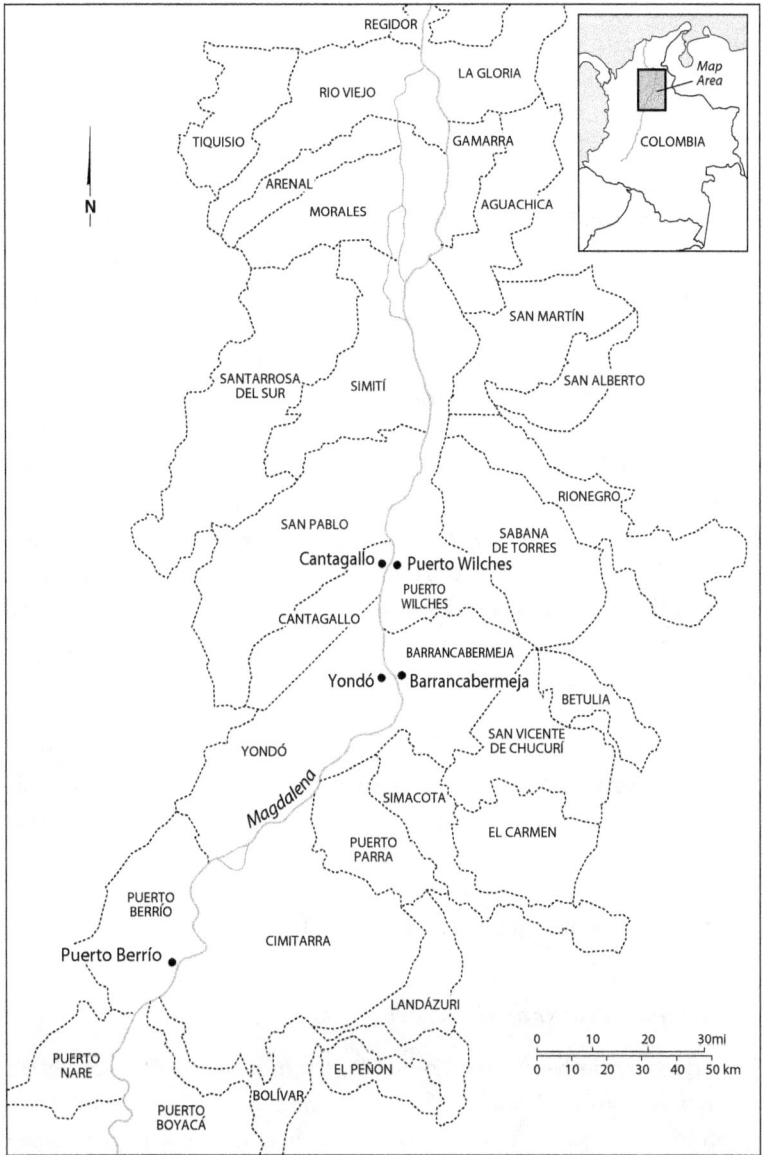

MAP 1.2 Map of the Middle Magdalena.

distance connections and how these connections transform social relationships and societies. It also poses tricky questions about national sovereignty. How, for example, does the creation of export-oriented enclaves concentrate power in the allegedly sovereign territory of the nation-state and make the extreme foreign exploitation, domination, and subordination of working people possible? How, too, does the accumulation of labor in these "strategic hamlets" of empire (see Kramer 2011: 1356) fuel radical popular struggles? This chapter examines the tense dialectic between corporate control and working-class formation and resistance that shaped the growth of the enclave and its ultimate demise over an approximately forty-year period from 1920 to 1960.

The chapter first explores the corporate effort to control space and concentrate labor in ways that allowed it to take on state-like characteristics in a frontier region and regulate the lives of people in the emergent enclave. It then considers how a heterogeneous group of working people—peasants, oil workers, and merchants—crafted new relationships to each other and created a militant political culture that enabled them to push back against the overweening power of the oil company and demand that the institutional state mediate conflicts with the corporation and better control the exploitation of natural resources. Finally, the chapter examines how popular struggles eventually contributed to the demise of the enclave and the nationalization of the oil industry. It demonstrates that processes of state and class formation involved intense conflicts over geography and capital accumulation, as well as the social relations and organizational forms through which working people came to understand and articulate their relationships to the oil company and the institutional state.

The Domestic Politics of a Foreign Enclave

In early twentieth-century Colombia, the notion of the monolithic state that regulated social life and monopolized violence within a given territory was less a reality than a claim asserted by Bogotá-based government officials. Colombia was a fragmented country of regions divided by high mountain ranges, turbulent rivers, and dense tropical forests. Highland elites were divided between the Liberal and Conservative Parties and sat atop regional social hierarchies, where they competed with each other to control national politics and the patronage and wealth-making possibilities that flowed from them. These interparty rivalries generated constant intrigue, unrest, and partisan hatreds. Even though the victors of political struggles acted in the name of the state, they could neither exercise direct control over the entire national territory nor monitor the population in a consistent manner, and they viewed the interior tropical forests, eastern plains, and Pacific and Caribbean coastal regions as ungovernable territories where Afro-Colombians and indigenous peoples existed beyond the pale of civilization.

The end of the Thousand Days War (1899–1902), a conflict between the Liberal Party and the Conservative Party, which the Conservatives won, enabled a tenuous peace to spread across the country that spurred the growth of commodity production. The national government funded infrastructure projects that tied some geographic areas to the world market and better integrated portions of the national territory. Coffee cultivation exploded in the central and western mountains; cattle ranching expanded on the Caribbean coast; sugarcane developed in the Cauca Valley; and foreign-controlled banana and oil enclaves arose on the Caribbean coast and in the Middle Magdalena River valley. The commodity boom and the Conservative government's willingness to finance road, railroad, and port projects gave rise to new spatial configurations of land, labor, and power that accentuated regional differences. Coffee and oil epitomized new configurations of class power and geography and illustrated how the expansion of capitalism was tied to particular regional dynamics.

By the late nineteenth century, coffee production had become Colombia's leading export commodity, spurring the colonization of new lands in the intermountain valleys of the western mountains. In the early twentieth century, settlers and entrepreneurs from Antioquia province propelled an expanding coffee frontier that became associated with the image of a democratic society of entrepreneurial small farmers defined by their Catholicism and "whiteness" (Applebaum 2003). Such racial imagery and cultural claims constituted the bedrock on which the coffee frontier was associated with "civilization" and on which the new commercial and entrepreneurial elites differentiated themselves from other developing frontiers, such as the Middle Magdalena (Arredondo 2005: 45–46). The cultivation and sale of coffee remained mostly in national hands, and the profits underwrote the development of light industry and expanded the domestic market for manufactured goods. Coffee production therefore never provoked the development of strong anti-imperialist sentiments as in the oil sector (Bushnell 1993: 169–74), and the social organization of coffee cultivation undermined the formation of the kind of collective solidarity that emerged in the oil zone. Coffee growing was based on family-centered, labor-intensive production arrangements on smallholdings. It was characterized by exceptionally high levels of exploitation, which drove a violent struggle for land among small-scale producers and workers and between them and elites to better their position or to avoid proletarianization. This contest, in turn, did less to foster collective values and challenge the status quo than to promote conservative individualism and strengthen Colombia's paternalist two-party political system, all of which undermined the growth of the Colombian labor movement (Bergquist 1986: 274–75).

Unlike coffee, oil represented the intrusion of foreign capital and the dominance of a North American corporate elite in the nominally national space of Barrancabermeja, and it fired collective struggles stoked by anti-imperialist nationalism. In 1919, Standard Oil's subsidiary, the Tropical Oil Company, received a territorial land grant—the DeMares concession—from the Colombian government to extract petroleum in a region where oil literally oozed from the ground and collected in surface pools. The concession completely surrounded the river port of Barrancabermeja and encompassed over 300,000 hectares, mostly covered in dense tropical forest that measured eighty kilometers long and forty kilometers wide. The TROCO operated only nominally under the jurisdiction of the Colombian government, which arrogated virtual sovereignty to it to pump oil, mobilize a labor force, and organize social life in and around Barrancabermeja. The subsequent development of the oil enclave was tied to the construction of roads and pipelines and the expansion of fluvial transportation that integrated the oil zone more tightly with world markets and the corporation's North American headquarters than with Colombia.

The rise of the enclave on the smooth surface of national sovereignty blurred the distinctions between the "foreign" and the "domestic," as the TROCO, with its infrastructure, technology, and capacity to concentrate a huge population of migrant workers, became a powerful actor in a sparsely populated region, where regional elites hoped that the modernizing impulse of market relations would transform the allegedly slothful ways of dark-skinned people who lived beyond the frontier of modernity. While it assumed some of the regulatory characteristics of a state, the TROCO never intended to replace the institutional Colombian state. The company's administrators recognized the importance of working with government officials, who saw the advent of foreign corporations as the harbinger of national "progress."[1] They understood that the institutional state remained the best way for them to secure the social, juridical, and administrative order that the TROCO needed to extract oil effectively and efficiently. In 1922, for example, the TROCO pressured state officials to make Barrancabermeja an independent municipality, even though the port town and its hinterland had neither the population nor the historical importance to meet the requirements for independent status. Part of the agreement to create a new, self-governing locality included the use of 5 percent of the TROCO royalties to finance services and infrastructure and to support the salaries of municipal officials.[2] Yet because the TROCO had constructed Barranca as a base of operations for oil extraction and refining and therefore owned most of the utilities, infrastructure, and services, the royalties were simply returning to corporate hands, and the new municipality quickly became dependent on the company for its budget (García 2006: 262; van Isschot 2015: 53–54).

The creation of corporate space through the crafting of a new municipality was key to solidifying TROCO power. Mayors served at the discretion of the company. According to a local Liberal Party member, "It was enough for the TROCO manager to call the governor of Santander and tell him to change the mayor, and the mayor was changed. . . . The Tropical was untouchable" (qtd. in Archila 1978: 63). Similarly, the institutional state provided the police and military forces—national, departmental, and municipal—that the corporation required to ensure labor peace in the enclave, a practice that made Barranca, from its inception, one of the most militarized towns in Colombia. In exchange, company watchmen, labor inspectors, and medical officials adopted hiring policies that favored the party in power (Roldán 2002: 117–18). The "boundedness" of the enclave was therefore shaped at the junction of wider networks of state and corporate power.[3]

The TROCO was the first and largest oil corporation to operate in the Middle Magdalena, where its production took off in the early 1920s, tripled between 1924 and 1925, and then increased another eightfold in 1926, after seventy-four new wells came online and the completion of a pipeline to the Caribbean coast enabled the company to ship oil abroad (Gibb and Knowlton 1956). The Standard Oil Company controlled this business from beginning to end. While the TROCO managed the drilling, another Standard Oil subsidiary (the Andian National Corporation) was charged with transporting the petroleum to the Caribbean coast and beyond, and still another subsidiary (Imperial Oil) refined the crude in Montreal. In an attempt to avoid charges of U.S. imperialism, all of these firms were registered in Canada. The TROCO did not act alone in the Middle Magdalena. Over the first half of the twentieth century, the British Lobitos Oil Field Company began oil explorations close to the nearby town of San Vicente de Chucurí; a couple of hours upstream, the Texas Oil Company extracted crude from a 127,000-hectare concession close to Puerto Boyacá; and across the river in the hamlet of Yondó, the Royal Dutch Shell corporation acquired a concession, in the 1930s, that encompassed 146,000 hectares. The concessions made Colombia a global player in the burgeoning oil industry, rivaling Mexico and Venezuela in the early twentieth century (Palacios 2006: 86).

The TROCO and the other oil companies did not begin operations on a blank slate. In the late nineteenth and early twentieth centuries, rapacious violence against indigenous peoples paved the way for the advent of the oil men. Fueled by metropolitan views of the frontier as geographically and temporally distant—an "empty space"—the hunting and killing of indigenous peoples was a widespread practice on Colombia's expanding internal frontiers (Bjork-James 2015). As early as the mid-nineteenth century, a boom in forest products—chinchona bark, palm nuts, rubber, and wood-based dyes—had attracted entrepreneurs and itinerant workers to the region and brought them into conflict with the indigenous Yariguíes. Entrepreneurs got hold of indigenous lands through the concession of *baldíos*—nominally uninhabited state lands—by the state, and immigrant workers, assigned to the construction of access roads through the forest, clashed with the Yariguíes. By the early twentieth century, on the eve of the oil boom, the Yariguíes had been mostly eliminated—either massacred, forcibly displaced, or relocated to Catholic Church–controlled settlements, where priests taught them Spanish and religion and sought to assimilate them. The physical disorganization and annihilation of the Yariguíes opened the door for immigrant workers and defeated Liberal soldiers, following the end of the Thousand Days War, to establish small villages along the banks of the Magdalena and its tributaries. The dense forest provided natural protection, and the availability of nominally unclaimed state lands offered the possibility of developing a livelihood (van Isschot 2015; Vega, Núñez, and Pereira 2009: 46–58).

The production of dry wood to fuel the steamboats that plied the long, navigable stretch of river between the Caribbean port of Barranquilla and the inland town of Honda set off a period of indiscriminate deforestation in the nineteenth century, and then the advent of the oil industry changed the Middle Magdalena forever. Petroleum exploration and production initiated an assault on the environment from which it never recovered. The oil companies dumped contaminants into the river and spewed sulfurous fumes into the air; they consumed more wood for the construction of houses and work encampments; and they spilled and leaked oil into the rivers, springs, and swampy marshlands. Oil fires became a new and terrifying hazard. As in Mexico and Venezuela, the oil men set in motion processes of migration, dispossession, proletarianization, and urbanization and a shift in land tenure arrangements unprecedented in regional history.[4]

Controlling Space and Concentrating Labor

The TROCO established its power in Barrancabermeja through the creation and control of space and the rigid regimentation of the lives of working people within the enclave. Race, gender, region, and national origin were key coordinates that guided how the TROCO regulated social life and organized its labor force. Yet corporate officials quickly discovered that their hands were not free to shape the enclave any way they chose. The concentration of thousands of migrants within the enclave and the exploitation of them generated tensions between the corporation's desire for control and working people's search for better, more comfortable lives. These tensions played out in the oil fields and in the daily lives of working people.

The corporation's early hiring policies reflected prevailing racist sentiments among company managers. During the initial phase of clearing forest, building roads, constructing buildings, and laying oil pipelines, the TROCO turned to men who lived in the area to fulfill its labor needs. These men, described as "a racial-lowlands mixture," were subsequently deemed unsatisfactory because they were "unaccustomed to the discipline of regular labor" (Gibb and Knowlton 1956: 374). As labor requirements intensified, the company sent contractors on recruiting missions to the predominantly Afro-Colombian Caribbean coastal provinces and the Antioquian highlands, where lighter-skinned individuals were considered "more robust of body and keen of mind" than the local population (Gibb and Knowlton 1956: 374). It also recruited West Indian workers known as *yumecas*. The West Indians' ability to speak English, their education within a colonial British system, and their previous work experience in the Panama Canal Zone or with Standard Oil operations elsewhere, such as Venezuela, made them attractive workers. In the opinion of company managers, the Caribbean contract laborers understood and accepted orders and were less likely to join labor unions. They filled intermediate positions in clerical and mechanical work between the Colombian labor force and the North American supervisors and drillers. Yet Colombian workers perceived them as part of the corporate elite because of their superior treatment and command of English (Vega 2002: 213–14), and, along with other sectors of Colombian society, some feared that the presence of West Indians would lead to racial contamination. On at least one occasion, for example, the local police chief opposed the company's plans to import a sizable contingent of Caribbean laborers because of worries about racial defilement (Archila 1978: 106–7; Valbuena 1947).[5] Corporate hiring practices, and sometimes even opposition to them, demonstrate how racist assumptions infused the recruitment and organization of a workforce and acted initially to hinder connections among immigrant laborers congregating in Barrancabermeja; it also illustrates what working people themselves had to overcome as they forged identities and alliances and maneuvered for position and power within the enclave's heterogeneous mix of migrant labor.

As the oil industry expanded in the late 1920s, contract labor was increasingly unnecessary. Personal and familial connections became the primary means of acquiring a job, as news of the relatively high wages paid in the oil zone circulated around Colombia, and migrants, who were mostly young, single men, came in droves. Older immigrants immediately incorporated new arrivals into an exhausting ten- to twelve-hour-a-day work regime that extended from Monday through Saturday, and not surprisingly, turnover was high, averaging 30 percent a month in the early years (Gibb and Knowlton 1956). Although some of the migrants came from declining gold mining towns in Antioquia or had moved from job to job in different locations, most of the newcomers shared a past as subsistence producers, and they were unaccustomed to the industrial labor discipline of the oil zone, where the workday began and ended with the blow of a whistle. These newly minted waged workers occupied an unusual position in early twentieth-century Colombia. Like their counterparts in Mexico and Venezuela, they were tied to an advanced capitalist industry that operated in an international arena, but they had grown up in an overwhelmingly rural society that had little connection to the oil industry and that moved to the rhythms of the agricultural cycle (Santiago 2006; Tinker Salas 2009).

Controlling the migrants posed a challenge for the oil company, whose expansionist and monopolistic ambitions clashed with the subsistence requirements of its workforce. Many workers combined wage labor in the oil fields with small-scale agricultural production on plots of public land as a means to offset the high cost of living in the enclave. The oil company claimed these lands, and even though it was not interested in agricultural production, it wanted to control access to the subsoil to ensure its right to the petroleum that lay beneath the surface. By monopolizing access to land, the TROCO also hoped to create a supply of local workers with no other means of survival but work in the oil fields. Resolving land disputes was a complicated matter because there was much uncertainty about the distinction between public and private lands, especially in frontier regions like the Middle Magdalena where settlers typically did not hold title to their properties but claimed rights through occupation and use (LeGrand 1986). The uncertainty arose, in part, from the government's own policies. On the one hand, the Colombian government supported the land claims of settlers in frontier zones because it sought to divert agrarian tensions from more populated regions of the country and build a class of small, rural proprietors in areas where the institutional presence of the state was weak. On the other hand, it had granted an enormous concession to the TROCO and recognized the company's right to exploit the land in areas where peasants had settled. Not surprisingly, when the provincial government had to choose whom to support, it sided with the TROCO and assigned more police to the enclave (Vega, Núñez, and Pereira 2009).

The TROCO, like other oil companies in the Middle Magdalena, attempted to construct sovereignty and regulate social life within its domain by issuing passes to workers and those settlers whose rights it recognized, granting them a form of pseudocitizenship, and then persecuting those who did not pass its test. Pedro Lozado, who grew up on the Texas Oil Company's concession near the river port of Puerto Boyacá, vented his annoyance at foreigners to me one day as we chatted in his home in Barrancabermeja, some sixty years after the oil company displaced his family. "We needed permission from foreigners, even though we were Colombians, to travel in the territory," Lozada recalled.[6] "It [the permit] was a little piece of cardboard—like an identity card—that carried the signature of the company manager and the commander of the army battalion. . . . If you didn't have this *pase* [pass]—they called it a pase—they made problems for you."[7] Similarly, in the Shell Oil Company's enclave of Yondó, across the river from Barrancabermeja, company passes had to be renewed every two months. One settler described the uncertainty of life on Shell's concession for those not approved by the company: "It was prohibited to cut trees or to prepare a field for cultivation because right there they would grab you and throw you in jail. There were personnel from the company who patrolled the forest and whoever they caught working [the land], they threw him off. . . . The forest guards went and brought the law to take the people away. They went and informed that '[people] are cutting forest in such a place' and the army and the police came and kicked you out" (qtd. in Murillo 1994: 190). And a Barrancabermeja resident, who disputed the TROCO's land claim, described the corporate vigilance in El Centro, the locus of oil operations in the municipality of Barrancabermeja: "The lands in El Centro were public [*baldíos*] . . . [but] the company, when it belonged to the gringos, didn't permit settlers. For example, you arrived at El Centro and they gave you a permit for a certain amount of time. If you didn't get work, they would not let you stay any longer" (qtd. in Archila 1978: 60). Like passports, the permits determined who could enter the territory over which the TROCO claimed sovereign rights and how long they could remain, and they operated hand in hand with rigid forms of spatial segregation.

In the early twentieth century, segregation was the norm in U.S.-based oil camps, and Barrancabermeja also developed clear spatial coordinates based on deep class, race, and national divisions. As a rising wave of impoverished immigrants crashed over the enclave, the company strove mightily to separate the unwashed masses from a small group of company officials, supervisors, and their families, and two distinct urban centers arose: El Centro and Infantas, where the oil was pumped, and Barrancabermeja, the municipal headquarters and location of the refinery. El Centro and Infantas, located twenty kilometers from the port town, contained a small, transient group of white U.S. and Canadian oil company managers, technicians, and their family members who lived in the *barrio staff* (staff neighborhood). The barrio staff was a clean, quiet redoubt that contained comfortable North American–style brick homes surrounded by shaded lawns. It was a place where foreign personnel found relief from the tropical heat in swimming pools and under covered verandas and enjoyed an array of services, including a hospital, a golf course, and a variety of sports facilities for their exclusive use. Fences separated the gilded ghettos of white, foreign personnel from impoverished, working-class encampments that grew up adjacent to them. In the work camps, basic services were nonexistent, and malaria, yellow fever, and intestinal disorders were pervasive. Rafael Nuñez described the residential layout: "There was an encampment that they called the *'yumecas'* camp, and another encampment where the common worker lived. And another encampment for the office workers. So we had segregation" (qtd. in Archila 1978: 45–46).

A segregated train connected El Centro and Infantas to Barrancabermeja, which was a collection of rudimentary huts, brothels, bars, and a few hotels in the 1920s. Although most of the oil workers lived in El Centro, more began to reside in the port after the opening of the refinery in 1926. Barrancabermeja also had a small fenced-in compound for foreign corporate personnel. The fences symbolized the hardening of race, class, and national boundaries that were dividing the enclave, which had no public services. The municipal government was unable to accommodate the health and housing needs of a growing population, which surged from nineteen hundred inhabitants in 1914 to more than twelve thousand in 1927, when Barrancabermeja acquired the largest concentration of urban proletarians in Colombia (Archila 1978: 44). Half of the urban residents worked for the TROCO, while most of the rest of the population was dependent on it in one way or another.

As the TROCO controlled social life through new forms of segregation, it also tried to exclude merchants from the enclave in order to monopolize commerce. The accumulation of labor in the municipality of Barrancabermeja had created a consumer market that stimulated new tastes and desires, which a multinational group of Syrian, Turkish, Palestinian, and Colombian merchants wanted to nourish with a range of foreign and domestic goods. Independent merchants developed wide networks of customers that extended into rural villages, and they made money from the small portion of oil wealth that trickled down to workers in the form of wages. One oil worker explained that it was possible to acquire a variety of exotic commodities: "Everyone here had clothing that was unavailable in the country: rubber ponchos . . . also bicycles, that's to say a range of things that were unknown. They drank whiskey, smoked American cigarettes, [sipped] champagne, everything that American civilization imported" (qtd. in Archila 1978: 61). Yet the merchants had to contend with the hostility of the TROCO, which, in the 1920s, operated company stores that sold goods to a captive work-force and controlled commerce well into the 1950s. Not surprisingly, relations between the retailers and the company were strained.

Amid the dance of consumer goods, sex was coveted more than any other commodity, and controlling workers' access to it formed another piece of the corporation's broader strategy to manage the lives of work-ing people. The high concentration of single men with biweekly pay-checks and few diversions created a market for sex workers, who came from around Colombia, the Caribbean, and Europe. Sexual fantasies based on the supposed exoticism and amorous qualities attributed to women of particular nationalities, races, and regional backgrounds were nurtured in the enclave, and when men returned from the work camps on Saturday night, the bars and brothels of the city came alive. Men and women drank, danced, fought, and had sex, as the oil workers escaped, albeit momentarily, from the repressive hierarchies of the oil fields, and it was not uncommon for long-term relationships to de-velop between them and the enclave's sex workers. Barrancabermeja thus acquired a special place in the imaginaries of corporate managers and governing elites, who viewed its plebeian, mixed-race population as promiscuous and ungovernable. The city became famous for *putas, plata, y petróleo* (whores, money, and oil), an identification that tended to associate all working women in the enclave with prostitution and provided the grist for several novels about the city (see Álvarez 1983; Jaramillo 1934; Restrepo 1999).

Colombian elites and foreign oil company managers created an as-sociation between the sex trade and the moral degeneracy and undisci-plined behavior that distinguished the Afro-Colombian and mestizo working class for them, and the TROCO's medical department initially adopted a punitive approach to employees who contracted vene-real disease. Although management allowed doctors to care for sick workers who were willing to pay for treatment, it docked the pay of absent workers with venereal disease and required them to pay a ten-dollar-a-day fee for hospitalization. When rates of infection increased, rather than decreased, the medical department reversed this policy and treated all sick workers equally, but to do so, it had to contend with strong arguments from within the company that the new dispensation would simply encourage men to go out and contract the illness (Gibb and Knowlton 1956). To improve the health and rectify the morals of a labor force viewed as degenerate, the TROCO and Royal Dutch Shell tried to control the time workers spent in Barrancabermeja. The TROCO restricted the workers of El Centro to Saturday night through Sunday morning. On the other side of the Magdalena, Shell limited its employees to Wednesday after work until early Thursday morning and Saturday until Sunday night, and it fired those who contravened this policy (Murillo 1994).

In contrast to the industrializing, highland city of Medellín, which *Life* magazine dubbed a "capitalist paradise" in 1947 (Farnsworth-Alvear 2000: 39), class conflict in Barrancabermeja was pervasive, raw, and violent. Unlike Medellín, with its conservative, Catholic elite who related to subalterns through ties of deference, clientelism, and religious moralism (Farnsworth-Alvear 2000), there was no national bourgeoisie that wielded moral authority and enmeshed working people in relationships of submission and obedience. An incipient elite of doctors, merchants, and lawyers had still not distinguished itself from workers, and a self-described group of notable families (*familias decentes*), so prominent in other Colombian cities, did not exist (Archila 1978: 153). Moreover, the Catholic Church exerted little influence over workers and peasants because it had ignored the largely Afro-Colombian and mestizo population of the Middle Magdalena and was therefore unable to broker conflicts effectively. In such a context, the TROCO field staff had difficulty developing cross-class relationships of respect and authority with workers. A relatively small, transient group of North American managers and supervisors translated oil company policy into daily practices, but these professionals and their families were unfamiliar with the cultural practices and social mores of Colombian workers. They were cosseted foreigners tied to a wealthy corporation that working people increasingly described as "imperialist." It is therefore not surprising that working people — oil workers, merchants, peasants, and sex workers — viewed corporate efforts to regulate their lives as arbitrary and heavy-handed.

Barrancabermeja's militant working-class political culture arose from the stark contrast between Colombians engaged in hard, dirty, dangerous work, housed in overcrowded work camps, and controlled by passes and North Americans involved in supervisory positions and sheltered within a residential setting that was unbelievably lavish for those beyond the perimeter. Despite the regional, racial, and gender differences that divided working people, and the different kinds of work—waged labor, subsistence agriculture, small-scale vending—that engaged them, the distinction between Colombians and "gringos" became most important. Oil workers, peasants, sex workers, and petty merchants had no common traditions to draw on as they confronted the harsh realities of the enclave. Because of their diverse backgrounds and, in some cases, prior involvement in a transient labor force that had begun to move around the country, they had to build new relationships and understandings among themselves. Archila argues that the mixing and mingling of migrants from all over the country in the crowded work camps of a foreign corporation and in the bars and brothels of the oil port generated an openness to different ways of life and to new ideas that laid the basis for a cosmopolitan culture to emerge in plebeian Barrancabermeja. As Luis Rojas, an early migrant, told him, "They never rejected me here; people from here were good. Better said, the people here are good because [Barranca] is a very cosmopolitan town. . . . A highlander [or] a Venezuelan comes here and nobody is rejected. Very cosmopolitan. That is why in a strike, nobody says 'you, why are you getting involved here'" (qtd. in Archila 1978: 113). The acknowledgment and taken-for-grantedness of cultural differences and the general absence of kinfolk to perpetuate values and traditions made Barranca an experiment in working-class cosmopolitanism that was unusual in twentieth-century Colombia. In addition, the stark contrast between the power of foreign managers and the relative powerlessness of Colombian workers nurtured forms of solidarity among oil workers and between them and the peasants and petty merchants who came to the enclave.

At the same time, new political discourses—socialism, anarchism, and communism—circulated among working people in the ports along the Magdalena River and provided concepts to understand corporate practices and interpret what was happening. "Imperialism," for example, was not an abstract concept in Colombia's oil and banana enclaves, as it likely was for artisans and peasants in the coffee zone, where the production and marketing of coffee was under national control; it was readily translated into the exploitation, indignities, and forms of exclusion that arose from the omnipresence of the TROCO and that diverse working people experienced in their daily lives. Anti-imperialist nationalism not only arose from authoritarian labor relations and bleak working conditions in the TROCO labor camps. It was also stimulated by the twenty-one-year U.S. occupation of Nicaragua (1912–33) and the 1903 loss of Panama to the United States, which prompted fears that the TROCO would steal Barrancabermeja and claim it as a U.S. possession. A 1928 banana strike and massacre of thousands of workers in the United Fruit Company–dominated enclave on the Atlantic coast further inflamed anti-imperialist sympathies, as the "banana zone" suffered from many of the same social and economic problems as Barrancabermeja. Anti-imperialist nationalism became a central tenet of the USO, Colombia's most powerful union that organized in the 1920s, as workers, peasants, and merchants pushed back against the control and abuse of the foreign corporation.

For all its rebelliousness, however, the political culture created by the first generation of migrants in the enclave was intensely masculine. Work in the oil fields—and the high pay relative to other occupations and other parts of the country—was the purview of men, who expressed their opposition to the TROCO through an aggressive, brash masculinity. A small number of women migrants found less well-remunerated work as cooks, laundresses, and domestic servants and gravitated to the underground economy of bars and brothels. Some of these women acquired a tenuous economic independence from men. Yet the nascent labor movement was mostly silent about these women in their capacity as workers because women's place, it was believed, was in the home with children, even though such a domestic ideal was beyond the reach of most migrant women in Barrancabermeja. For example, when the Communist Party railed against the exploitation of women who labored as "servants" of the TROCO, it was because women's work outside the home was perceived as dividing the proletarian family and leaving children abandoned (see Archila 1991: 118n71). Much more than domestic service or other kinds of female labor, sex work received more attention from a number of intellectuals who wrote novels about early Barrancabermeja, but the authors tended to exoticize prostitution. They said little about how prostitution exposed women to sexual violence, nor did they comment in great detail about the dearth of rights and protections that characterized sex work. In the prolific writings of Gonzalo Buenahora, for example, prostitutes were repeatedly discussed, but less was written about either the conditions in which they worked or the other kinds of female labor in the enclave. Like Buenahora, most novelists and commentators chose to mythologize the relationships between oil workers and prostitutes in which women's unpaid domestic labor subsidized the oil economy.[8]

At this point, it is worth recalling E. P. Thompson's point that classes "do not exist as separate entities, look around, find an enemy class, and then start to struggle" (1978: 149). On the contrary, people find themselves enmeshed in struggles that they cannot avoid, and out of these battles, which are multiple and complex and involve multiple ways of working, a sense of commonality may or may not emerge that defines them as a class. Thompson places great emphasis on the formative quality of struggle, as working people maneuver to build alliances and to define newly forged collectivities in opposition to more powerful groups. His emphasis is always on the making of connections and alliances over time, as well as their periodic undoing (Thompson 1963, 1978). Thompson's perspective helps us understand how a heterogeneous mix of working people in Barrancabermeja crafted new forms of solidarity through struggles to improve working conditions and end the suffocating strictures on daily life imposed by the TROCO. They did so by constructing new relationships that reached across their regional differences, by organizing a powerful union, and by reaching out to political parties and movements—the Partido Socialista Revolucionario (Revolutionary Socialist Party, PSR), the left wing of the Liberal Party, and the national popular movement spearheaded by Jorge Eliécer Gaitán—to channel their demands and to involve the Colombian state more directly in resolving conflicts with the oil company. In the process, they would redefine the spatial configuration of the oil industry in Colombia.

Building Popular Power under Conservative Rule

During the 1920s—the fourth decade of Conservative Party rule in Colombia—economic liberalism and political authoritarianism set the narrow boundaries of Colombian democracy, which allowed men to vote but did not recognize the rights of workers to organize unions and to engage in strikes.[9] Government officials and elites subscribed to the liberal dogma that the state should not intervene in social and economic affairs and left the resolution of labor disputes up to employers and workers. In Barrancabermeja, this policy meant that the TROCO enjoyed a free hand in disciplining and repressing its workforce, but if labor conflicts became too big for the corporation to control alone, they became "public order problems" that then involved the police and the military.

In 1926, the PSR formed independently of Liberal or Conservative Party control. A precursor to the Communist Party of Colombia, the PSR represented the most important expression of popular political organization with a national projection, and its rapid rise put it in competition with the Liberal Party for representation of the nascent labor movement. The PSR's leaders—Raúl Eduardo Mahécha, Mario Cano, Tomás Uríbe, and Ignacio Torres Giraldo—adopted a nationalist stance and a vernacular form of socialism that was flexible and amenable to adopting the popular language of protest. They organized unions and led strikes up and down the Magdalena River, including Barrancabermeja. A lawyer by training, Raúl Eduardo Mahécha first came to Barrancabermeja in 1922, when he offered his services to resolve land and labor disputes with the TROCO and founded the Sociedad Unión Obrera, which operated in clandestinity for several years but eventually became the powerful oil workers union, the USO. Initially composed of peasant settlers whom Mahécha organized through the provision of low-cost basic necessities, the Sociedad Unión Obrera, in 1923, counted three hundred peasants among its members, an early indication of the close ties that were developing between peasant settlers and oil workers in the enclave. Mahécha then reached out to the oil workers through *Vanguardia Obrera*, a newspaper founded by him that denounced the TROCO and the deplorable working conditions and extolled the oil workers as the embodiment of the Colombian nation (Vega 2002: 250). Like *Vanguardia Obrera*, a vibrant alternative media of newspapers and broadsheets played an important part in the circulation of new ideas that became part of Barranca's emergent political culture.

The Sociedad Unión Obrera led two oil strikes in 1924 and 1927. These strikes defied a national ban on union activity, formed part of a larger strike wave that disrupted the oil and banana enclaves, swept through many of the port towns along the Magdalena River in the 1920s, and demonstrated the growing unity and organizational power of diverse working people in the enclave. The strikes confronted the TROCO with a series of worker demands that underscored the miserable conditions in the oil fields and challenged the company's right to organize and control the enclave for the private accumulation of capital. Oil workers sought to ease the intense control that the TROCO exercised over their lives by asserting the right to read the press in the work camps and insisting on the distribution of meals in company facilities "without the presence of the national police, as is the practice, which humiliates Colombian workers and places them in the position of convicts in the work camps" (Vega 2002: 225). They also demanded recognition of their union, wage increases, improvements in food and hygiene, an eight-hour workday, and Sunday as a day of rest. During the strikes, workers carried red flags emblazoned with three 8s that symbolized eight hours of work, eight hours of study, and eight hours of rest (Vega 2002: 226). Workers' demands echoed those set out by labor movements in the industrializing countries of North America and Europe and reflected the concerns of nascent proletarians in Mexican and Venezuelan oil enclave economies (Santiago 2006; Tinker Salas 2009). They expressed an incipient internationalism that transcended the confines of the enclave and identified common problems shared with working people elsewhere.

The strikes did not focus only on winning higher wages and better working conditions, however. Even as former peasants identified themselves as "oil workers" and distinguished themselves from the diverse stew of laboring people who had settled in Barrancabermeja, they projected their growing power in support of petty merchants and peasants and were, in turn, supported by them. Although scholarship and journalistic accounts about the enclave era in Barrancabermeja have focused on the oil workers and ignored other aspects of social life in the enclave, Colombian historians Renán Vega and Mauricio Archila drew on government documents, oral histories, and newspaper reports to show that strikes cast in the language of labor united various groups within the enclave and did not just involve the oil workers. Oil workers supported the right of merchants to operate on company territory and opposed the TROCO's attempt to monopolize trade by excluding merchants from its compound. Some merchants, who depended on workers for business, repaid their solidarity with funds to support the oil strikes. In addition, because many oil workers were themselves semiproletarianized peasants, or recently dispossessed of their lands, backing the land claims of rural cultivators blended easily with demands for better conditions in the oil fields.[10] Peasants previously organized by Mahécha, in turn, provided food—yuca, plantains, squash, and rice—to sustain strikers. Finally, the city's numerous sex workers, who relied on oil workers' salaries, operated soup kitchens in Barrancabermeja during labor protests, when the bordellos closed (Archila 1978, 1991; Vega 2002).

The strikes also demonstrated an early effort to scale up demands and make common cause with working people in the port towns of the Middle Magdalena. When, in 1927, the protests of three thousand oil workers in Barrancabermeja provoked stevedores who shipped the oil and pipeline workers to declare sympathy strikes in other port towns, government officials reacted with alarm, as the protest wave surpassed the boundaries of the enclave. Minister of government Jorge Vélez told the Congress that "in the beginning the strike's only object seemed to be stopping work, but then it acquired a more aggressive disposition . . . and lately its character is frankly riotous and subversive" (Government of Colombia 1927: 4). Because of the strike's "vast projections," the government imposed martial law in Barrancabermeja and four other municipalities along the river. It also expelled Mahécha and other strike leaders from Barrancabermeja and imprisoned them for ninety days in the highland city of Tunja (Government of Colombia 1927). Containing resistance in the enclave, isolating leaders, and disrupting broader popular alliances were all means used by the government to discipline an increasingly restive working class and limit the scale of working-class activism.

The 1927 strikes were followed, in 1929, by the PSR-led uprising known as the Revolution of the Bolsheviks, which united rural peasants and urban workers in the Middle Magdalena towns of San Vicente de Chucurí and Puerto Wilches and the highland coffee center of El Líbano in a revolt that envisioned the "total annihilation of capitalist society" (Sánchez 1976: 72). The peasant-worker alliances at the root of the uprisings differed from the more typically agrarian movements of the time and became a feature of popular struggles in Barrancabermeja during much of the twentieth century. Moreover, the stories and memories of the protagonists enhanced a rebellious, plebeian political culture that was distinguishing itself from both the fenced-in, expatriate bastions of the TROCO, where corporate personnel tried to reproduce a tropical version of the "American way of life," and the Catholic conservatism of Colombian elites, who embraced the church's creation of labor unions as a bulwark against communism.[11]

The labor strikes in the multinational enclaves and the peasant unrest, most powerfully expressed in the Revolution of the Bolsheviks, created a crisis of hegemony for the Conservative Party and energized the revolutionary left. Yet working people in Barrancabermeja were still unable to pull themselves out from under the boot of the TROCO's repressive rule. Calls for an eight-hour workday, which had become widespread in the industrializing countries of the global North, and anti-imperialist nationalism sounded esoteric in the overwhelmingly agrarian societies of Latin America, and they could not serve as a rallying cry beyond the relatively circumscribed zones of multinational control.[12] Yet as Charles Bergquist (1986) argues, the strikes and upheavals of the 1920s pushed the Liberal Party to change its approach to governing and to intervene in the management of "social problems" in order to block an upsurge of more revolutionary demands. With the fall of Conservative rule and the advent of the Liberal Republic (1930–46), working people developed a more favorable view of the institutional state, which they hoped would intervene in the arbitration of conflicts with the TROCO. A new phase of popular struggle developed as working people, who had reached beyond their differences to imagine themselves as Colombians and sometimes as workers (obreros), envisioned a larger role for the Colombian state in the administration of the country's oil wealth and the regulation of working conditions.

The Advent of the Liberal Republic and Gaitanismo

As the Great Depression deepened poverty and raised new questions about laissez-faire capitalism, the advent of the Liberal Republic, marked by four presidential periods from 1930 to 1946, raised hopes about popular political participation and state arbitration of the class conflicts that roiled across Colombia. Working people in Barrancabermeja and along the Magdalena River thought that they had found an ally in the Liberal government, after the 1930 presidential election of Enrique Olaya Herrera ended thirty years of Conservative domination. Olaya Herrera (1930–34) and especially his successor, Alfonso López Pumarejo (1934–38), cultivated working-class support through the promulgation of reforms and a discourse of labor-capital harmony that sought to control and institutionalize the labor movement. Most of the important labor legislation, such as the recognition of labor unions and the right to unionize, the eight-hour workday, and the forty-eight-hour workweek, was enacted during López Pumarejo's Revolution on the March, which aimed to modernize Colombia along the lines of Roosevelt's New Deal. Moreover, Colombia's first national-level labor federation — the Confederación de Trabajadores Colombianos (Confederation of Colombian Workers, CTC) organized with Liberal, Communist, and Socialist participation but quickly confronted government attempts to make it a client of the Liberal Party. The left wing of the Liberal Party took over labor issues and prevented the formation of powerful left-wing parties, like those that emerged in Chile (Safford and Palacios 2002: 288–96). Yet despite its efforts to regulate and tame the labor movement, López's pro-labor policies appealed to workers, while setting off alarms among Conservatives, who did not believe that workers should have rights or be protected by the state. Conservatives asserted that the president's revolution was a front for communists, and even mainstream Liberals worried that López was selling out to leftist causes.

Barrancabermeja was a center of political effervescence in the 1930s. The Middle Magdalena was a bastion of liberalism, but the Partido Comunista de Colombia (Colombian Communist Party, PCC) was founded in 1930 with a majority membership of former PSR militants, and in 1933, labor lawyer Jorge Eliécer Gaitán briefly abandoned the Liberal Party to establish the Unión Izquierda Revolucionaria (Revolutionary Left Union, UNIR), before returning to the Liberal fold in 1935. Although most of the oil workers in El Centro backed the López wing of the Liberal Party, the Communist Party extended its reach into the refinery (Almario 1984), and its members filled some leadership positions in the USO. In addition, Gaitán's condemnation of the 1928 massacre of striking banana workers in the United Fruit Company enclave raised his profile in Barrancabermeja. In practice, little separated rank-and-file communists, the Lopista wing of the Liberal Party, and gaitanistas, despite the ideological battles that often divided party leaders (W. J. Green 2000). According to Rafael Nuñez, a resident of Barrancabermeja at the time, "Here socialism and liberalism were confused. The socialist and the liberal had more in common than the socialist and the conservative. But this was without an understanding of the exact ideas, without a distinction between what was liberalism and what was socialism" (qtd. in Archila 1978: 151).

Many working people in Middle Magdalena believed that López and his administration stood for Colombian sovereignty, even though he never developed a nationalist posture regarding the oil industry, and that he would back their conflicts with the oil companies, shipping firms, and other entrepreneurs (e.g., Arredondo 2005). In 1934, three years after the 1931 promulgation of Law 83, which legalized labor unions, the government recognized the Union Sindical Obrera. The USO, however, continued to operate clandestinely because the TROCO behaved as if national laws did not apply in its concession. Yet a widely shared sense that the government supported oil workers' struggles moved more workers to join the union at a time when the Great Depression obliged the TROCO to make deep cuts in the workforce and reduce the wages of those who remained. Rising unemployment in the enclave created a crisis for small merchants, and it generated frustration among the jobless who often had little to return to in their regions of origin. The worsening economic context, the widespread view that the TROCO exploited its workforce, and the belief that the government was on their side fueled two major strikes, in 1935 and 1938, in which many of the workers' demands focused on the TROCO's refusal to abide by existing national labor laws (Vega, Núñez, and Pereira 2009).

The strikes of the 1930s had mixed, and mostly unfavorable, results. Some five thousand workers struck the TROCO in 1935, and, as in the past, merchants and peasants provided the strikers with money and food, while urban artisans, domestic servants, and urban transporters also allied with the USO. *Barranqueños* organized "union kitchens" to provide free meals to those no longer receiving a wage, and as more than one person observed, even the "muchachas," or prostitutes, came out in solidarity. Julio Morón, who witnessed the strike, described the broad-based support: "The conditions in Barrancabermeja were unique. . . . To speak against the strike was to lose your business or to have to leave Barranca because in that moment . . . nobody could be a scab, the person who was a scab had to keep it to himself inside the company" (qtd. in Vega, Núñez, and Pereira 2009: 195). Such statements reflected the broad legitimacy of popular demands and the sense of empowerment felt at the time.

Although the government did not repress the 1935 strike and forced the TROCO to cede ground to workers for the first time, it denied the USO the right to negotiate directly with the company and sent ministers to develop a solution to the conflict with TROCO representatives for which it then took credit. And when workers struck again in 1938, the national government had completely abandoned the practice of intervening in labor conflicts, while the local and provincial governments actively repressed the strikers, making it easier for the company to manipulate workers through appeals to regional differences and by red-baiting labor leaders. The 1938 strike ended in complete failure with the USO divided and weakened, and it raised questions about future alliances with the Liberal Party. Relying on an elite-dominated political party to support its struggles and represent its concerns beyond the spatial confines of the oil enclave was proving problematic for the USO.

By the 1940s, the hopes inspired by the Liberal Republic were dead. In his second term as president (1942–45), López Pumarejo repealed the eight-hour day, and his successor, Liberal Alfonso Lleras Camargo, crushed a Communist-led port workers' strike in Puerto Berrío and the union, the Federación Nacional del Transporte Marítimo, Fluvial, Portuario y Aéreo (National Federation of Maritime Transport, River, Port and Air, FEDENAL), which was the only Colombian labor federation to have won a closed shop. Elites, too, were less inclined to tolerate labor reforms and launched a new offensive against workers and radical peasants, while the USO entered a period of rebuilding. Despite an unusual level of solidarity and institutional power constructed in Barrancabermeja, working people had been unable to escape the Liberal Party's move to incorporate and declaw the labor movement, and following the defeat of FEDENAL, they were isolated until the rise of *gaitanismo* offered the last and most significant chance to scale up popular demands and claim national power.

After the brief experience of UNIR and an electoral defeat in 1935, Gaitán returned to the Liberal Party and forged a national popular movement on its left flank that crossed class and ethnic lines. Gaitanismo brought a broad swath of peasants, artisans, workers, and sectors of the middle class together in a movement that challenged Colombia's elites and was not afraid to talk about class struggle. The rise of Gaitán—a lawyer, senator, and mayor of Bogotá—within the Liberal Party represented the apogee of the left-Liberal tradition of popular organizing in the twentieth century. As the nation's most famous labor lawyer whose condemnation of the 1928 massacre in the United Fruit Company's banana zone propelled his rise to national prominence, Gaitán advocated the expansion of Liberal social and economic programs, such as agrarian reform, and his juxtaposition of the political nation (*país político*) and the real nation (*país nacional*) referenced the divisions between a wealthy elite and "the people" that divided Colombia (W. J. Green 2000). His independent run for the presidency between 1946 and 1948 carried the hopes of many peasants, artisans, and workers in the Middle Magdalena.

For people like Pedro Lozada, who was coming of age on a rural homestead upriver from Barrancabermeja, Gaitán embodied his dream of a different country. Lozada explained to me in 2007 how "Gaitán launched his presidential campaign around a program that was going to support the oppressed. That is to say poor people. He asked that the worker retain part of what he produced for a business and that peasants should be landowners. The peasant who works the land [should own the land] and not those people who live in Bogotá in a three-story house . . . and don't even visit their haciendas because they have people working on them."[13] Lozada's comments illustrate how concerns about livelihood activities, from controlling the fruits of one's labor to gaining rights to land, connected peasants and workers and found political expression in the movement led by Gaitán, whose ability to unify a broad, mass following and challenge property relations sent shock waves through establishment circles, including the Liberal Party itself.

Gaitanismo, however, was not strong enough to outlast Gaitán, who was shot dead by a gunman outside his Bogotá office on April 9, 1948. The end of gaitanismo forestalled the consolidation of a political movement that connected working people in different parts of the country in united political action. Years later, the death of Gaitán would be widely remembered as the onset of La Violencia, a twelve-year period of extreme conservative reaction to the radical promise of gaitanismo in which thousands of Colombians died. Terror disorganized worker and radical peasant organizations and ensured that class and ethnic conflicts remained within the clientelistic political structures of Colombia's two-party system (Hylton 2006: 39–50).

La Violencia and the Nationalization of the Oil Industry

After Gaitán's assassination, riots devastated Bogota, while more organized and politically significant uprisings broke out in Barrancabermeja and other radical strongholds, where revolutionary juntas and worker-peasant militias briefly seized power (Arredondo 2005; Díaz 1988; Sánchez 1983). Barrancabermeja experienced a brief, ten-day period of "popular power" that came on the heels of a fifty-day strike in which the resurgent USO demanded the nationalization of the Colombian oil industry. Barranqueños declared the Conservative-led central government illegitimate and set up a revolutionary junta composed of communists, liberals, and supporters of Gaitán. The junta named a new mayor — Rafael Rangel, a Liberal Party member influenced by communist ideas (Díaz 1988). Rangel, in turn, authorized workers' militias, armed with weapons seized from the police and the TROCO, to prevent pillage and maintain order, as enraged groups of mourners tried to kill Conservatives and oil company representatives and burn the churches. The oil workers made common cause with the junta by enforcing a ban on alcohol and seizing control of telephone and telegraph communication, the water supply, and the police. They also organized the defense of the city through the distribution of small arms manufactured in the TROCO's workshops, the digging of trenches along the Magdalena River, and the mining of the port (Sánchez 1983: 129–37).

The so-called Barranca Commune, combined with uprisings up and down the Magdalena River, demonstrated the political power and the insurrectional leanings of a broad sector of the population inspired by Gaitán. It united oil workers, residents of Barrancabermeja, and peasant leagues from the Opón River, who had long opposed the TROCO's control over produce markets, against the TROCO, local clerics, and the Conservative-led government in Bogotá. Because of the strength of the labor movement and the predominance of Liberalism in the Middle Magdalena, the government was less able to manipulate partisan divisions, as it did more successfully in areas where Liberal and Conservative networks competed for power (Roldán 2002: 112–14). Yet because popular power was dispersed in export enclaves and a few cities, the insurrections remained isolated occurrences and were quickly suppressed by the military.

The city's experiment with direct democracy came to an end at the negotiating table, after government planes threatened to bomb the city and workers vowed to blow up the refinery in retaliation. Yet after the negotiation of an agreement that allowed the military into the city, the accord was subsequently violated, and the provincial government backed a military crackdown. The repression dismantled popular power and pushed the mayor and others to join forces with newly forming Liberal guerrilla insurgencies that sought to overthrow the Conservative regime and return Colombia to Liberal Party rule (Sánchez 1983: 129–37). The repression also targeted the labor movement. The Conservative government suppressed trade unions through restrictions on protest and freedom of association, and it banned the USO between 1951 and 1957, when a company union was created to replace it; the oil workers would not strike again until 1963. Radical popular movements like the Barranca Commune never became strong enough to transcend regional strongholds, make common cause with opposition movements elsewhere, and create an independent political party to champion the cause of radical nationalism and working-class politics on a national scale. The accumulated power of Colombian oil workers remained rooted in the Middle Magdalena, even as their demands resonated well beyond the oil fields.

At a time when Third World nationalist struggles were rattling the chains of empire and striving to wrest greater national control over the resources exploited by multinational corporations, working people in Barrancabermeja created the conditions "from below" for the nationalization of the oil industry. Decades of popular struggles against the TROCO had created a heterogeneous, contentious working-class political culture that was nationalist, anti-imperialist, and infused with socialist notions of the common good. Through the production, practice, and valuation of solidarity within both the oil enclave and the Middle Magdalena region, working people challenged the TROCO's right to exploit labor, control national resources, and claim a series of rights and privileges for its foreign managers and supervisors that were not available to Colombian workers. In 2009, oil worker Ramón Rangel explained his understanding of the early labor struggles to me: "Maria Cano, Raúl Eduardo Mahécha, and the others created a consciousness that, adding up everything that they overcame, cemented a very solid base [in Barrancabermeja]. That's to say, to defend what is national above everything else. That is one of the legacies that they and the first generation of oil workers left us. . . . Little by little a political consciousness developed that has formed us here in Barranca and that we inherited. We inherited it because the struggle has been permanent, continuous, and without rest."[14]

Oil workers, however, never became the symbol of the Colombian labor movement as they did in Venezuela. Oil production in Colombia was overshadowed by the coffee economy and the conservative individualism associated with it, and demands for labor rights did not always resonate with Colombians elsewhere. Moreover, working people in Barrancabermeja were stigmatized for their rebelliousness, and popular movements, most notably gaitanismo and the Barranca Commune, were disrupted and disorganized. Consequently, Barrancabermeja's radical political culture remained isolated, even though the oil workers' position within a prominent industry, and the alliances they built locally, compelled national elites and foreign corporations to contend with them.

Yet by the late 1930s, the tide had started to turn. Following the Mexican government's 1938 expropriation of foreign oil companies and the nationalization of the oil industry, preventing "another Mexico" became an obsession among corporate executives (Santiago 2006: 8). Colombian industrialists were forced to rethink how they wanted oil produced in Colombia, how they would deal with Colombian oil workers, and how they would safeguard private property, if they wanted to avoid revolutionary upheavals at home (Bucheli 2006). Therefore, when the TROCO's concession expired in 1951, a law established that a new state oil company—ECOPETROL—would acquire it. This legal move soothed elite sensibilities because it avoided the disruptions of expropriation and sidestepped the kind of worker participation in the national oil company that had taken place in Mexico. It also addressed the oft-expressed desire of workers that oil production take place under national control. Although the TROCO did not immediately hand over control of the Barrancabermeja refinery to ECOPETROL, growing nationalism, intensified union activity, and a government search for more export revenue eventually persuaded the TROCO, in 1961, to relent and to cede control of the refinery to the Colombian government. The pillars of the enclave economy were crumbling.

The contests between labor and capital that gave birth to the enclave in the 1920s contributed to its demise in the mid-twentieth century, when power relations and patterns of capital accumulation were remapped. The era of the foreign-dominated export enclave was not ending only in Barrancabermeja; it was in decline everywhere. In Mexico and Venezuela, the governments nationalized the oil industries in 1938 and 1939, respectively. On Colombia's north coast, the United Fruit Company relocated banana production from Santa Marta, where the company had owned land, hired workers, and run plantations since the early twentieth century, to Panama and the Colombian province of Urabá, where it subcontracted production to a provincial elite (Chomsky 2008: 189). The United Fruit Company also pulled up stakes on Ecuador's south coast, where peasants and workers had placed it under siege and contract farming was replacing corporate-owned estates (Striffler 2002).

The creation of ECOPETROL in 1948, the reversion of the TROCO's concession to the Colombian state in 1951, and the nationalization of the refinery in 1961 inaugurated a shift in the relationship between oil workers, other working people in Barrancabermeja, and the Colombian state. Nationalization marked the start of more direct state intervention in the stewardship of the economy through the promotion of import-substitution policies and agricultural modernization (Safford and Palacios 2002), and Barrancabermeja changed from a foreign-dominated enclave economy to a state-run oil town in which workers labored for the state. Although ECOPETROL represented a crowning achievement of decades of popular struggle for many barranqueños, the departure of the TROCO did less to end class conflicts than to shift them to a new register. The expansion of the Colombian state, the intensification of capitalist development in the countryside, the influx of ruined peasants to Barrancabermeja who could not find work in the oil industry, and the narrowing space for political participation amid a deepening cold war reshaped the social geography of political struggle. Chapter 2 explores these processes.

TWO

COLD WAR

CRUCIBLE

. . .

By the middle of the twentieth century, Barrancabermeja had changed from a foreign-dominated export enclave to a "state-run company town," and the creation of ECOPETROL represented the fulfillment of one of the oil workers' principal demands: greater national control over and regulation of Colombia's oil industry.[1] Oil workers had achieved strong workplace bargaining power within an industry vulnerable to strikes and disruptions in the flow of oil, and they had transformed an arbitrary labor system in which foreign supervisors set the terms and conditions of work into a labor regime regulated by the state. Together with a heterogeneous mix of ruined peasants, petty merchants, and socialist labor organizers, oil workers had modified the rules on which contests over capital accumulation and class formation took place in Barrancabermeja. They had done so through the transformation of Barrancabermeja into a center of radical democratic political sensibilities and the organization of a powerful union, the USO.

Yet years of Conservative rule in the aftermath of Gaitán's death and the Barranca Commune had forced them to pay a heavy political price. During the 1950s, the suppression of the USO, the persecution of labor leaders, and the creation of parallel unions tied to the Catholic Church debilitated the labor movement and ruptured Barranca's culture of solidarity, but with the fall of the brief dictatorship of Rojas Pinilla (1953–57), the labor movement inhaled once again and embarked on a process of reorganization. As they emerged from a decade of Conservative Party power and repression, oil workers severed the imposed ties to clerical, parallel unions and began a new strike wave between 1959 and

1964, and a new generation of migrant workers, who clamored for jobs and public services, pushed into the city to join them.

But the ground had already shifted. As the lives of ordinary *barranqueños* unfolded within a city freed from the yoke of corporate domination and Conservative Party rule, the National Front outlawed solidarity strikes in an effort to undermine the reemergence of regional worker solidarity, and it routinely resorted to anticommunism to discredit leaders, workers, and organizations that did not abide by its policies. Moreover, the relationship between rural migrants and the state foundered over issues of urban development, labor rights, and state repression. New hopes, concerns, and dangers emerged that people could not address in exactly the same ways as in the past. Oil workers and migrants discovered that they had to develop new alliances, understandings, and practices in order to advance their claims on the powerful, and over the course of the 1960s and 1970s, they remade their relationships with each other, again.

Urban residents confronted the Colombian state and the national bourgeoisie much more directly than in the days of the TROCO. They did so at a time when the National Front government (1958–74) was pursuing a program of capitalist modernization through import-substitution industrialization that did not open the political arena to greater working-class participation. Brokered in 1958 between the Liberals and the Conservatives, the National Front was an institutional compromise to end La Violencia and establish a stable basis for capitalist development in which the parties divided legislative and high administrative positions equally, and the presidency rotated between Liberals and Conservatives. According to Marco Palacios (2006: 171), it represented "the golden age of gentlemen's agreements between the leadership of the state and the quasi-corporative trade associations" of industrialists, landowners, merchants, and bankers. Spurred by the cold war, National Front governments initiated a limited program of investment in public services that sought to co-opt a growing middle class through a set of policies that expanded and subsidized higher education, broadened access to health care and housing, and responded to pent-up consumer demands. Under the National Front, the public sector expanded, and unions among public sector employees—for example, teachers, health care workers, telecommunications employees—grew between 1959 and 1965 from 5.5 percent to 13.4 percent of the economically active population (Palacios 2006: 179).

Yet because peasants and working people in general had little political power, the National Front was less concerned with supporting small-scale agriculture and food production in the countryside or providing social services to the ruined peasants pouring into urban neighborhoods than with using state policies to incorporate the middle class into an expanded sense of national citizenry. Although it never developed a Keynesian welfare state, its limited public investments and reforms were somewhat successful in broadening the notion of social citizenship and winning a tenuous legitimacy. The National Front also managed to integrate some working-class Colombians into its modernization project through the creation of neighborhood action committees known as *juntas de acción comunal* (JACs), which channeled funds for community development through the creation of clientelistic relationships with the Liberal and Conservative Parties, and which I discuss more in chapter 6. The National Front, however, did not offer a long-term solution to endemic poverty, political marginalization, and enduring violence. By consolidating institutional power in the hands of the ruling class, the National Front reasserted the exclusionary nature of Colombian politics and delegitimized any expression of social conflict. It suppressed memories of La Violencia and continued a well-established pattern of political marginalization in which reformist concerns could only be raised on the left flank of the Liberal Party (Chernick and Jiménez 1993; Palacios 2006).

In Barrancabermeja, tensions between the aspirations of urban migrants and the National Front, as well as the continued repression of the labor movement, shaped urban conflicts in which demands for the provision of public services to poor urban neighborhoods intertwined with those of the increasingly radicalized USO. They periodically erupted into large-scale mobilizations known as "civic strikes" (*paros cívicos*), which brought the city to a standstill and became the archetypal form of protest in the mid-twentieth century.[2] The civic strikes exposed how the National Front's program of capitalist modernization was creating new forms of poverty and wealth, and they revealed the Colombian state's inability to completely pacify working people or incorporate them as fully entitled citizens of the nation.

This chapter examines the remaking of class relations in Barrancabermeja from the era of civic strikes in the 1960s and 1970s to the advent of neoliberalism in the 1990s. During this period, amid the contrapuntal forces of the cold war, longtime residents and new arrivals pushed against the seams of the National Front's political straitjacket and that of successor governments over public services, labor rights, and the organization of political life. The juxtaposition of destitute immigrant neighborhoods and a profitable, state-owned company with its well-paid workforce laid bare the state's role in the production of inequalities and the differential entitlements of citizenship that flowed from them. It also exposed the deepening divide between waged and unwaged workers. Diverse working people found common cause in the insistence that the state live up to its promises of development and modernization. As they constructed new networks, relationships, and organizations to advance their deeply felt concerns, they created a new configuration of class power that challenged the National Front as the sole source of legitimacy and that underscored the inadequacy of static categories, such as formal sector/informal sector or urban/rural for understanding changing class relations. My history of Barrancabermeja in this period demonstrates how diverse working people—peasants, unwaged urban immigrants, and wage laborers—built new alliances that updated earlier forms of class struggle created in the TROCO period. It points to the rising importance of neighborhood-based livelihood struggles and their connections to oil worker protests over working conditions at the point of production, as barranqueños pushed the state to fulfill its promises of modernization, and conflicts over the organization of power and capital accumulation shifted gears.

Mid-twentieth-century capitalist modernization produced a range of new and remade relationships, and in Barrancabermeja, unwaged urban immigrants became more common than oil workers because violence and the expansion of agrarian capitalism destroyed peasant livelihoods and forced ruined rural dwellers to reconstruct their lives in the city. Destitute migrants raise new questions for scholars about the changing experiences of labor in Barrancabermeja and what they mean for processes of class formation. Migrants were not separated from capitalism or from the so-called formal economy, even though they were excluded from many of the rights of citizenship—for example, health care and education—won by oil workers through social struggles with the oil company and taken for granted by elites. Their casual labor as part-time construction workers, domestic servants, itinerant vendors, and petty commodity producers generated value and kept the city running. They also played a key part in popular movements that sought to reclaim some of the wealth produced in Barrancabermeja and to assert their rights as citizens in what had become a state-run company town. This perspective runs counter to scholarly arguments that suggest that unwaged migrants are not "workers," that their lives are shaped by "informality," and that therefore their struggles are politically distinct (e.g., Fischer 2014).

Examining the experiences and the history of differently categorized workers is important as working people began to assess what they had in common and develop a common cause. As they pushed against the exclusionary practice of the National Front, the logic of anticommunism increasingly framed urban militancy within a deepening cold war context, while growing militarization fueled repression and spurred the formation of guerrilla insurgencies that sought to overthrow the state. The polarizing dynamic of popular mobilization and repression generated rising levels of resentment that ignited extreme forms of state and paramilitary terror at the end of the twentieth century. The terror aimed to destroy the left, roll back the gains of working people, and deepen exclusion. It was closely connected to a radicalized alliance of nouveau-riche drug traffickers, the patrician agrarian bourgeoisie, merchants, multinational corporations, and the military that was deeply threatened by the muscular flexing of popular power and that aimed to make the Middle Magdalena more hospitable to capital.

Agrarian Transformation, Urbanization, and the Accumulation of Labor

The contours of popular struggle in Barrancabermeja changed as a new generation of uprooted peasants streamed into the city and doubled the urban population between 1951 and 1964. Driven out of the countryside by violence, the expansion of agrarian capitalism, the erosion of small-scale agriculture, and the failure of the Colombian state to enact significant agrarian reform, the migrants chased hopes of a job with ECOPETROL and dreams of comfortable urban lives. The National Front enacted a modest 1961 agrarian reform law that aimed to palliate the class conflicts unleashed by La Violencia. The reform authorized the expropriation of unproductive estates and their redistribution to peasants who possessed little or no land. It received encouragement from the United States as a means to stamp out the revolutionary fires ignited by the Cuban Revolution of 1959. Yet few estates were broken up. Large landlords fended off calls for land redistribution by modernizing their properties with development assistance from the Alliance for Progress, a social, economic, and military aid program inaugurated by President John F. Kennedy, in 1961, to vaccinate Latin Americans against communism (Bushnell 1993: 234). Credit and technological assistance allowed them to increase productivity. Yet in some areas, it also allowed them to expand at the expense of smallholders, who received less institutional support and were encouraged to migrate to frontier regions and stake out new claims to unsettled state lands (*tierras baldías*), which were far from markets and good roads. As a result, the national share of foodstuffs produced by peasants declined from two-thirds in the 1960s to one-third in 1980 (Chernick and Jiménez 1993).

The agrarian reform was particularly weak in the Middle Magdalena, where the agricultural frontier was closing. Unclaimed state lands were less available than in the past, and lands once colonized by Andean peasants fleeing La Violencia had been purchased or taken over by cattle ranchers and large landowners, who converted them to cotton, rice, and soybean production (Molano 2009: 37; Zamosc 1986: 28) and then employed displaced smallholders as seasonal wage laborers. When peasants received land titles, it was typically to lands that they already occupied. For example, one of the most important land transfers followed the 1967 seizure of some 160,000 hectares that once belonged to the Shell concession, across the river from Barrancabermeja. As ECO-PETROL prepared to nationalize the holding, peasants occupied it and declared the land public property, which the Colombian land reform institute was subsequently pressured to cede to them (Zamosc 1986: 43). Yet this case was exceptional.

Even before the Alliance for Progress provided new impetus for the consolidation of large landholdings, landlords, local government officials, and oil companies in the Middle Magdalena had represented a source of pressure for peasant settlers struggling to carve productive farms from the heavily forested lands, and as early as the 1950s, the PCC had begun to organize peasants as a form of "self-defense." Although best known for organizing self-defense movements in the coffee zones of Tolima and Cundinamarca that became "independent republics" and then bastions of FARC support, the PCC also had considerable influence around the towns of Puerto Berrío and Puerto Boyacá to the south of Barrancabermeja and around Puerto Wilches to the north. The Communist attention to rural smallholders grew out of a vision of radical agrarian democracy, articulated by rural people themselves, that focused on peasant land rights, participation in local organizations, control over the market, freedom from onerous labor obligations, and education and other rights of citizenship (Chernick and Jiménez 1993; Pizarro 1989). For young men like Pedro Lozada, the party changed their lives.

Lozada joined the PCC in 1953, after the Texas Petroleum Company forced his family off the land that his parents had settled in the 1930s. Nearly sixty years' later, he remembered, as if it were yesterday, when the army jailed his father for challenging the multinational's right to the family property. His father was heading to town, he recounted, when soldiers detained him and took him to an army base, where they forced him to sign a rental contract with the corporation. Texas Petroleum had become ever more mired in land conflicts with the growing number of settlers who generally did not recognize the multinational's land claims, and it adopted a strategy in which it offered peasants the option of renting land in the hope of getting them to indirectly accept its right of ownership (C. Medina 1990). Its offers, however, were not always accepted voluntarily. Lozada described how the company's inspector of forests came to the army base bearing the rental papers for his father to sign. "The contract was fictitious," Lozada asserted, "but the company was claiming the land, and there was nothing fictitious about that. The same thing happened to [my father's friend]. We became the company's tenants, rather than owners of the farm [finca]."[3] Soon, however, even this tenuous arrangement collapsed, when a company manager gave his father a nominal fee for the improvements on the property and told him to vacate. The loss of the land broke up Lozada's nuclear family: his brother left to work on an hacienda farther upstream; his father moved to Puerto Berrío; and Lozada moved to a village near Puerto Berrío, where he married and created a livelihood through fishing and seasonal agricultural labor. Neither Pedro, his father, nor his brother would ever possess their own land again, and many years later, Pedro would join a wave of displaced migrants flowing into Barrancabermeja.

The anger and humiliation over the loss of the family land pushed Lozada into a life of politics and spurred a long affiliation with the PCC, which, he explained, "told us that the company had no right to abuse the settlers." The party encouraged peasants not to sign the rental contracts, and according to Lozada, it "began to cut away the spiderwebs" that clouded his understanding of the world. The party taught him "to value people, to support others, to be a humanist, and to understand what social class I belonged to. I didn't know that Colombia was divided into social classes and that one powerful class—the rich—imposed its will on the rest of the people . . . so, the poor—peasants, workers, and fishermen—are the majority and the day that they organize, we can take power away from the oligarchy and form a country where there are equal conditions for everyone. . . . And it's true, with time that is what we started to do."[4] Indeed, the PCC offered Lozada and other peasant settlers a form of solidarity that rejected the notion of inequality as God-given and downplayed the intense partisan hostilities that divided Liberals and Conservatives at the time. "They told us, look, the Conservatives kill the Liberals because they are red [the color of the Liberal Party], but the blood of Conservatives is also red," Lozada explained.[5] Through the PCC, Lozada found an alternative to the intimidation and abuse of the oil company and developed a stronger sense of his own ability to analyze social life, to see beyond the mystifying veil of Catholic orthodoxy and the parochial confines of partisan hatreds, and to act on the world in order to change it. The party also helped him locate his own aspirations within an expanding network of national and international movements and to feel connected to them.[6] "The orientation went over well," Lozada remembered about an early PCC meeting that he attended. "We were already mad . . . and they explained to us why [all of this] was happening. I liked the party and very soon it was everywhere."[7] Although the Communist Party and its cadre of peasant militants could not stem the expansion of agrarian capitalism and the rural-urban migration that were reworking both the countryside and the cities, the enthusiastic support that the party received from Pedro Lozada and other peasants spoke to the government's failed agrarian policies and to the lack of support for the National Front in the countryside.

As peasants migrated to Barrancabermeja, where neither ECOPETROL nor the private sector could provide jobs to everyone who needed one, the PCC backed their struggles to create livable neighborhoods. Migrants settled unoccupied lands on the city's northeastern and southeastern fringes. They did so through large-scale occupations that could involve hundreds of people and that usually took place under cover of darkness. Labeled invasions (*invasiones*) by the state and land reclamations (*recuperaciones de tierra*) by supporters, these settlements were opposed by the municipal government, which on occasion sent security forces to dislodge the immigrant occupiers. A longtime Communist Party activist recalled: "The Communist Party . . . was very strong in the northeast of Barrancabermeja. . . . It had a really good process of community and leadership formation, and it supported the immigrants [*recuperadores de tierra*]. Several neighborhoods grew up with its support, which was aimed at organizing people, legalizing the settlements, and turning them into neighborhoods with basic services and municipal transport."[8] The peasants, fisherfolk, and casual laborers also received some organizational and material support from other political parties, such as the Frente de Izquierda Liberal Auténtica (Front of the Authentic Liberal Left, FILA) and the socialist branch of the Alianza Nacional Popular (National Popular Alliance, ANAPO), which aimed to broaden their constituent bases in Barrancabermeja by appealing to the new arrivals. In addition, the Catholic Church's community outreach program (*pastoral social*) began to address the problems of immigrant neighborhoods through new development projects, sustained engagement with local residents, and pressure on municipal officials. These political parties and the Catholic Church brought immigrants together and became important referent points for them.

As the immigrant shantytowns exploded over the red clay hills and through the ravines that once constituted the city's rural hinterland, wood and bamboo huts were separated from the city center of the refinery, the municipal government, and the USO by a railway line that ran like a sutured scar along what was once Barrancabermeja's eastern boundary. Dusty, unpaved roads turned into quagmires in the rain and became dark at night; streams of black sewage flowed through open ditches; and mosquito-infested marshes were the only source of drinking water, when the Magdalena River dropped below a certain level. The burgeoning warren of makeshift dwellings became known as "the other Barranca," which was eventually connected to the urban center by an elevated bridge that arched over the railway. Much like the TROCO's fence in an earlier era, the bridge symbolized the old and new forms of segregation and inequality in Barrancabermeja.

The state did nothing to alleviate deepening urban segregation. Rather, it aggravated the divisions with the construction, in 1969, of two new neighborhoods for oil workers. Galán and El Parnaso showcased a series of neat, two-story white houses connected to a sewer system, an electrical grid, and a water main. Located near the city center,

FIG. 2.1 ECOPETROL's oil refinery in Barrancabermeja.

they were only a short walk from the municipal stadium and the Club
Infantas, a recreational center with swimming pools, athletic facilities, and meeting rooms created for the exclusive use of ECOPETROL
management, workers, and their families. The ECOPETROL managers
and technicians had already moved into the residences once occupied
by TROCO officials in the former *barrio staff*, and when the company
expanded the refinery in the 1970s, it recruited more midlevel supervisors and engineers to oversee the process. The arrival of the new hires
drove up the price of urban land and expanded a small elite that had
begun to distinguish itself from working people as early as the mid-
1940s, when institutions such as the Hotel Pipatón, the Chamber of
Commerce, the Rotary Club, and the Fishing and Hunt Club were established (Archila 1978: 158–59). For many poor barranqueños, it was becoming increasingly clear that the advent of the state was not living
up to their expectations, as they remained excluded from its largesse.

Ninety percent of Barrancabermeja's economic output came from
ECOPETROL, but the oil company provided employment for only 2 percent of the city's residents (van Isschot 2015) at a time when Colombia
was one of the most rapidly urbanizing countries in Latin America. Immigrants represented 70 percent of the urban population in 1970. They
had come primarily from the Atlantic coast regions, the plains of Bolívar province, Antioquia, and other parts of Santander. Most were poor,
displaced peasants and fisherfolk who either contented themselves

with periodic, temporary jobs with ECOPETROL, if they were lucky, or turned to unremunerative forms of petty commerce, which most did. An ECOPETROL-commissioned study of Barrancabermeja found that the city retained many of the characteristics of an enclave. Very few small and medium-size businesses had emerged to service the oil industry, and according to the report's authors, ECOPETROL functionaries, who often maintained their primary residences in other cities, contributed to a profound apathy about urban problems, especially the lack of basic services and the woeful state of transportation (Contreras 1970: 65). In addition to this indifference, the report noted that "the conflictive fame of the human factor" (the oil workers) aggravated an already "not very positive investment environment" (Contreras 1970: 135).

Worries about the conflictive "human factor" were amplified through the lens of the cold war, which turned anticommunism into a much more lethal ideology. Anticommunism united diverse regional elites, who feared a return of the instability and class warfare of La Violencia, and it justified the use of violence against critics of the status quo. It also bound Colombian elites to sectors of the middle class and tied them to North American and Latin American ruling classes elsewhere, as regional conflicts were absorbed in a global, U.S.-backed, anticommunist crusade (Safford and Palacios 2002). Yet with the exception of cities such as Santiago, Chile, where the Chilean Communist Party's ties to residents and its skilled local leaders played a direct role in the politicization and organization of some shantytowns (C. Schneider 1995), fears of urban radicalism were mostly exaggerated.[9] But they were not misplaced in Barrancabermeja, where the development of new social and political networks in migrant neighborhoods, the looming presence of the USO, and the absence of right-wing political parties or social movements rooted anxieties about communist infiltration and rebellion in firmer soil.

Elite paranoia about the radical inclinations of oil workers coexisted with a profound antirural bias that informed perceptions of peasant immigrants. Although rural prejudices were not new in Colombia, they gained traction at a time when modernization theory placed emphasis on the traditional backwardness of peasants and agrarian economies and located the fount of transformative growth in dynamic, industrial urban sectors, such as the oil industry. Evaluated through traditional/modern or rural/urban analytic categories, migrants and shantytowns exemplified backwardness and traditionalism. Their poverty supposedly arose from the unchanging values, practices, and understandings that peasants brought with them from the countryside. A Ford Foundation technician, for example, wrote about a shantytown (*tugurio*) on the outskirts of Bogotá as follows: "The living setting in the *Barrio* resembles that of the living setting of the poor peasants' *ranchos* and the complex of cultural norms of rancho life have essentially been transposed into the tugurio's urban setting and have been found inoperable." He concluded that "the peasant's dignity is buried in urban poverty's abyss" (Schulman 1967: 191). Such prejudicial views of the peasantry informed the remedies that the Ford Foundation and other U.S. development organizations prescribed for Colombia, remedies that focused less on ending economic inequality than on attacking the alleged backwardness of peasant culture.

Visions of rural backwardness and urban breakdown perceived through the lenses of static dichotomies could not account for the fluidity of changing class relationships. The families of many poor, urban working people had always been dependent on family members living in rural villages, small towns, and cities in order to survive.[10] In addition, ties between the urban-based USO, left political parties and movements, and rural peasant organizations had a long and continuing history. For example, a 1963 study of Barrancabermeja and its environs conducted by the University of Wisconsin's Land Tenure Center noted the participation of rural settlers in a series of peasant leagues, influenced by the left and in contact with the USO, that had arisen from settlers' antipathy toward ECOPETROL and absentee hacienda owners. Peasant resentment emerged from a number of concerns. Much like the TROCO, ECOPETROL attempted to control the movement of people within the former TROCO concession by erecting barriers that hindered travel between rural villages and their urban, administrative centers. In addition, there were no clear distinctions between "industrial" and "rural" areas, and the company routinely evicted peasant settlers without adequately compensating them for improvements to the land. Settlers also believed that ECOPETROL should provide health and educational services to them, and they resented large absentee landlords who operated in the interstices of the oil wells. These landlords paid low wages for clearing pasture and were known to push settlers off lands cleared for food cultivation in order to expand their holdings (Havens and Romieux 1966: 101–24).

The new political struggles and social movements that roiled across the Middle Magdalena in the 1960s and 1970 reflected working people's changing relationships to each other and their new engagement with the state. In addition to challenging how the nationalized oil company extracted profits from its workers, working people protested the ways that class power was organized in the living spaces of the city and challenged dominant assumptions about the relationship between citizens and the state. Sometimes waged and unwaged workers acted together; at other times, they moved along parallel tracks. Their shifting alliances were most visible in a series of labor and civic strikes that wracked Barrancabermeja in 1963, 1971, 1975, and 1977.

Building Popular Power and Confronting the State

In 1963, a two-day civic strike, prompted by the dearth of public services, and a forty-three-day labor strike erupted in Barrancabermeja within the space of a few months. The protests were possible because of the already well-established radical democratic movements—trade unions, peasant leagues, and incipient urban civic groups—in the oil port. They laid bare the problems bedeviling residents who produced an enormous amount of the nation's wealth but received very little of it in return. The strikes, and the state's belligerent response to them, established the rudiments of future collaboration between labor, immigrants, and peasants. They punctured the consensual façade of the National Front by calling attention to the exclusion that it was creating and dismissing any pretense that it represented a democracy.

The 1963 civic strike was waged over a series of demands for better living conditions, such as paved roads, a new public hospital, a municipal slaughterhouse, electricity, and especially potable water. It was the high degree of popular organization that enabled working people to direct their concerns to state officials. Although the involvement of urban squatters was less apparent than in years to come, the tradition of political organization and the vitality of political life in Barranca extended to the new arrivals, who, in many cases, had prior experience in rural peasant organizations. The city had also become "the worker capital of Colombia," with unions representing a large percentage of its population, including peasants, construction workers, fishermen, painters, railroad workers, shoe shiners, teachers, and lottery ticket vendors, as well as the oil workers. There was even a union, the Sindicato de Bares y Cantinas (Union of Bar and Cantina Workers), that sought ways to improve the working conditions of the city's prostitutes, despite the state's refusal to recognize their profession.[11]

A growing sense of entitlement among those people who were not included in the state's modernizing agenda emerged from the 1963 civic strike, which received support from a cross-class coalition. The coordinating committee that organized the strike included ex-functionaries of the municipal government; representatives of the church, commerce, and the radio; and local leaders from the Provivienda neighborhood, an urban shantytown established with the help of the PCC in 1960. It also counted among its participants militants from the left-leaning Movimiento Revolucionario Liberal (Liberal Revolutionary Movement, MRL). Led by Alfonso López Michelsen (son of the former Liberal president), the MRL included intellectuals, former Communists, and veterans from Rafael Rangel's Liberal guerrilla movement. The strike shut down the city. Stores closed, banks ceased operations, transportation ground to a halt, and the airport canceled flights. The government declared a state of siege, and the protest ended a day later in bloody confrontations between protesters and three thousand soldiers sent to Barrancabermeja to restore order.

The repression of the civic strike was a harbinger of what was to come three months later, when oil workers struck ECOPETROL during contract negotiations. The labor strike—the first under the National Front—did not erupt over contractual disagreements. Rather, tensions and simmering dissension in the wake of the civic strike had been building between workers and ECOPETROL over a range of seemingly minor concerns, such as ECOPETROL's denial of benefits to workers' common-law wives, the suspension of a union member who sought medical care in the Soviet Union,[12] and the use of dilapidated buses, provided by a subcontractor, to transport workers' children to school (Vega, Núñez, and Pereira 2009). Workers also demanded the removal of corrupt ECOPETROL officials, especially general manager Luis Aurelio Díaz, whom the union accused of being bourgeois, displacing peasant settlers to enlarge his own property, selling overpriced meat to the oil company, and a series of other offenses (Havens and Romieux 1966: 43). The oil company was seemingly unable to manage these concerns because, according to University of Wisconsin researchers, its cumbersome bureaucratic structure impeded communication between different levels of management in Barrancabermeja and Bogotá. Moreover, local functionaries generally knew neither the oil workers nor the region particularly well because they came from other parts of the country, and they made judgments about working people in accord with class-based stereotypes (Havens and Romieux 1966: 132).

The spark that ignited the forty-three-day standoff was the firing of several people accused of stealing from the company store. In response, the USO shut down the refinery, and workers locked up the store manager. The strike then devolved into a violent confrontation between protesters and the state in which the labor politics of the National Front were on full display. The governor of Santander sent troops to quell the protest and declared the USO illegal. The mayor imposed a curfew, suspended the sale of alcohol, and censored the press's ability to report on events. Protest organizers, including all the leaders of the USO in Barrancabermeja, were arrested. Even though labor legislation enacted under the National Front prohibited sympathy strikes, oil workers from Shell in Casabe and Texas Petroleum in Puerto Boyacá went out in support of those in Barrancabermeja. It was, however, peasant solidarity that enabled the Barrancabermeja workers to endure. As they had done in the past, peasants provided food to the protesters throughout the strike. Their support arose from prior collaboration with the USO, which had long insisted that ECOPETROL purchase peasant products through its company store and treat rural people in its clinic (Vega, Núñez, and Pereira 2009: 247). Yet government officials refused to see the protest as the outgrowth of valid concerns; the sinister hand of "communist manipulation," they insisted, lay at the root of the disorder. In this way, urban political dynamics were increasingly interpreted through the lens of the cold war.

Finally, in August 1963, a settlement was reached, and workers returned to the refinery, but the strike—and the civic strike that preceded it—had left a legacy of bitterness. The military repression and the refusal of the state to recognize protests as a legitimate part of a democratic society soured relationships with the National Front, which many working people had once understood as a constructive attempt to restore peace and democracy in Colombia. Relationships between the popular organizations—the USO, peasant groups, and new urban associations—and state institutions, especially ECOPETROL and the security forces, took on a more hostile quality. The frustration, anger, and feelings of impotence left in the wake of the strikes were not resolved. They fueled a deepening polarization of social life and stoked the radicalization of some oil workers and urban activists, who began to think that peaceful social change was impossible. Such sentiments fueled the formation of rural guerrilla insurgencies that advocated the overthrow of the state.

Social conflicts in the Middle Magdalena could not escape the grip of the cold war. The United States relentlessly opposed left-wing political movements and leaders it assumed were connected to Cuba and the Soviet Union, even if no evidence existed to link them to these countries.[13] The U.S. government took it as axiomatic that the Soviet Union and its Cuban ally were out to destabilize Colombia and the rest of Latin America and to spread communism throughout the Western Hemisphere, and local and regional tensions became defined within the context of the United States' global campaign against communism. Yet in Colombia, the cold war was less a fight against Cuban and Soviet proxies than a concerted effort by Colombian elites to disrupt challenges to the placid veneer of the National Front and prevent them from spreading. As the military sought ways to quell rural unrest, it began to speak of the Middle Magdalena as a region that stretched along the river between La Honda in the south and Gamarra in the north (van Isschot 2015: 59), and, with U.S. support, it started to develop counterinsurgency programs that combined military repression and development initiatives to eliminate dissent.[14]

Through the training, arming, and financing of Colombian security forces, the United States internationalized state-sponsored violence in the Middle Magdalena. It did so by working through the Colombian state and integrating the national military into a repressive, hemispheric security apparatus under its supervision (Gill 2004). The United States' National Security Doctrine then assigned Colombian security forces the task of policing the national territory for alleged "subversives," while the United States assumed the role of shielding the hemisphere from Soviet intrusion. In this way, the illusion of nation-state sovereignty was preserved, reinforcing the idea of the state as locus and container of claims and legitimizing powerful class interests, while silencing the marginalized voices of peasants, workers, and poor urban dwellers.

Although inspired in part by the Cuban Revolution, the emergence of an armed, conspiratorial left in the Middle Magdalena arose primarily from simmering tensions over poverty and social exclusion in the aftermath of La Violencia and the National Front's use of repression to contain them. The two largest insurgencies—the ELN and the

FARC—put down deep roots in the Middle Magdalena. Unlike the Liberal guerrillas of La Violencia, who sought only to reestablish Liberal Party rule, the ELN set its sights on overthrowing the state and replacing it with some variant of socialism. Founded a short distance from Barrancabermeja in 1964, the ELN drew inspiration from the Cuban Revolution, Christian humanism, and regional experiences of collective struggle, such as the Liberal guerrillas, the Barranca Commune, and the Bolshevik uprising. Many ELN founders had suffered persecution during La Violencia, and members of their families had either belonged to the Liberal guerrillas, participated in the Bolshevik revolt, or arisen from the youth wing of the MRL. For example, ELN cofounder Fabio Vásquez had belonged to the MRL, and the father of another ELN cofounder, Nicolás Rodrígues Bautista, had taken part in the Bolshevik uprising. Several radicalized clergy, such as Camilo Torres and Manuel Pérez Martínez (Cura Pérez), came to the ELN from the Golconda movement, which had arisen among Colombian Catholic clergy who began to question church teachings as a result of the Second Vatican Council (1962–65), a meeting of the world's bishops that called for the renewal of the Catholic Church through more direct engagement with the "world." The insurgency thus drew on various social and political expressions of discontentment specific to the Middle Magdalena, as well as the energizing force of the Cuban Revolution and the new openness of one sector of the Catholic Church.

The ELN chose the Middle Magdalena as a staging ground for its revolutionary struggle because of the tradition of popular resistance, especially the close ties between the oil workers and the peasantry around Barrancabermeja (C. Medina 2001: 78–79), and it built much of its strength in former strongholds of the 1950s era Liberal guerrillas.[15] The ELN made alliances with students at the Universidad Industrial de Santander in Bucaramanga and with oil workers of the USO. Ricardo Lara Parada, leader of the ELN, was himself the son of a Barrancabermeja oil worker. A former guerrilla, who joined the insurgency in the late 1960s, described how Barrancabermeja trade unionists supported the rural guerrillas: "In addition to raising issues about imperialism and workers' rights in their union struggles, they sent supplies to us and helped to organize actions, such as the theft of weapons, in the city. In a couple of cases, the entire union directorates supported us."[16]

Yet during the 1960s and most of the 1970s, the ELN remained isolated in the countryside, where it was consumed by internal divisions and nearly annihilated by the army in 1973 (Broderick 2000). The insurgency made little effort to organize Barrancabermeja's shantytowns until the 1980s, and, with the exception of the USO, it largely ignored the strategic importance of Barrancabermeja and its militant civic organizations and trade unions. It also eschewed the formation of a political party because of rigid adherence to the notion of an armed vanguard (*foco*) borrowed from the Cuban Revolution. Middle-class ELN leaders believed that revolution would begin in the countryside and that through their example of commitment and sacrifice, they could inspire support among the peasantry to overturn the old order and usher in a socialist transformation of Colombian society. In this vision of guerrilla strategists, urban working-class organizations, most prominently the USO, would only operate as a support base for the rural insurgency, but such a strategic vision was seriously flawed. The expansion of large-scale capitalist agriculture and the erosion of subsistence agriculture were evacuating the countryside. Peasants — the wellspring of insurgent visions of revolutionary change — were migrating to the cities, and Colombia was becoming one of the most urbanized countries in Latin America.[17] Nevertheless, the importance of organizing the cities — especially a militant oil town like Barranca — was largely ignored until much later.

While the ELN drew much of its early support from middle-class university students and militant clerics, the FARC enjoyed a deep well of peasant sympathy in the frontier colonization zones of southwest Colombia (Chernick and Jiménez 1993), but at a 1966 conference, it designated the Middle Magdalena as a strategic growth area. Although it established the IV Front in 1968, its presence was limited to the organization of rural, self-defense communities until the 1980s, when it expanded with an infusion of money derived from taxes levied on cocaine traffickers in its southern stronghold (Pizarro 1991). As the FARC's power grew in the Middle Magdalena, the insurgents also financed an increasing number of columns, or "fronts," through the collection of "war taxes" from wealthy landowners whom they kidnapped and harassed. The practice of kidnapping, however, eventually extended to others who were less well-off, such as small shop owners, peasants, and street vendors in the region's small towns and villages, and turned many potential supporters against the guerrillas, with deadly consequences.

As the rise of rural insurgencies set off government alarms, a sector of the Catholic Church was reassessing the church's historic ties to the powerful. Catholic priests, nuns, and lay catechists influenced by the changing winds within the Catholic Church dedicated themselves to a new kind of pastoral work that focused less exclusively on religious training than on the development of neighborhood-based organizations that addressed the pressing needs of poor residents, especially women and youth. What came to be known as liberation theology reinterpreted scripture by focusing on the exploitation and suffering that poor people experienced in their daily lives. It found institutional expression in the Second Vatican Council and then took sharper political form in the 1968 bishops' conference in Medellín, where adherents to this political current called on the church to adopt a "preferential option for the poor" and dedicate more resources and services to poor neighborhoods and villages.

In Barrancabermeja, the new pastoral work was facilitated by the creation, in late 1962, of the Diocese of Barrancabermeja, which united fourteen municipalities in the provinces of Santander, Bolívar, and Antioquia. Newly graduated seminarians from the Pamplona seminary in North Santander province came to Barrancabermeja (van Isschot 2015: 60) and began pastoral work in the emerging northeastern neighborhoods, such as Primero de Mayo, Providencia, Miraflores, Versalles, and La Esperanza, where they affiliated with the Church of Nuestra Señora de los Milagros. The most influential priest was Eduardo Díaz, whose father was an ECOPETROL manager. During the early 1960s, Díaz had lived with his family in the barrio staff of El Centro before attending the Pamplona seminary. He then returned to Barrancabermeja in 1970 to take up pastoral work. Díaz and another priest, Nel Beltrán, created a cadre of catechists known as the Unidad Dinamizadora del Programa to carry out the church's grassroots pastoral work in Barrancabermeja's emerging immigrant neighborhoods. Díaz not only played a key role as a community organizer when he led the parish of Nuestra Señora de los Milagros but also emerged as an important interlocutor between the government and the urban social movements in the 1970s.

Because of the almost complete absence of schools in the shantytowns, the church established the Colegio Camilo Torres, named after a prominent Colombian cleric who died fighting alongside the ELN, and a generation of young activists passed through it. One of them was a future trade union leader named William Mendoza. "I lived in a very poor neighborhood," he explained, "and I got very involved with political activism through a priest, who was the principal of my high school.

He believed in liberation theology, and we [students] used to go with him and other priests to their little farm, where they taught us about the ideas in Karl Marx's *Capital* and about liberation theology."[18]

Yolanda Becerra, an alumna who graduated in the late 1970s, described how "in high school, we [students] were linked to all the social networks of the neighborhoods, and I became involved with a literacy program for adults. . . . The church has something that you don't get in other kinds of political education: *mística* [mystique]. It is an education so solid that one remains committed for life."[19] Becerra, who was the daughter of peasant migrants, would go on to become the director of the Organización Femenina Popular (Popular Feminine Organization, OFP), which grew out of a series of church-sponsored mothers' clubs in 1972. The OFP was one of the most important fruits of the church's engagement with residents of the northeast, and it would soon become a key link in the network of grassroots organizations that were developing in immigrant neighborhoods. Becerra became politicized through involvement with the surge of destitute migrants who were rapidly transforming northeastern Barrancabermeja, where her family lived. "A strong housing movement developed in which women played an important role in the takeover of land," she explained. "When the police and the army came to evict them, women and their children put up the resistance because, at the time, they were less likely to be harmed than men. All of this moved us and the parish of Nuestra Señora de los Milagros to start thinking about how to organize women."[20] The absence of water, electricity, and schools placed a heavier burden on women for whom the management of the household was the primary responsibility, and for Becerra and others, organizing women was a way to strengthen what they understood as "the popular movement." More than an earlier generation of female migrants, shantytown women started to play leading roles in the popular protests that shook Barranca in the 1970s, and women's work became a focus of organizing initiatives.

In the late 1960s and 1970s, a revolutionary tide washed over Barrancabermeja and the rest of Latin America, and the city became a hotbed of political projects and ideas of the left. Liberation theology and revolutionary Marxism contributed to this upsurge of political organization. Both emphasized structural injustice and the need to transform society, and both required commitment to a set of core beliefs. Looking back, a retired high school chemistry teacher commented in 2010,

"I came to Barrancabermeja in 1971 because I thought that the revolution was going to happen here."[21] Eduardo Díaz noted how, in 1975, a social shift took place among the women of the OFP, who began to see themselves less as individuals learning a skill under the church's tutelage than as participants in a popular movement with transformative political demands.[22] Yolanda Becerra recalled that the OFP "participated in the coordination of the civic strikes and that [involvement] began to create some noise within the church. . . . We began speaking about autonomy and that the organization must be autonomous from the church. We had to create strong movements that were not at the service of the church."[23] The politicization of a generation of young people like Yolanda Becerra generated a way of understanding the world and participating within it that animated hope and nurtured beliefs that immediate alternatives were available.

Many residents of Barrancabermeja understood the cold war as a pretext, elaborated by the United States and its Colombian allies, to repress efforts to expand social well-being and democratic processes. Their sense of possibility on a broad scale, along with the growing organizational muscle of oil workers and urban squatters, nurtured the basis of an astonishingly radical political culture that had emerged in the 1920s and 1930s and was reconfigured around new class alliances in the 1960s and 1970s. This political culture valued solidarity, held that social change was possible, and had the capacity to nurture collective action. A retired oil worker recalled how the 1970s civic strikes built on and intensified popular solidarity: "After every strike, in spite of the state repression, the consciousness of the oil workers and the consciousness of the people became more powerful. The parallel development of a city and a union as powerful as the USO created a very solid, very critical political consciousness that demanded improved public services."[24] The social movements — trade unions, women's groups, student organizations, and peasant leagues — insisted on equality, land reform, labor rights, and the rights of citizenship from the state, and the contour of collective politics took on a sharper edge during the 1970s.

The Civic Strikes of the 1970s

The USO and urban civic groups were the driving force behind two major civic strikes, in 1975 and 1977, that focused on the continuing absence of social services, especially the enduring problem of potable water in a city where the average temperature hovered in the upper nineties. The oil industry had polluted rivers, streams, and marshes for decades, and water flowed through the taps for only a few hours of the day. What came out was putrid, malodorous, and unfit for bathing. Even in the hotels, a room with or without a shower made little difference. People were forced to purchase mineral water for cooking, and not surprisingly, gastrointestinal infections were rampant (Vega, Núñez, and Pereira 2009).

Through the biannual agreements that it signed with ECOPETROL in the 1960s and 1970s, the USO not only secured more rights and benefits for union members but also obtained agreements from ECOPETROL to provide community services that included two public schools, health services, and sewerage. A longtime resident recalled that "there came a moment when Barranca and the USO became one. People felt a claim, a right, to ECOPETROL."[25] Many working people believed that the oil wealth produced by ECOPETROL belonged to the Colombian people and that, as Colombian citizens, they should receive a larger share of its profits in the form of public services. The USO responded to these yearnings. It aimed to fulfill the democratic promises of trade unionism enmeshed in society by addressing aspects of working-class experience not dealt with in the workplace. This was not a straightforward process, however.

In 1971, the USO suffered a bloody, devastating strike that sapped its power and weakened the leadership. Thirty-six workers, including the entire union directorate, were tried in a secret military court (*consejo verbal de guerra*) and sentenced to prison terms.[26] For the next few years, the union had to regroup, a generational transition took place, and its politics grew more radical. A new group of young workers known as the Mechudos (Longhairs) moved into positions in the refinery. Influenced by the Cuban Revolution and the ELN, these youngsters were impatient with the pace of change and did not shy away from direct confrontation with the National Front. A member of this cohort told historian Renán Vega, "We had leftist thinking, that the country had to change definitively, that we had to free ourselves from any imperialist yoke" (qtd. in Vega, Núñez, and Pereira 2009: 309). For the first time in its history, in 1976, the USO organized under the banner of a trade union confederation—the Communist-dominated Confederación Sindical de Trabajadores Colombianos (Union Confederation of Colombian Workers,

CSTC)—that was not connected to the Liberal Party, after President Alfonso López Michelsen legalized the CSTC.

The USO subsequently declared itself an alternative political project, one sustained by revolutionary nationalism and the defense of national resources for the entire population. This position enabled the USO to forge alliances with diverse working people and mobilize them (Vega, Núñez, and Pereira 2009). Doing so was a challenge. Oil workers viewed themselves as the product of capitalist modernity. They lived more comfortable urban lives than the founding generation of oil proletarians, and they were better educated and enjoyed more social security than the legions of ruined peasants settling the urban periphery, who they often characterized as less modern than themselves. Yet the oil workers also saw themselves as the defenders of an important natural resource and part of the *pueblo* (people). In addition, despite the differences between a full-time, well-paid oil proletariat linked to a strategic, global industry and the unemployed and underemployed immigrants of the urban periphery, a common thread linked both groups: the desire to control their work and the products of their labor and to reside in neighborhoods in which potable water, electricity, schools, health clinics, and paved roads were available to everyone.

The USO downplayed the differences between its members and urban squatters; indeed, some oil workers lived side by side with immigrants in the northeast sector, where they suffered from the same lack of services along with the rest of the population. The union created unity through a political program that supported peasants affected by oil exploration; contributed union funds to the development of infrastructure in poor neighborhoods; advocated for the extension of benefits to temporary ECOPETROL workers; and backed the civic struggles of the urban poor (Delgado 2006). For example, one resident recalled how "in the northeast, the USO organized a kind of strike among brick makers. It propelled a whole movement to demand better working conditions for them. This was one way that people in the northeast became articulated to the labor movement in Barranca."[27] The presence of unionized workers in immigrant neighborhoods, or their connections to friends and relatives in these settings, provided a core of established, politicized individuals with ties to left political parties and movements. Activist priests resident in the northeast also facilitated relationships between the USO and barrio residents and helped to overcome some of the social differences and political factionalism that divided activist groups with similar goals.

By 1975, the USO had recuperated from its 1971 defeat and became involved with a civic strike, which was actually two protests, held three weeks apart, that centered on water and demonstrated civic unity. A broad cross section of groups—women of the OFP, students, trade unionists, merchants, some professionals, and peasants from the Asociación Nacional de Usuarios Campesinos (National Association of Peasant Landholders, ANUC)—organized the events, which were even supported by the bishop, who proclaimed in a widely circulated statement that the water in the city was too polluted to be any good for blessings. And even though water was the central focus of the strike, other demands—for example, streetlights and an end to peasant repression in the countryside—reflected the diverse composition of the organizing committee. The strike ground the city to a halt. Daily assemblies in the Parque Infantil drew large crowds; neighborhood committees (*comités de barrio*) connected residents to the central strike committee; and civil guards (*guardias cívicas*) organized residents, distributed leaflets, coordinated actions at the neighborhood level, and maintained order. Although the sustained power of grassroots organizing pushed the national government to commit to the improvement of the urban water supply and address other concerns, including the land claims of regional peasant groups, social unrest did not end with the strike. The governor named an army colonel mayor of the city, and even though the colonel did not remain in the position for long, his appointment was indicative of the unrest and growing militarization of Barrancabermeja (van Isschot 2015).

When the city erupted again, in 1977, the military response was brutal. A two-day civic strike, organized by the USO and urban civic groups, took place in solidarity with a sixty-five-day oil worker strike. Once again, the governor of Santander installed an army colonel in the mayor's office, and thousands of soldiers descended on Barrancabermeja to put down the protests, just a few months after a national-level civic strike had paralyzed the country, received huge support from residents of Barranca, and united the country's three trade union confederations (Liberal, Catholic, and Communist). Few people escaped the repression, and anyone who even sympathized with the USO was thrown in jail.

Oscar Romero was a high school student at the time. He later recalled that he "couldn't remember anything bigger. There was support from everywhere—even the merchants." Oscar and other students collected food donations for striking workers, set up barricades, and picked out the spies, known as *patevacas*. They coordinated with the USO and supportive city council members who backed the protest, despite the mayor's opposition. One of the city council members was his father, a former USO leader who had been fired after the 1963 strike. Oscar recalled how his father left home every morning of the strike as if going to work. He would then meet secretly with strike leaders to plot strategy and publish a clandestine news bulletin. On at least one occasion, the police raided the family home and carried away items that they considered subversive, including Oscar's Cuban flag. When the strike finally ended, some 277 ECOPETROL workers were fired; only 1 was ever reinstated. One worker summed up a widely shared sense of what had happened: "We had prepared for a strike and had to confront a war."[28]

Out of the protests of the 1970s, a series of coordinating committees (*coordinadoras*) formed to connect social and political groups in the city. These coalitions gave birth to the Coordinadora Popular de Barrancabermeja, which organized a civic strike in 1983 and became a model for similar organizations in other Colombian cities. Although the organizers were the same as those who had led earlier struggles, they conceived of the Coordinadora as a more permanent link between Barrancabermeja's expanding immigrant neighborhoods, the USO, popular movements, and political parties, a relationship that went beyond the episodic coordination of civic strikes. The Coordinadora included the USO, as well as left-wing political parties, unions, members of the Catholic Church, and representatives of women, peasant, and student organizations. It became the regional interlocutor with the government, which was forced to recognize it, and because of its deep popular roots and political clout, the Coordinadora also provided visibility and respectability to peasant mobilizations that took place under its umbrella (Molano 2009: 56). The Coordinadora thus expanded the geography of working-class power by connecting peasants, oil workers, and migrants to a broader field of organization, struggle, and solidarity.

For many working-class barranqueños, the experience of solidarity through involvement with a network of grassroots organizations provided a sense of dignity and entitlement and a feeling that they were making history. Working people saw hope for change through the resurgent power of popular protest in Barrancabermeja, as well as the 1979 victory of the Sandinistas in Nicaragua and the possibility of an FMLN victory in El Salvador. The political work of numerous unions, squatter groups, student organizations, and peasant associations generated a strong sense of "altruism, commitment, and capacity to struggle" among the people affiliated with them (Vega, Núñez, and Pereira 2009: 309). It gave rise to what Greg Grandin (2004: 180–81) calls "insurgent individualism," in which individuality and solidarity merged through collective politics. Individual men and women developed a new sense of self rooted in a larger social collectivity as they engaged the state and linked personal aspirations to national and international concerns. Yet these new and remade relationships, as well as the sense of power and entitlement that emerged from them, would come under increasing strain.

In 1978, Liberal president Julio César Turbay (1978–82) enacted the National Security Statute, which imposed extreme restrictions on civil liberties, censored media coverage of armed conflicts with the insurgencies, and granted new powers to the military, which could detain anyone suspected of "subversive" activities. This hard-line policy further narrowed the parameters of political action in the Middle Magdalena. Although it was directed at the growing power of the FARC, ELN, and other insurgencies, it served less to blunt the expansion of the guerrillas than to further polarize social life, as militarization closed off peaceful means of change and bolstered a feeling among many barranqueños that the insurgencies represented a legitimate political option and an alternative to the repressive Colombian state.

The 1970s represented the apogee of Barrancabermeja's radical popular movements, which, despite the severity of repression, forced the Colombian state to grant concessions, but the lights began to dim in subsequent years. Political violence intensified and crashed over the Middle Magdalena like an endless cresting wave for the next two and half decades. Physical displacement, massacres, extrajudicial executions, extreme forms of torture, and disappearance set the tone of a prolonged dirty war that heated up in the 1980s and ravaged Barrancabermeja and the Middle Magdalena into the twenty-first century. Violence and the wholesale divestment of the social relations, property, and organizations through which working people crafted their livelihoods and channeled their demands to the state were central to the defeat of a working class that had achieved considerable organizational

power. Escalating violence spread fear and insecurity; it fractured social networks and destroyed unions, peasant associations, and political parties; and, most important, it disorganized social life and made
working people available for incorporation into new relationships of
inequality.

"They Killed People at Any Time of the Day"

Pedro Lozada was one of tens of thousands of peasants violently displaced from their homes in the 1980s. Some thirty years after the
Texas Petroleum Company had expelled his family from its homestead, a dirty war carried out by paramilitaries in collusion with the
military, local entrepreneurs, and drug traffickers gathered steam in
the Middle Magdalena. Communist Party militants like Lozada as well
as anyone suspected of supporting the insurgencies were targeted and
often killed. Lozada recalled a day when the local radio station announced a meeting at the army's XIV Brigade headquarters to organize a response to guerrilla harassment. "The meeting," he insisted,
"was to form a death squad in Puerto Berrío and to organize merchants
and ranchers." Reports of extrajudicial executions and massacres upriver around Puerto Boyacá were already circulating, and daily life in
and around Puerto Berrío was growing more and more insecure. "They
started to kill anyone who belonged to a civic organization, a union,
or a neighborhood committee," Lozada said. "They killed people at
any time of the day and in any place."[29] Despite warnings from neighbors that unidentified men had come looking for him, Lozada did not
leave until a municipal official sent him a note that his name was on a
paramilitary hit list. Then, dressed in a disguise, he, his wife, and their
small children fled. Two older sons remained behind. The Lozada family
would eventually settle in Barrancabermeja, along with other forcibly
displaced peasants from the Cimitarra River valley, southern Bolívar
province, and communities along the Opón River. The arrival of hungry, traumatized peasants raised anew worries about political violence
among urban residents, intensified animosity toward the state, and
overwhelmed the city's ability to cope with so many refugees.

The Middle Magdalena town of Puerto Boyacá became the epicenter
of the dirty war. Around Puerto Boyacá and in much of the southern
Middle Magdalena, drug traffickers had bought up large tracts of land
to launder their profits and gain entrée into the blue-blooded Colom-

bian oligarchy. Yet much like their old-guard counterparts, who viewed them with suspicion and referred to them disdainfully as the *clase emergente*, the drug-traffickers-turned-landlords became the subjects of guerrilla extortion demands and kidnapping attempts. Hatred of the insurgents solidified an alliance between a rising group of nouveau riche, narco-entrepreneurs, cattle ranchers, urban merchants, and the Texas Petroleum Company, a subsidiary of TEXACO. In 1983, the mayor of Puerto Boyacá and Liberal Party members created the Asociación Campesina de Ganaderos y Agricultores del Magdalena Medio (Association of Middle Magdalena Ranchers and Farmers, ACEDEGAM), with financial support from the Texas Petroleum Company, other businesses, and drug traffickers, to wrest peasant support from the guerrillas. The association created some thirty "patriotic and anti-Communist schools," as well as health clinics and peasant cooperatives (Dudley 2004: 68), but it was essentially a façade for the recruiting, financing, and training of paramilitary groups with names like Muerte a Secuestradores (Death to Kidnappers) to combat the guerrillas (C. Medina 1990). Unlike in the 1990s, when they operated as standing armies, the 1980s era paramilitaries acted like hit-and-run death squads that were integrated into military intelligence networks, which permitted the Colombian military to deny any knowledge about or connection to their activities and to deflect charges from international human rights organizations that state security forces violated the human rights of Colombian citizens. Military officials gave them free rein to engage in the unsavory acts of a dirty war. The mercenaries gathered information on unions, opposition political parties, and peasant organizations and then carried out attacks on their leaders and supporters under direction from the military. The repression did less damage to the guerrillas than to unarmed civilians, who were easier targets, and it eventually eliminated the left from the political playing field in the Middle Magdalena.

As counterinsurgent paramilitary violence unraveled social life in the rural Middle Magdalena, the government of Belisario Betancur (1982–86) broke with the hard-line strategies of his predecessors and negotiated a cease-fire with the FARC that ended with a peace agreement in 1985. As part of the peace accord, the government agreed to decentralize certain governmental decision-making powers to provincial and municipal authorities and to allow the local election of governors and mayors. Although city councils and provincial assemblies had long been directly elected, the Colombian president had appointed mayors and governors since the nineteenth century. Betancur's decision to open up the political process was motivated by a strategic calculus that political decentralization would pacify the insurgents (Castro 1998). It was also a concession to the FARC, which had demanded political and economic decentralization for years in its periodic negotiations with the government.

Political decentralization served less to pacify the insurgents than to intensify regional tensions. The FARC had had some success organizing peasants, and with the devolution of political power, the insurgents demonstrated their political appeal through the formation of a new party—the Unión Patriótica (Patriotic Union, UP)—to mark their entry into electoral politics, even as they clandestinely armed for war. The UP candidates performed well in both national and local elections, and their success alarmed the regional bourgeoisie. The UP and the direct election of mayors and governors sharpened the concerns of the security forces, the bourgeoisie, and the Texas Petroleum Company that the balance of power would tip in favor of the guerrillas and their supporters. Old-guard ranchers claimed that the military was not doing enough to protect them from the predations of the FARC, and they suspected peasants of supporting the guerrillas. At the same time, the political opening raised the expectations of marginalized groups that their concerns about land reform, services, infrastructure, and public education would receive serious discussion (Romero 2003).

Political decentralization in the Middle Magdalena served only to aggravate armed competition in the context of a counterinsurgent war. Landowners had long claimed a right to "self-defense" in a region where the organization of private militias to protect property rights was established during La Violencia, and they backed a neofascist political movement called Movimiento de Reconstrucción Nacional (Movement of National Reconstruction, MORENA), with ACEDEGAM at its core. With its close ties to the paramilitaries and the security forces, MORENA declared its support for "Christian values" but dedicated itself to the physical elimination of the UP.[30] In the 1988 elections, MORENA candidates gained control of the mayoralties in six small towns of the Middle Magdalena, including Puerto Boyacá, where a sign on the road into town proclaimed the river port "The Antisubversive Capital of Colombia." At the same time, the intensification of U.S. counterinsurgency wars in Central America undermined any negotiated solution to the Colombian conflict. The United States ignored paramilitary drug trafficking and alliances with the Colombian security forces and criminalized the FARC with the label "narco-guerrillas," erroneously suggesting that the insurgents were at the center of the illegal narcotics trade. "The war on drugs" then became the axis around which U.S.-Colombian relations turned. Counterinsurgency and political decentralization would, in time, facilitate the far-right capture of provincial and municipal elected offices and lead to the privatization of the institutional state, as paramilitaries and their backers used public office to siphon off state funds, monopolize public contracts, and legalize their possession of stolen lands (see chapter 5).[31]

The escalating political violence transformed the countryside, which had become a center of peasant protest in Colombia. It displaced peasants who had fled La Violencia and colonized the region in the 1940s, 1950s, and 1960s, depopulating what had become guerrilla strongholds by the 1980s. As legions of traumatized refugees placed the terror on public display for urban residents, they were among the first to speak about human rights violations in Barrancabermeja. The insurgencies subsequently became urbanized, as the guerrillas followed their support bases into the city. In the 1980s, the ELN embarked on a period of expansion with funds obtained from the extortion of foreign oil companies along the Colombian-Venezuelan border, where new oil discoveries had been made. Similarly, the FARC was flush with money from the taxation of drug traffickers, who purchased coca paste—the basis of cocaine—from peasants in the FARC's southern stronghold, and it expanded into numerous municipalities around the country. The ELN and the FARC, as well as smaller guerrilla groups like the Maoist Ejército Popular de Liberación (Popular Liberation Army, EPL) and the M-19, composed of FARC and Communist Party dissidents, organized urban militias (*milicias urbanas*) in the northeastern and southeastern districts of Barrancabermeja.[32] Composed mostly of young people from the barrios, the militias supported the insurgencies with information about the movement of security forces, logistics, and the organization of political activities. The militias represented a belated attempt to plant the insurgencies in urban soil (see chapter 3), but despite the sympathy for the guerrillas, especially the ELN, in Barrancabermeja, the insurgents never really abandoned the position that revolution would happen in the countryside.

It should come as no surprise that the insurgencies found a well of popular support in Barrancabermeja. By the 1990s, the ELN's identification with urban residents had become so complete that guerrillas no longer adhered to the compartmentalized organizational structure that protected the identities of local cadres. A resident explained: "There was a time when you could walk into some of the neighborhoods of the Northeast and stand in the middle of the street and shout out, 'Who is the commander of the ELN in this neighborhood?' and people would tell you. Everyone knew the guerrillas, and people trusted them and each other."[33] For urban people accustomed to repressive police and military tactics during the labor and civic strikes that rattled Barrancabermeja, the guerrillas offered a form of protection. Evangelina Marín, a member of the Coordinadora, explained that "many people considered the time of the guerrillas to be one of military accompaniment for them. . . . The fact that the militias were able to maintain a presence for thirteen years in such a small city is because people accepted them and supported them" (2006: 356). Such support was not universal, and it changed over time, but for much of the 1980s and early 1990s, the guerrillas were either welcomed or tolerated, and they became part of the social fabric of working-class Barrancabermeja.

The guerrillas' daily presence in the barrios differed from other Colombian cities, where insurgents moved in and out of working-class communities but never established a permanent relationship with their inhabitants. One longtime resident of La Esperanza neighborhood remembered that even if people were not involved with the guerrillas, the insurgents were their sons, daughters, husbands, friends, lovers, and acquaintances, and they were tolerated, if not always actively supported, for reasons of personal connection. Echoing these observations, a social movement leader said that "the culture of the guerrilla was part of the life of civil society. That doesn't mean that all civilians were guerrillas, but the guerrillas were part of our lives, part of our culture. Everyone struggled and lived together in one way or another."[34] Another longtime political activist, who reflected on the period, insisted that "whether you were actually a guerrilla, a collaborator, or simply a social movement member with no connection to the guerrillas, people more or less wanted the same things. This is not to say that everyone always agreed with the guerrillas; they [the guerrillas] sometimes made decisions that hurt the popular movement. But people in the Northeast were proud to have a guerrilla commander spend the night in their home, and they saw the insurgents as a political alternative."[35]

Relationships with the insurgents were not seamless. The ELN, for example, frequently backed the demands of labor, whether or not it was asked to do so, while extorting corporations, kidnapping managers, and destroying physical plants when its demands were not satisfied. A president of the USO addressed the awkward relationships between the union and the insurgencies when he acknowledged that his union shared political sympathies with the guerrillas: "This union, besides engaging in collective bargaining, is political in nature. It openly confronts the oil policies of different governments. This concern of ours has led, in some way, to a certain coincidence with the insurgent movement. One of our rallying points is national sovereignty, and this has also been a rallying point for the insurgent movement . . . but this does not mean that we literally agree with all of the activities that the guerrilla develops in this country" (*El Tiempo*, January 29, 1997, qtd. in Delgado 2006: 143). Many oil workers did not support repeated guerrilla bombings of ECOPETROL's oil and gas pipelines because they believed that the assaults posed a threat to their jobs. And when the insurgents publicly sided with workers during contract negotiations and labor strikes to legitimate their violent methods, newspaper pundits, public officials, and the security forces quickly condemned what they perceived as an unholy alliance between the unions and the guerrillas. These accusations were especially pernicious given the guerrillas' decision to combine legal and illegal forms of struggle, known as the *combinación de todas las formas de lucha*. The deeply controversial *combinación* strategy had individuals acting on behalf of the insurgencies in trade unions, popular organizations, political parties, and Christian base communities.[36] It lent credence to accusations that insurgents operated within legal community organizations, and it enabled the military to justify targeting union and civic organizations and exposing unarmed civilians to state repression.

Moreover, although guerrilla involvement with unions, neighborhood councils, and civic groups varied, it raised prickly questions about autonomy that caused friction. "They [the guerrillas] didn't manage to understand that there were organizations capable of constructing autonomy," complained the head of one group to me in 2007.[37] Others asserted that the guerrillas were simply trying to use the popular organizations as "echo chambers" for their views. Guerrilla encroachment on the autonomy of popular organizations almost certainly undermined the appeal of these groups to nonmembers and made the guerrillas themselves appear intrusive and disrespectful. Because of these tensions, historian Álvaro Delgado (2006: 139) called the insurgents the "uncomfortable allies" of trade unionists in the Middle Magdalena, although such discomfort extended beyond the unions to other groups as well.

The presence of three insurgencies in a city known for its militant social organizations made subduing Barrancabermeja, especially the USO, an important paramilitary objective, and during the 1980s and 1990s, the Middle Magdalena entered a spiraling vortex of violence that would eventually unravel working-class Barrancabermeja. Regional-based paramilitaries accrued enormous power and autonomy through ties to the cocaine traffic, and they federated, in 1997, under a national umbrella organization called the Autodefensas Unidas de Colombia (United Self-Defense Forces of Colombia, AUC), which attempted to centralize under its command the various paramilitary groups that operated in the country. The FARC and the ELN grew militarily stronger from the rents extracted through extortion and kidnapping and spread beyond their traditional strongholds, but military strength and territorial control did not translate into greater political support. In many cases, the insurgent expansion had less to do with their increasing popularity than with the heightened capacity to intimidate.

When an AUC affiliate—the Bloque Central Bolívar (Central Bolívar Bloc, BCB)—seized control of the city in the early twenty-first century, after years of massacres, threats, and extrajudicial executions, it drove the final nail into the coffin of a once vibrant, heterogeneous working class. The paramilitaries dismantled the ideological and institutional framework that tied residents to each other, and they stunted popular demands that the state care for its citizens through the provision of decent wages, safe and democratic working conditions, and public services, and that it protect national resources from foreign despoliation. Barrancabermeja changed from a city that had long received displaced victims of the violence to one that became a source of displacement.

The brutal power of reactionary violence remade class relationships. It lubricated the dispossession of working people, propelled the disorganization of their lives and organizations, and spread fear and insecurity, all of which facilitated the incorporation of traumatized survivors into new relationships of power over which they had little control. Political terror made the Middle Magdalena governable in the interests of capital and opened the doors to foreign corporations eager to invest in the region's abundant natural resources. It also transformed how state power was organized, enacted, and understood. In the next chapters, we turn to a more detailed examination of the unmaking of class and the restructuring of the state in Barrancabermeja.

THREE

TERROR AND
IMPUNITY

. . .

May 16, 1998. It was Saturday night in Barrancabermeja, a weekend evening like many others. As the sun dipped below the western horizon and the torrid heat of the river valley slowly abated, the city began to shift gears. People spilled into corner bars and discos in the working-class districts of the northeast and southeast, where a mix of salsa and vallenato music blared into the streets. Families gathered on patios or moved chairs onto the sidewalks to escape the accumulated heat of their homes, while young couples, friends, and relatives set out on strolls, taking in the social life that came alive after sunset. The Protestant faithful, whose numbers had expanded over the last two decades, attended services in storefront churches, where the exhortations of preachers and the entreaties of the repentant mixed with the rhythms of guitar music and floated to the heavens. Many residents of the southeastern Maria Eugenia, Divino Niño, and Campín neighborhoods headed to a bazaar that local people had organized in a high school soccer field to raise funds for a Mother's Day celebration.

Sixteen-year-old Yesid Peña was sitting in front of his home with other teenage members of a Bible study class, not far from the congested bazaar. He was a quiet youth, a homebody according to his father, who preferred the company of a few friends to the commotion of the soccer field. At around 9:00 PM, two armed men approached from the street and forced Yesid and another boy to accompany them at gunpoint. A startled dog began to bark, alerting his father, who was inside watching television, that something was wrong. At first, the elder Peña recalled, he thought that the men were police checking the youngsters' identification, but he quickly realized that something more sinister was afoot. No sooner had he put on his shoes and gone out to the street than he saw a pickup truck carrying men in bulletproof vests. Yesid had vanished, and splayed on the street near the bazaar lay a corpse with its throat slit. Peña heard shots and yelling. A neighbor told him to get out of sight or he would be killed, too, and for the next half hour, Peña and his wife cowered in the neighbor's home.

Despite what he had seen, Peña still thought that his son was in police custody. Yet when he and his wife made their way to police headquarters, the officer in charge denied any knowledge of Yesid's whereabouts and treated their requests for help with indifference, even though, according to Peña, "you could still hear shots being fired." Disgusted, the couple continued to the headquarters of the Departamento Administrativo de Seguridad (Department of Administrative Security, DAS), Colombia's premiere security service, where the reception was even worse. "They [the DAS officials] were having sort of a party," Peña remembered. "They were drinking and had women inside. . . . They laughed in our faces and didn't offer any kind of help." For the rest of the night, Peña and his wife searched for their son in a hired taxi amid a torrential rainstorm, but it was only over the next few days that the outlines of the tragedy became clear: a heavily armed paramilitary force had driven into the neighborhood in three pickup trucks, and it had killed seven people in the bazaar and disappeared twenty-five others, including Yesid Peña.[1]

In the aftermath of the massacre, Barrancabermeja exploded. The USO, together with other union, religious, and popular organizations, called a five-day civic strike to pressure the government to investigate the attack and locate the missing people, and it denounced the military for allowing the paramilitary incursion to happen, despite having advanced warning. Schools, the oil refinery, and banks closed, and two days after the assault, ten thousand people accompanied the funeral procession for the seven murder victims, shouting antiparamilitary slogans. The mercenaries reacted with threatening graffiti in several neighborhoods and declared the strike leaders "military targets." A week later, Colombian president Ernesto Samper gave a speech in Barrancabermeja in which he said that the government knew who was responsible for the assault and that it was trying to determine the fate of the abducted. The commander of a regional paramilitary group, the Autodefensas de Santander y Sur de César (Self-Defense Forces of

Santander and South César), subsequently claimed responsibility in an interview granted to a national newsmagazine. He stated that, in addition to the seven people murdered at the time of the assault, his forces had killed all of the kidnapped victims in the days following the abductions because of their alleged ties to the guerrilla militias that operated in the city. He also vowed to continue the attacks (Amnesty International 1999).

Echoing Colombian writer Gabriel García Marquéz's classic novel *Chronicle of a Death Foretold*, Jaime Peña and many other *barranqueños* insisted that the paramilitary foray represented a massacre foretold (*una masacre anunciada*). Local military and police commanders had received warning that the paramilitaries planned to carry out a massacre, and on the day of the incursion, an army officer ordered the establishment of a twenty-four-hour checkpoint on the main access road to the city's southeastern neighborhoods. Yet shortly before 9:00 PM, the military units returned to their barracks, and the checkpoint came down. The paramilitary forces then entered the city to begin the assault on the southeastern districts (Amnesty International 1999).

The massacre initiated the paramilitary shift from targeted individual assassinations, used against journalists and labor and civic leaders since the 1980s, to a full-scale invasion and occupation of Barrancabermeja in the early twenty-first century. Although many people had refused to believe that the paramilitaries would ever gain a foothold in a city noted for its radical tradition, the disorganization of Barrancabermeja's working class and the rise of an extreme form of neoliberal, "gangster" capitalism had been under way for several years. The massacre therefore constituted less a rupture with the recent past than an early indication that the long years of dirty war and neoliberal economic restructuring were reaching a violent denouement. Yet because of its sensational impact, the carnage of May 16 indelibly marked popular memory. It divided the history of the dirty war into "before" and "after" May 16, 1998, and signified the initial consolidation of a new, neoliberal economic era characterized by radical insecurity, the triumph of free-market policies, and the victory of the counterinsurgent right, which would take over the institutional state and much of civil society in the early years of the twenty-first century. It also demarcated the end of one period of urban history in which radical democratic movements clamored for labor rights and the rights of democratic citizenship, and a rebellious political culture nurtured collective action.

In this and subsequent chapters, we turn to an exploration of how political violence and neoliberalism unmade Barrancabermeja's working class during the 1990s and early 2000s, a time when paramilitary armies seized control of small towns, urban neighborhoods, and rural hamlets across the country (e.g., Cívico 2012; Hylton 2010; Taussig 2003), while burgeoning U.S. military aid made them stronger by shoring up their allies in the army and the police. Violence and economic restructuring redefined the geography of power, tore people from social networks, refashioned political subjectivities around individual survival strategies, and reconfigured how working people advanced their claims on the state. Understanding the unmaking of the working class affords on important perspective on how the organization of capital accumulation changed and processes of state formation veered to the far right.

This chapter focuses on the paramilitary takeover of the city, especially the most violent period between 2000 and 2003, when the homicide rate was among the highest in the world.[2] Paramilitaries of the BCB, one of the largest and most lethal groups that operated in Colombia, unleashed violence on behalf of an emergent narco-bourgeoisie to destroy unions, expel the guerrillas from the city, and dismantle Barranca's scaffolding of working-class solidarity, and they did so with the knowledge and support of the state security forces. The chapter first discusses the intensification of violence amid the growing liberalization of the Colombian economy, which working people in Barrancabermeja opposed because of the multiple ways that it eroded their livelihoods. It then explores how the terror and impunity that defined the paramilitary occupation provoked a collective trauma for working people that enabled the mercenaries and those they served to weaken, disorganize, and, in some cases, obliterate working-class institutions, as well as the social relationships and understandings that undergirded them. It argues that the crisis-induced fragmentation of the social order "unmade" class by killing or displacing popular leaders, destroying networks of solidarity, and privatizing individual experiences of terror. The repression deprived people of the ability to talk about or do anything about what was happening, and it disrupted the ability of working people to reproduce the material and emotional relationships that were necessary to care for themselves and each other, that gave meaning to their lives, and that enabled them to imagine the future.

Poor urban residents became more vulnerable to the manipulation and domination of the new masters of the city, who crushed opposition to subcontracting and the withdrawal of the state from social welfare activities. Chapter 4 takes up the specific example of Barrancabermeja's Coca-Cola workers. It explores how political violence and neoliberal restructuring dismantled a "labor elite" that had begun to enjoy the rights and protections won in previous labor struggles, and that constituted a small but vital part of Barrancabermeja's activist political culture. Together, chapters 3 and 4 demonstrate how late twentieth-century and early twenty-first-century paramilitary terror emerged as a consequence of working people's opposition to free-market policies, their demands for public services, and their insistence that the state attend to the needs of its citizens. The wrath of the regional bourgeoisie drove political violence, which dismantled working-class power. Violence simultaneously created the conditions for neoliberal capitalism to prosper through the reorganization of social and economic life on more unequal and authoritarian terms.[3]

The Evil Twins: Neoliberalism and Political Violence

During the 1980s and 1990s, political violence and neoliberalism became intertwined in the Middle Magdalena, and the future of Barrancabermeja's working people unfolded within a vicious dialectic in which the resurgent power of popular movements and the accumulating force of reactionary violence generated rising levels of terror and desperation. Peace talks with the guerrillas and the local election of mayors initiated by the Barco administration in the 1980s, and the convening of the National Constituent Assembly to rewrite the Colombian constitution in 1991, had spurred the renewed organization and unification of popular forces to take advantage of the possibilities offered by political decentralization and the democratic opening. The labor movement unified under the umbrella of the Central Unitaria de Trabajadores (Unitary Workers Central, CUT) in 1986, bringing the majority of unions from three competing federations, as well as a group of independent unions, together for the first time. New social movements—the Unión Patriótica and A Luchar, which were electoral fronts for the FARC and the ELN, respectively—formed from the commitment of guerrilla groups to lay down their arms and participate in the political process, and in the 1980s, they won control of a majority of union directorates.

In addition, the Constituent Assembly brought together a broad spectrum of left political forces—indigenous, labor, religious, and demobilized guerrillas from the M-19, EPL, and Quintín Lamé insurgencies—to produce a new, more democratic and inclusive Colombian constitution (Valencia and Celis 2012), even though the FARC and the ELN refused to participate. The new constitution deepened the political decentralization initiated during the Betancur administration by devolving administrative and fiscal functions to the municipalities. The rationale was twofold: to make funds available to newly elected authorities so that they could respond to the needs of constituents for infrastructure development, water, trash collection, and other public services, and to pacify the insurgencies by incorporating them into the political system (Ballvé 2012; Castro 1998). Yet as we saw in the previous chapter, the groundswell of popular organizing and rising expectations about addressing pent-up popular concerns through a more open political system radicalized right-wing regional power holders, who felt threatened by the growing popularity of the legal left and the challenge that decentralization posed to their vested interests. A resurgent left spurred closer alliances between regional elites and the security forces and fed the expansion of paramilitarism, which was financed by the explosion of the illegal cocaine traffic. Decentralization did less to tame the insurgencies and make the political field accessible to greater popular participation than to intensify regional conflict and facilitate the configuration of new, scale-spanning geographies of power under the control of paramilitaries and their civilian allies. Although it arose from particular Colombian circumstances, decentralization was fully compatible with the free-market policy reforms endorsed by the United States, the International Monetary Fund, and the World Bank that, throughout the 1980s and 1990s, drove more and more working people into poverty around Latin America and the world.

Unlike other countries forced by crushing international debt to adopt the free-market reforms that constituted what came to be known as the "Washington consensus," Colombia did not carry a significant debt burden due, in part, to the massive, albeit illegal, profits of the cocaine industry that flowed into the country. The specter of default, the loss of global economic credibility, and the domestic consequences of becoming a "pariah" state in the eyes of global financial institutions were thus ineffective in leveraging the opening of the Colombian economy. The administration of César Gaviria (1990–94) agreed to implementing a series of free-market policy reforms only after President George H. W. Bush offered a substantial cut of the $2.2 billion Andean Initiative to fight drug trafficking. In 1990, the government then passed a series of laws that legalized temporary labor contracts and made it easier for employers to hire and fire workers (Law 50), created a private pension system and expanded private health care and social security (Law 100), deregulated trade and lowered tariff barriers (Law 49), liberalized financial institutions (Law 45), and decentralized public spending (Law 49). In addition, between 1989 and 1994, the large-scale privatization of state-owned enterprises began. These policies were maintained and expanded throughout the 1990s and became key to the violent economic strategies of the Uríbe administration (2002–10).

As President Gaviria opened the country to market forces, paramilitary groups in the Middle Magdalena, the eastern plains, Córdoba province, and the Urabá region of northeast Antioquia province were already establishing the framework for a national-level counterinsurgent organization and a new concentration of power that united drug-traffickers-turned-landlords, cattle ranchers, traditional politicians, and regional elites in a far-right alliance. With profits from the illegal cocaine traffic, these regional-based paramilitary entities, whose most important leaders came from the drug cartels, morphed from roving death squads into standing armies that outgrew their role as the military's clandestine enforcers. The majority of them federated, in 1997, under the umbrella of the AUC, but their power remained rooted in the regions, where they constructed new nodes of development centered on mineral extraction, African palm cultivation, and, most important, the cocaine traffic.

These new geographies of power were forged through predation and dispossession. Paramilitary commanders disputed territorial control with the guerrillas, murdered or displaced anyone alleged to sympathize with the insurgents, and amassed an enormous amount of wealth and power for themselves and those they served through the theft of land and the displacement of the inhabitants. They did so as the United States' Andean Initiative was followed, in 2001, by Plan Colombia, authorized by President Bill Clinton and providing $1.3 billion in mostly military aid. Although officially described as a counternarcotics program, Plan Colombia strengthened paramilitary power by channeling money and arms to its main ally, the Colombian security forces. It did not target areas in northern Colombia where paramilitaries supervised the shipment of cocaine out of the country but fumigated the southern coca fields of peasant cultivators who supported the FARC.

At a moment when paramilitarism was gaining momentum and wrapping itself in the cloak of counterinsurgency, neoliberal reforms aimed to roll back the hard-won popular gains from earlier rounds of class struggle and make working people more "manageable." Mercenaries awash in drug profits stepped in to repress challenges to the emergent economic order, as conflicts over labor rights, landownership, the privatization of public enterprises, national sovereignty, and the control of decentralized municipal budgets ignited around the country. Paramilitary violence undergirded the opening of the economy through the repression of working people, labeled "subversives" for their opposition to neoliberal economic reforms, the theft of their lands, and the assassination of their leaders. It was the midwife of neoliberalism and fueled a new phase of territorial reconfiguration and capital accumulation.

The enactment of neoliberal economic policies prompted an increase in unemployment, economic precariousness, and insecurity in Barrancabermeja, where state workers represented a substantial sector of the workforce. Workers in petroleum, telecommunications, education, transportation, health care, and fertilizer manufacture all faced the threat of privatization and either job loss or new contracts on less favorable terms. With the partial privatization of ECOPETROL, foreign oil companies signed contracts with the government to provide specific services and operations. These contracts resembled the early twentieth-century TROCO concession but on even worse terms, that is, the contracts could be extended indefinitely, until the exhaustion of the oil field, with no requirement that the oil field eventually revert to state control. And as state entities were privatized, the cost of public services—telephone, electricity, health care, and so forth—increased. In addition, the rise of subcontracting diminished the power of the USO and other unions and opened the door for private contractors with ties to the paramilitaries to exert greater control over the labor force. In the midst of growing precariousness, new stores opened in the city center and in small regional towns displaying flashy imports, such as clothing, expensive sneakers, and electronic equipment, that became a way of laundering illegal drug profits. The dance of commodities tantalized working people, but the gaudy imports generally remained beyond their grasp, as civil war and economic restructuring drove people deeper into poverty.

By the end of the 1990s, paramilitaries had weakened the ELN in the Middle Magdalena and, according to local activists, thoroughly infiltrated its forces in Barrancabermeja, but the paramilitary presence in the city was still limited and not pervasive enough to be considered an occupying force. This situation changed in late 2000, when a commander of the BCB announced over the radio that the mercenaries intended to take control of the city. Some one thousand fighters then laid siege to urban neighborhoods, starting with Miraflores in the northeast and taking control of them one by one in an orgy of violence. Within only a few months, the BCB had expelled the guerrilla militias, and its commanders had become the new lords of the city. A report by the Center for International Policy, based on a March 2001 staff visit, found that, with the exception of the downtown and the area around the oil refinery, five and a half of Barrancabermeja's seven districts (*comunas*) were under BCB control (Isacson 2001).

Impunity and the Paramilitary Takeover

When a journalist asked BCB leader Rodrigo Pérez Alzáte why taking Barrancabermeja was important, the paramilitary chief alluded to the disruptive power of organized labor, noting the capacity of the USO to organize labor strikes that shut down the city and affected the entire country. "This municipality is the biggest oil port in the country, the carburetor of Colombia. ECOPETROL, the state oil company, has a union, the USO, that was infiltrated by the ELN for a long time. When the subversives wanted to paralyze the country, the union organized a strike leaving Colombia without fuel, in only 48 hours" (Aranguren 2001: 257). Crushing the USO and expelling the ELN guerrillas from a working-class stronghold represented an important victory for the BCB. The USO strongly opposed government plans to privatize the oil industry and objected to the national enactment of neoliberal policies. More important, the USO was a critical resource for working people because it had the power to inflict economic damage beyond Barrancabermeja. Because of the centrality of oil to the Colombian economy, an oil worker strike had national implications that increased the spatial field of worker power, a fact that paramilitaries like Pérez Alzáte understood well.

Impunity underwrote the BCB takeover of Barrancabermeja and gave form to the new political, economic, and social order that the mercenaries set out to create. It constituted more than simply getting away with murder. Impunity was an aspect of both power and powerlessness forged within the clash of opposed, unequal political forces. Widespread exemption from any form of accountability protected the perpetrators of massive human rights violations who acted in the service of an emergent narco-bourgeoisie, while creating and maintaining exclusion, disorganization, and fear among working people. In Barrancabermeja, impunity not only allowed paramilitaries to move unimpeded throughout the city and avoid accountability for their crimes; it also enabled them to abuse urban residents over and over again because residents could do nothing about what was happening. Brutal violence with no negative consequences for the instigators engendered chaos in people's lives, severed them from their ties to each other, and created the conditions for the establishment of new, authoritarian relationships that undergirded the further accretion of wealth and power.

The BCB takeover would have been impossible without the collaboration of the security forces, who looked the other way as the mercenaries committed atrocities and rarely took action against them. Barrancabermeja had long been one of the most militarized cities in Colombia. The army based two battalions in Barrancabermeja: Nueva Granada and Heroes of Majagual; the navy monitored traffic on the Magdalena River from another base; the National Police had three bases, including one in the northeast quarter; special intelligence arms of the police (Seccional de Policía Judicial e Investigación) and the military (B2) conducted surveillance operations; and a division of the Attorney General's Office, the Cuerpo Técnico de Investigación (Technical Investigation Corps), oversaw police investigations. Yet despite the presence of multiple state security forces, these entities routinely denied any knowledge of the paramilitaries and their activities. In Barrancabermeja, as well as other conflicted Colombian regions, the paramilitaries formed such an integral part of the armed forces' counterinsurgent strategy that Colombians referred to them as the army's "Sixth Division" (Human Rights Watch 2001).

Impunity was, in fact, an important strategy of the Colombian armed forces. Upholding the pretense of Colombian democracy would have been impossible with the army massacring, displacing, and torturing other Colombians, but by outsourcing the disreputable aspects of a dirty war to clandestine, illegal armies whose existence they denied, the armed forces contained and ultimately crushed the insurgencies and the radicalizing trajectory of popular democratic movements in Barrancabermeja and the Middle Magdalena. Impunity turned out to be the whitewash that obscured the relationship between the legitimate, official state and its illegitimate, unofficial counterpart, and it played an important part in the radical right turn that processes of state formation were taking in the Middle Magdalena (see chapter 5).

As urban neighborhoods shifted from guerrilla to paramilitary control, residents found themselves immersed in a living hell. They began to notice hooded men walking through the streets at night and then discovering, or hearing about, mutilated corpses that appeared in public places the next day. Mercenaries dressed in civilian clothing stationed themselves on street corners to monitor the comings and goings of local people, and the blep-blep sound of their two-way radios left no doubt that the menacing figures were integrated into a larger, partly invisible force. Walking down the street became fraught with peril for urban residents, as firefights could erupt out of nowhere at any time. Parents were afraid to send their children to school, and those who did worried about what would happen after they arrived. Traveling to work became an ordeal, too. Taxi and bus drivers refused to enter certain areas, forcing residents to walk. Fearing for their lives, many residents—especially those who had openly collaborated with the insurgents—sold their homes and fled to another city, but because the mayhem had driven down property values, they often earned little on home sales to begin anew. Other families did not have time to sell their property and simply abandoned their homes; still others were forcibly evicted by the paramilitaries. The BCB rented commandeered dwellings to collaborators who arrived from other areas under its control, or it used them as command centers or places to inflict torture.

Human rights defenders, armed only with cell phones, relayed accounts of the paramilitary terror unfolding in Barrancabermeja's working-class neighborhoods to local, national, and international human rights organizations. They represented Colombian organizations, such as the Corporación Regional para la Defensa de los Derechos Humanos (Regional Corporation for the Defense of Human Rights, CREDHOS), that had organized, in the 1980s, in response to intensifying state and paramilitary violence against the left. They also worked for internationally based NGOs, such as Peace Brigades and

Pax Christi, that established a presence in Barrancabermeja during the 1990s, when human rights activism was gaining traction as a new form of international solidarity.

Despite the pressure of human rights activists on army and police commanders to stop the mayhem, the security forces either did not respond to the paramilitary incursion or delayed the deployment of forces, thus aiding and abetting the mercenary advance. Human rights organizations reported that even when police sent out patrols, stationed armored vehicles near poor neighborhoods, and searched houses, they avoided locations where the paramilitaries kept hostages or conducted operations, and they ignored civilian pleas for help (Human Rights Watch 2001). As one individual explained, "When the paramilitaries came into Barranca, everyone knew that they stayed with the army battalion. And we knew what cars they used, where they ate, and even what prostitutes they had sex with. It was so obvious that sometimes we even told the authorities and gave them the addresses, but they didn't do shit."[4]

The experience of William Mendoza, a Coca-Cola worker, CREDHOS activist, and president of the local affiliate of SINALTRAINAL, illustrates the license that enabled the mercenaries to seize control of Barranca's working-class neighborhoods and the corresponding inability of residents to stem the violence. On a January morning, Mendoza was showering on the back patio of his home in La Esperanza neighborhood. It was still early. The sun had barely risen, as the northeast sector of the city stirred to life in the relative coolness of the morning. Luz, William's wife, had sent their daughter to the corner store for eggs and bread, and the smell of coffee floated in the air. Mendoza rarely ate breakfast at home. On most days, he would have already left the house, but on this particular morning he was angry at Luz and wanted to reassert his domestic authority, so he insisted that she cook breakfast for him.

He had just finished dressing when his daughter walked through the front door, looking ashen and distraught. The store was full of armed men, she reported, and there were others positioned all around the block. The news passed through Mendoza like an electric shock. Peering cautiously out the window, he saw male figures dressed in blue jeans and black T-shirts walking up and down the street. The young men were not local residents. Without wasting a minute, he grabbed his cell phone and began to call a network of human rights activists, fearing that, as the armed men went door-to-door hunting down alleged "subversives," they would discover his identity and kill him. "If those guys were going to come into my house, I was going to shoot with them [*volar plomo con ellos*]," he told me several years later. "I knew that they had come to kill . . . , Lesley, and if they got me alive, they would subject me to the worst torture imaginable."[5] Because of his long career as an outspoken trade union leader, and as a member of a prominent regional human rights organization, Mendoza had good reason to be afraid. The paramilitaries, as well as their shadowy supporters in government, in the security forces, and among regional elites, tended to lump any critic of the status quo together with the insurgents.

Yet despite repeated calls to the police by human rights activists, as well as assurances from the police that a helicopter would soon fly over the neighborhood, nothing happened. Mendoza and his family cowered in their home for over an hour and a half, fearing the worst. When the police finally arrived, an officer asked Mendoza if he knew a human rights defender whom, he claimed, the security forces were under instructions to extract from the neighborhood. Because Mendoza suspected that the police were collaborating with the mercenaries and knew that the officer was referring to him, he denied knowledge of such a person and seized the opportunity to pile his wife and their children onto a motorcycle and leave along a route that the police had begun to cordon off. "I left," he said, "like a soul that the devil takes." But even though Mendoza survived, his life would never be the same again.

The BCB took over La Esperanza and began a reign of terror like that which had already engulfed other urban neighborhoods. Unlike many unionists and human rights activists, Mendoza did not leave Barrancabermeja. He slept in different places for several months and eventually sold his house and moved closer to the center of the city, where, he believed, the paramilitaries operated with less impunity than in the northeast. Two bodyguards began to accompany him everywhere he went. Coherence and predictability vanished from his life, and the routines and practices that once defined it became memories. Terror and the impunity that enabled it transformed his life into a recurrent nightmare as Mendoza, along with other labor leaders, became the targets of paramilitary fury because of their real or alleged ties to the insurgencies and leadership positions.

The BCB had become the most powerful mercenary force within the

AUC at a time when the distinction between drug trafficking and the counterinsurgent war had become irrevocably blurred. It controlled the narco-economy in much of the country, and seizing Barrancabermeja offered it an opportunity to expand its domination of the illegal cocaine traffic, a point I discuss further in chapter 5. Ever since the days of the TROCO, Barrancabermeja had been the nerve center of the Middle Magdalena with access to an Atlantic port, and it was located along major highways that crossed the country. As a vibrant commercial center, Barranca offered mercenaries the opportunity to launder drug profits, control traffic on the river, and project themselves into the coca-growing zone of southern Bolívar province. In addition, its oil refinery produced 75 percent of the nation's gasoline, which represented a lucrative source of rent for anyone who could organize the theft of the gasoline from ECOPETROL pipelines.

Although the collusion of the state security forces made the paramilitary takeover possible, the BCB also took advantage of divisions and betrayals among the insurgents to wrest control of the city from them. For example, by the 1990s the EPL, a Maoist splinter group formed in 1967, had been nearly decimated in Barrancabermeja and throughout the country by military and paramilitary attacks, which had killed its more left-wing leaders and leveraged the group's political reorientation. As the reconfigured national leadership sought to negotiate accords with the paramilitaries, many of the EPL rank and file switched sides and exposed other guerrillas and their supporters to the BCB.[6] But the EPL was not alone. "Many from the FARC switched sides," explained an elderly woman whose neighborhood had been under FARC control, "and it wasn't just the boys [muchachos]. It was the commandants, too. This was the ugliest thing that happened at the time. It was really ugly. It was the worst environment that we saw [and] that's why many people say that you can't believe in anything. What happened is a disgrace."[7] The overwhelming violence and power of the paramilitary assault, strengthened by the collusion of state security forces, pushed many guerrillas to betray their support networks in order to save their own lives or for the benefits that collaboration with the paramilitaries appeared to offer.[8] Their behavior sowed a sense of panic, as most people had some type of interaction with them through family or neighborhood ties, a business deal, school, a friendship or romance, or simply because they said hello to each other in the street. Few people were free from possible exposure.

Not surprisingly, the desertions and betrayals created a deep reservoir of cynicism and disillusionment that erased the ability to hope, or to "believe in anything," and they stoked feelings of revenge. After describing to me in considerable detail how a friend fingered him as a guerrilla, one individual said quietly, when I put my notebook down, that if he ever saw the man again, he would kill him. It was clear that the dirty war had not only created pervasive fear; it also taught people to hate.

The guerrilla betrayals of each other and their support networks only solidified popular resentment of the insurgents, which had been accumulating for a number of years. The insurgents' righteous political demands that had unified, inspired, and politicized some urban residents over the years had devolved into little more than ossified slogans, as young *milicianos* behaved less like the vanguard of a political alternative—or even as Colombian Robin Hoods who robbed multinationals and redistributed the booty among the poor—than like arrogant delinquents who took advantage of people like themselves. One longtime urban resident, who had supported the insurgents in his youth, described the gradual decomposition of the ELN guerrillas and their loss of legitimacy:

> There was, first, the decade of the 1970s when the insurgencies were way out there in the mountains. That was a very romantic time, a moment of strong support. . . . The second moment came when the guerrilla arrives in Barrancabermeja and sets up its urban networks, more or less between 1985 and 2000 and with a strong, armed urban front. During the first ten years, 1985 to 1995, the guerrilla is close to the people, the guerrilla works with the neighborhoods, the guerrilla goes hand in hand with the social organizations, the guerrilla, in one way or the other, is seen by residents as part of themselves, of their daily life. But the third moment of the guerrilla is their degradation, from 1995 to 2000. The insurgents become more like an occupying force and degenerate into common criminality. They start to assassinate people, to extort, to rob, and sectors of the FARC also decompose quickly. In their desire to grow, the ELN had let anyone join up and given them no political education, and this made military infiltration much easier. Some business leaders went to visit the commandants in the middle of 2000 and told them what was happening. They told them that if the insurgents didn't stop what was

going on, they were going to the paramilitaries. And those guerrilla chiefs did nothing.[9]

One elderly resident who had once collaborated with the FARC commented that their "proposal had always been to change the state, for a substantial change for the Colombian people," but "that was converted into a kind of common criminality. They killed a lot of innocent people and extorted a lot."[10]

When the FARC demanded protection payments from multinational corporations, the practice did, at times, build popular support, but when onerous extortion demands—or requests for "contributions"—were directed at the guerrillas' own supporters, they eroded the insurgents' legitimacy. Richani, for example, cites a case in Barrancabermeja in which three multinationals planned to build an electric plant in 1997. Operating through a neighborhood council with the support of local people, the FARC demanded that the companies pay $2 million for a vocational school and $150,000 for a jobs-creation program as a condition for the right to operate (Richani 2002: 80). Yet so-called contributions were also exacted from small merchants, the same group that once supported the labor struggles of the USO and the civic strikes of the 1970s. Much like the multinationals, these shop owners, whose margin of profit was not large, viewed their payments less as contributions to a transformative social project than as protection from the guerrillas themselves. Neighborhood merchants complained, too, of milicianos who entered their establishments and refused to pay for services rendered. Not surprisingly, many of these shopkeepers initially welcomed the arrival of the paramilitaries.[11] The BCB's commander, Rodrigo Pérez Alzáte, explained, "The best way to win territory from the subversion consisted in going block by block to win over people asphyxiated by the extortion. We started in Comuna 2, the commercial center of the city. People there were 'vaccinated' from every side" (Aranguren 2001: 256). Yet the paramilitaries would soon become infamous for practicing their own form of extortion.

Guerrilla extortion and then increasing resort to kidnapping, selective assassinations, and bombings in heavily populated civilian areas raised questions about the political projects that the guerrillas claimed to represent. Attacks on banks, police stations, and other establishments angered civilians affected by the mayhem, and the increasingly harsh and arbitrary "justice" meted out by the guerrillas to alleged informants and others who ran afoul of them served only to further alienate the insurgencies from the population. One resident of La Esperanza neighborhood, for example, recounted how an ELN insurgent murdered his brother for smoking marijuana. "They killed him because . . . he was supposedly a drug addict who could influence other boys to smoke dope, too. But who are they to come and judge another person who has problems, especially when there are worse cases among [the insurgents]."[12] By the late 1990s, the guerrillas were providing their urban militias with little political education about what they were supposedly fighting for, and they devolved into criminal protection rackets, essentially abandoning the urban working class to the paramilitary right.[13] Because of the inability or unwillingness of local commanders to control criminal behavior within their own ranks, thuggery overwhelmed any remaining vision of revolutionary transformation.

The understanding and practice of solidarity that had characterized Barrancabermeja's working-class political culture was defeated by the degradation of the insurgencies and a paramilitary victory that rested on savage violence, and what remained of it was ravaged by neoliberalism. The dismantling or weakening of unions and civic organizations suppressed opposition to neoliberalism. A new generation of working-class youth who came of age at the end of the twentieth century confronted a stark world of limited job opportunities, on the one hand, and new forms of consumption and a lack of political alternatives, on the other hand. Although these youngsters had the benefits of some education, the liberalization of the economy, the constriction of manufacturing, and the creeping privatization of public entities reduced legal employment opportunities, which had also grown less secure for members of their parents' generation, some of whom had found work— albeit often part-time—in the oil industry and in the city's small factories, businesses, and public sector (see chapter 4). Amid deepening economic insecurity, the explosion of the cocaine economy dangled the symbols of wealth and status before the eyes of young people.

The expansion of organized crime, tied to the export of cocaine, fed on the growing reserve of un- and underemployed youth in a city where the unemployment rate was 30 percent. Young men who toiled in the underground economy processing cocaine paste, selling small quantities of drugs, and harvesting coca leaves in the nearby mountains of southern Bolívar province earned more than their counterparts in the legal economy. The "easy money" from the drug traffic and the conspicuous consumption fueled by it clashed with notions of solidarity and Christian commitment that had once formed part of Barranca's political culture, and it nurtured a resentful individualism. In addition, the paramilitaries enticed recruits with cell phones and monthly salaries well above what they could earn from legal employment; indeed, the foot soldiers of paramilitarism generally lived better than rank-and-file guerrillas because they were not persecuted by the state. Under these circumstances, "nothing," Forrest Hylton notes, "could have been less likely to lead to armed insurrection than 'popular militias,' which often became indistinguishable from predatory youth gangs" (2014: 87).

Following the BCB takeover, the chaos that enveloped working-class neighborhoods and the fissures that opened in people's lives deepened a crisis that rendered daily life incoherent and unpredictable. Women and children bore the weight of this crisis with particular difficulty. Many young women found themselves widowed after the death or disappearance of husbands and companions. Forced to raise children alone without the support of a male breadwinner, they faced the prospect of falling deeper into poverty. Those who sought justice learned hard lessons about the nature of impunity. For example, Amelia González, a mother of two young children, lost her husband in a paramilitary massacre three years before the BCB took over the city. Together with five other women, whose husbands were murdered at the same time, González reported the crime to the police, and a suspect whom witnesses identified as one of the perpetrators was arrested and placed in jail. Then, after the BCB takeover, paramilitaries summoned the six widows to a meeting in an occupied neighborhood. As González recalled, "They told us that we had to gather in a park, and then they blindfolded us and put us in a taxi. They took us to a house . . . [and] then the commandant appeared. He was horrifying and I could not look at his face, which was hideous. He was surrounded by his boys and there were shovels and picks. I thought the worst." Another man identified himself as a lawyer and instructed the women to withdraw their criminal complaint. Doing so would ensure that the case was dropped. "I was terrified for my girls," recounted Amelia, "because they depended only on me."[14] Amelia González had no choice. If she wanted to ensure that her daughters had a mother to care for them, she had to decide between survival and the dim prospect of justice for her husband's murder. The brutal disorganization of the working class extended to the rupture of intimate familial relationships. It not only placed a heavier economic burden on women like Amelia González; it obliged some of them to choose between life and death.

Impunity limited what people could do alone and with others. It created a crisis that gave rise to a new configuration of imperatives and possibilities over which working people had little control, and it destroyed any sense of stability that poor urban residents had established in their lives, a stability that was necessary to organize their livelihoods, to do whatever was necessary to get through the day, and then to repeat it again and again. Claiming a modicum of stability and coherence had never been easy for most inhabitants of Barranca's poor neighborhoods. Many residents had already suffered the trauma of forcible displacement once, and sometimes twice or even three times, losing all of their possessions, witnessing the deaths of loved ones, and having their ties to home severed. Moreover, some degree of uncertainty and unpredictability had long been integral to the lives of people who had not yet been directly touched by the counterinsurgent war. Even before the advent of neoliberalism, unwaged workers in particular had to deal with chronic financial instability, inadequate health care, precarious housing, and political exclusion, which produced a state of constant apprehension about what was around the next corner. Violence and economic restructuring deepened that uncertainty, which spread to once relatively secure unionized workers, and it eroded the capacity of people to organize their lives and livelihoods in such a way that made social reproduction possible and that provided enough autonomy to allow them to shape the future. All of this was an essential part of the restructuring of class relationships in Barrancabermeja.

Although claiming an everyday life—and not just a daily existence of one thing after another—had always been a high-stakes struggle, some people had managed to create, or re-create, a relative sense of stability and continuity in which the horizon of their expectations for the present and the future could expand.[15] This sense of security arose from the capacity of people who had suffered trauma and displacement to forge new relationships of cooperation that congealed around making a living. These ties, and the expectations and obligations associated with them, constituted a first step toward stitching together the tattered social fabric and generating a sense of hope that life could be lived on one's own terms. Unfortunately, moments of relative stability were too often short-lived, as remade alliances and forms of assistance were destroyed over and over again, and crisis became an integral part of visions of the future.[16]

Pedro Lozada and his family, for example, were among the first group of displaced peasants to seek refuge in Barrancabermeja in the early 1980s. Forced from Puerto Berrío by paramilitaries, the family fled downriver to a small mining town, where they settled for several months until the FARC kidnapped the mine owner and the army arrived. "The displacement was really hard for me," Lozada related years later. "And when the army came, it searched people going to the mine as well as returning to town. And because we were from Puerto Berrío, the army, of course, knew that we had fled. [The soldiers] were all over those of us from Puerto Berrío. They even came to our homes, investigating and asking questions." Feeling that their lives were in jeopardy, the family set out again, this time to Barrancabermeja. After traveling for three days on the river, they arrived hungry, tired, and with little but the clothes on their backs. "It was a real adventure," Lozada said. "I really can't explain how we dared to set out on the river without knowing what we were doing. We were going to Barranca but had no idea what we would do there. . . . The first few days [in the city] were really, really hard. In spite of the solidarity—we lived from the solidarity—there were times that we went hungry."[17]

Over time, however, the Lozada family gradually carved a place for itself and staked a precarious foothold. It did so with the solidarity of a number of groups and organizations, including the USO, the Communist Party, and the Catholic Church, that found ways to assist those uprooted by the rural violence, and with the support of other displaced peasants from the same region. Lozada's wife found work as a laundress in a health clinic, and Lozada labored as a night watchman. They also laid claim to an urban lot through a land "recuperation" and constructed a home. Their sense of relative stability was short-lived, however, as the paramilitary takeover turned any sense of continuity upside down and ruptured many of Lozada's newly established relationships in the port city. He fled once again, as the chaos and violence that so regularly intruded into his life reappeared. For Pedro Lozada and his family, crisis was less an exceptional situation—a brief interruption in an otherwise settled life—than a manifestation of the radical insecurity that, for more than half a century, had constantly undermined their ability to create a livable life.

The disintegration of the social order gave rise to a new political subjectivity in which self-interested individualism replaced a more capacious understanding of self, one tied to solidarity with others through a "collective politics that looked to the state to dispense justice" (Grandin 2004: 14). This new sensibility grew out of the betrayals and divisions that the relentless violence had created in people's lives. Trust evaporated. In 2007, one man explained to me: "When you walk past an unknown person, you always go on the defensive. It's not the same anymore. If somebody comes around asking if you know so-and-so, nobody will admit to knowing [the person] because you don't know who is asking or why they are looking for him."[18] Social life grew more privatized and isolated as the left public sphere shrank and a welter of autocratic, personalized relationships became more important to the livelihood strategies of working people. People turned inward or to evangelical churches, and away from politics, to find solutions to their problems. They were increasingly remade as autonomous individuals, dispossessed from their relationships to each other, and felt bitter, passive, and in despair. Such mistrust arose not only from what had happened to people but also from what they had done — or been forced to do — to each other. Violence created unsustainable tensions for those in the line of paramilitary fire. It forced people to betray others like themselves, as they desperately sought ways to survive in a violent new social order that had still not fully emerged. Betrayal was the solvent of social solidarity, and its corrosive power was worse when inflicted by an acquaintance, a workmate, or a close friend. It violated the certainties and expectations that people held about each other, and it bred suspicion and feelings of isolation, diminishing their capacity to talk about what was happening and formulate a response. Rumors of paramilitary hit lists, atrocities, and so-called social cleansing campaigns aggravated the sense of menace and created a climate of fear.

The Dynamics of Fear

Most barranqueños who resided in the northeastern and southeastern districts of the city experienced a deep sense of physical insecurity during the most intense months of fighting in late 2000 and 2001, when the BCB routed the insurgencies. The rituals and routines of daily life became fraught activities, as firefights often erupted out of nowhere and political allegiances were in flux. People felt terrified. Yet once the fighting abated and daily life became, in the words of one man, "normal between quotation marks," fear—an emotion aroused by the real or imagined sense of imminent danger or harm—gripped some people much more tightly than others. Those who lived in former guerrilla strongholds, or who aided the guerrillas by stashing arms in their home or allowing an insurgent to spend the night, as well as those who participated in activist unions, human rights committees, or left political movements, faced grave physical danger. It is important therefore to examine the circumstances that generated fear and connect them to the actual experience of it (or not) among different kinds of people.[19]

Unlike those individuals and institutions that expressed opposition to the paramilitaries, there were many people, such as the merchants discussed earlier, who welcomed the arrival of the BCB and the end of the abuses suffered under the guerrillas. And other men and women, if they did not actively support the BCB, accepted it as the lesser evil—the latest group of armed overlords to dominate their neighborhoods—and found ways to adjust to life under BCB rule. One trade union leader, for example, observed that people had few difficulties with the paramilitaries as long as they "do what they say. That means going from home to work, agreeing to participate in their marches and meetings, showing up when [they] announce through the neighborhood councils that there will be a trash cleanup, not complaining about the high cost of electricity and the absence of public services, and, above all else, not organizing other people who might challenge the power of the paramilitaries."[20] Indeed, the paramilitaries rewarded supporters with jobs in construction, park maintenance, transportation, and, of course, a range of illegal activities (Loingsigh 2002). Some urban residents therefore benefited from paramilitary largesse. They made the accommodations and concessions that were necessary to carve a place for themselves within paramilitary-controlled patronage structures, which began to take shape under BCB control (see chapter 5), and which minimized, at least for a time, the fear that became "a way of life" for surviving members of the opposition.[21]

Residents of Barrancabermeja's northeastern and southeastern districts were under constant surveillance. The paramilitaries transgressed the boundaries that had once delineated guerrilla-controlled territory and that even the security forces had been hesitant to breech, unifying the city under their control and mapping new spaces of fear onto it. Paramilitaries clad in civilian clothing, or informers paid by them, monitored the ebb and flow of social life in the barrios and kept tabs on the arrival and departure of passengers at the bus terminal, the river port, and the airport. Taxi drivers and young men with motorcycles were also recruited as informants and admonished to report on what they saw and heard as they moved about the city. They watched union activists, neighborhood leaders, human rights defenders, and members of left-wing political parties more closely than others, aiming to break any remaining links among the insurgencies, political parties, or social movements that challenged their power.

Trade union leader Juan Carlos Galvis, for example, often opened his home to me during my trips to Barrancabermeja because he, like other threatened activists, felt safer in the company of foreigners, especially North Americans and Europeans, who came to Barrancabermeja with international human rights organizations to accompany threatened leaders of urban popular organizations. Galvis had survived an attempted assassination, after hidden assailants ambushed his car as it was passing through a ravine, and his wife, Jackeline, had barely evaded a paramilitary attempt to murder her in a small river town where she traveled in her work as a human rights defender. Early one evening, I returned to their home—an apartment on the top floor of a three-story building—and found Jackeline distraught. The neighbors had alerted her to a man standing in front of the building, she explained, and he had been there for quite some time. I had seen him— an individual in his twenties, wearing blue jeans and a short-sleeved shirt—when I entered the building but had not paid special attention to what he was doing. "He shouldn't be there. There is no reason for him to be hanging around on the street," Jackeline insisted. Although she had already called the police, more than a half hour had passed with no response. I called again, and when a voice answered at the end of the line, I explained the situation in my foreign-accented Spanish and insisted that the police themselves had to understand the seriousness of the problem, as the family had been threatened before. Yet the police never came. Fortunately, the man on the street eventually departed, but he left behind a sense of uneasiness and insecurity. Who was he? What was he doing on the street? Who, if anyone, told him to be there? This was how fear worked. It fed on uncertainty and anxiety and called forth past traumas. Impunity enabled fear to blossom and to envelop the Galvis household within a constant state of menace that would eventually become unbearable.[22]

Fear also enforced a deafening silence about what had happened and continued to happen, and only in exceptional cases, such as the Galvis family, did people find ways to fight back against it.[23] More typical was the silence described to me by a female activist who discussed daily life in a northeastern neighborhood during 2007, after the BCB had officially demobilized. Although we talked in the privacy of her home, she made only oblique reference to "those people" (*esa gente*) when referring to the paramilitaries, and she repeatedly lowered her voice when describing the human rights violations perpetrated by them in her neighborhood. She explained that many of her neighbors maintained a resolute silence because of what might happen if they complained, and others had left for fear of paramilitary reprisals. A family across the street, she said in a hushed tone, lost a son; the paramilitaries disappeared him because he was a guerrilla. But now, "they don't say anything," she whispered, putting a finger to her lips and glancing toward the door.[24] Silence divided people from each other, undermining their ability to understand what was happening and to devise strategies to deal with the social "order" created by the dirty war, and it opened the door for dominant explanations of the urban violence that placed the onus of responsibility for the mayhem on the guerrillas and the social movements to take root.

Those most targeted by the paramilitaries increasingly found that they had to depend on individuals known to the paramilitaries to prove their "innocence," which meant no ties to the guerrillas or trade unions, popular organizations, human rights groups, or left-wing political parties. Much like Spaniards in the immediate aftermath of the Spanish Civil War described by Susana Narotzky and Gavin Smith (2006), working-class barranqueños needed a guarantor to remain alive, keep a home, maintain a job, and move about the city. Finding such a person was not only a difficult task; it also created new vertical relations of power and dependency.

In the early days of the BCB occupation, for example, as the paramilitaries sought to consolidate their control, commanders typically sent emissaries to summon trade union leaders and others suspected of guerrilla entanglements to meetings in which they laid out new rules of social engagement and advised them to keep a low profile. Worried that they would never return from such meetings alive, some, like William Mendoza, refused to attend and then bore the full brunt of paramilitary oppression. Others, however, leaned on the support of individuals known to the paramilitaries to negotiate the terms of new relationships with the occupiers. Andrés Mosquera, a state telecommunications worker and union leader, agreed to meet with a commander who wanted to question him prior to the privatization of the telecommunications company. Because he "had nothing to hide from them," and perhaps because he felt that the consequences of defiance were too severe to ignore, Mosquera decided that it was in his best interest to talk to the mercenaries. Emissaries took him to a home in an occupied neighborhood of the northeast sector, where Mosquera met the local commander, who was accompanied by bodyguards and a woman known to Mosquera. Much to Mosquera's horror, the paramilitary accused him and other telecommunication workers of plotting to sabotage the company, of having ties to the guerrillas, and of belonging to a "bad union for the company," one that publicly protested its impending privatization. As the charges and accusations mounted and the meeting seemed to spiral out of control, the woman insisted that Mosquera had no ties to the insurgency and vouched for his upright behavior. He subsequently credited his survival to her intervention, which, in turn, facilitated the establishment of new ground rules for his union leadership that included no protests, no strikes, and no public statements against the company.[25] Such pressure on trade unionists points to how intimidation played a key part in the decline of working-class power, the privatization of state-controlled entities, and the rise of neoliberalism.

Finding a guarantor to negotiate the paramilitary occupation presented special problems for gay men and women. Homophobia was deeply ingrained in social life and officially condemned by both popular religious traditions—Catholic and evangelical Protestant—that competed for adherents in working-class districts. The BCB sought to reassert rigid gender, generational, and sexual hierarchies after years of violence, and the repression of homosexuality formed part of this agenda, which was quietly welcomed by some residents who saw homosexuals as the purveyors of sexually transmitted diseases. The paramilitaries lumped homosexuals, prostitutes, and the always expandable group of "communists" (i.e., social justice advocates; peasant, labor, and student activists; and critics of the status quo) into one category—the disposable ones (*los desechables*)—which then facilitated the use of lethal violence against them. Many gay-friendly venues and nightspots shut down in the wake of the occupation, and gays and lesbians, including those who had already endured painful coming-out experiences within their families, churches, schools, and workplaces, found themselves forced to negotiate their very existence with a violent group of armed mercenaries.[26]

Carmen Villamizar, for example, was a lesbian in her thirties who lived in the Miraflores neighborhood, one of the first places occupied by the paramilitaries after they entered the city. Villamizar lived on a narrow street in a small home that, like other houses in the northeast, shared a wall with the dwellings on either side. She had operated a beauty parlor and a small dry goods store from the front of her home for more than a decade, and she was well known to her neighbors, most of whom were aware of her homosexuality. At the time of the paramilitary incursion, she lived openly with her young lover but worried about their safety. Paramilitaries clad in civilian clothing constantly passed along the street in front of her home, and sentries monitored the comings and goings of residents from every street corner. One of the men directing the offensive was a former ELN guerrilla-turned-paramilitary named Wolman Said Sepúlveda, known to residents by the alias Don Oscar. Sepúlveda had installed himself in a house down the street from Carmen's home, where he lived with a woman named Dora who was reputed to be his lover.

Dora and Villamizar were friends, and Dora had urged Carmen to speak directly with Sepúlveda about the relationship with her partner, assuring her that all would be well. Carmen hesitated for some time before seizing the opportunity one day after catching a glimpse of him on the street, as she and her companion passed on a bus. "One day, without planning," she said,

> I had the opportunity to meet Wolman down the street where he maintained himself. I saw him down there, and it was easy to just get off the bus. He was with his bodyguards but stepped away from them to talk to me. So I said, "Don Oscar, I come to talk to you because the truth is that there are rumors around that you don't like gays and lesbians. And I know that you have heard about me. People in the neighborhood call me Carmencita [little Carmen]. I am Carmencita to everyone in Miraflores. And what's more, you can ask Doña Dora about me." . . . What he told me was "Look, Carmencita, what I don't like are these dikes who entice men to sleep with them and then rob them. . . . That is what I am not going to permit. And

yes, I will punish that. But if you live your life behind the doors of your home, nobody is going to bother you." And that's how it was.[27]

By drawing on her friendship with his lover Dora, and displaying subservience through the use of the honorific "Don" to refer to Sepúlveda and the diminutive of her own name, Carmen managed to clarify a set of ground rules for her coexistence with the paramilitaries. These rules prohibited any public displays of lesbian sexuality, which had to remain concealed behind the walls of her home, and they left unchallenged Sepúlveda's characterization of lesbians as women who abuse and rob men. During the months that followed, Villamizar said that she "had [her] parties and meetings behind closed doors [*de la puerta para adentro*]. And when we went out at night in a taxi—taxis still had to keep their interior lights on—they [the paramilitaries] always stopped the taxis, but when they saw that it was me, they said, 'It's Carmencita, let her pass.' . . . They communicated from block to block [on walkie-talkies] and said, 'Here in the taxi is Carmencita,' and they let me pass because they knew that it was me."[28] The search for guarantors was one way that men and women tried to ensure their survival and renegotiate the terms of daily existence after the paramilitary takeover. Although it worked as an individual tactic for some people, the recourse to guarantors forced men and women to swallow their dignity, endure humiliation, and deal with new, unsettling dependencies and power dynamics, as their individual security turned on the willingness of another to vouchsafe their political credentials and good names to the new urban lords.

The collective politics that had once sustained individual lives through the experience of social solidarity was fractured by the combined force of paramilitary and state violence, which severed social relationships and created fertile ground for neoliberalism. The dirty war dismantled the network of trade unions, civic organizations, left political parties, and guerrilla insurgencies that had shaped and given meaning to working-class life for many years and protected some people from the full impact of the market. Impunity-driven violence ruptured social solidarities and remade men and women as autonomous individuals, who had to confront new, life-threatening vulnerabilities on their own. Yet the fear, betrayals, and lack of trust that arose amid the chaos generated by paramilitary domination made it nearly impossible for working people to do anything about what was happening to them.

With notable exceptions, working people turned away from collective politics and demands that the state provide them with decent jobs and livable neighborhoods and dedicated themselves to individual survival strategies. In these ways, Barrancabermeja's working class was unmade in the late 1990s and early 2000s, and the conditions were created for the incorporation of working people into new, authoritarian relationships on terms that accommodated the accumulation strategies of an emergent alliance of paramilitaries, drug traffickers, traditional politicians, large landowners, and neoliberal entrepreneurs.

FOUR

UNRAVELING

. . .

In late December 1996, paramilitaries shot SINALTRAINAL leader Isidro Gil dead. He was standing in the entrance to the Coca-Cola bottling plant in Carepa, a small town in a region of vast banana plantations and cattle ranches that hugs the Panamanian border and the Caribbean sea known as Urabá. Another Coca-Cola worker, Osvaldo Torres, was having breakfast in a kiosk outside the plant at the time and saw two men drive past on a high-powered motorcycle. The individuals circled back and forth several times before pausing briefly to exchange words with a man standing nearby. Torres grew worried. Since 1994, he had borne witness to the rising arc of violence across Urabá and had lost his brother, who also worked for Coca-Cola, to paramilitary assailants. "When I had to leave town and make a delivery," he told me, "I saw a lot of things. The paramilitaries would stop the trucks carrying workers to the banana plantations and leave fifteen or twenty dead bodies on the road. They would cut off their faces."[1] Not surprisingly, when Torres noticed the men on the motorcycle, he had no doubt who they were and went into the plant to express his worries to Gil. The two men talked for a moment, but then as a large metal gate opened for a delivery truck to leave, the assassins seized the moment to pump two bullets into Gil, who died immediately.

In the aftermath of the killing, the paramilitaries persecuted other members of the SINALTRAINAL directorate, forcing them to write letters of resignation from the union on company stationery, and then faxing the coerced statements to headquarters in Bogotá. Fearing for their lives, union leaders fled Carepa, and the SINALTRAINAL local ceased to exist. The men insisted that the decimation of the local took place with the complicity of company managers, whom workers had observed talking to paramilitary leaders in the plant cafeteria prior to the attack on Isidro Gil. Many rank-and-file trade unionists, who constituted the plant's approximately ninety full-time workers, were fired; most had logged more than ten years with the Coca-Cola Company and had received a range of benefits, such as health care and paid vacations. Average wages in the plant dropped from $380 a month to $130, and new hires received short-term contracts of three to four months with few, if any, benefits.

Displaced workers faced hard times in the months and years that followed. Union directorate member Adolfo Cardona tried to lose himself and his family in the sprawling working-class communities of southern Bogotá, where war refugees from all over the country had settled, but his search for peace and anonymity was short-lived. After neighbors told him that strange men had been asking about him, he entered a government protection program and then applied for asylum in the United States, where he resettled and found a job cleaning toilets at a Chicago airport. Like Cardona, Osvaldo Torres fled to southern Bogotá, but after being hunted down and accosted on a bus, he and his family moved again. Some fired rank-and-file Coca-Cola workers who did not leave Carepa secured temporary jobs on the banana plantations; others tried to set up small business; and still others purchased trucks from the Coca-Cola Company to become independent distributors, until the corporation cut back their routes and they could not make enough money to pay off the trucks.

The dramatic events in Carepa mirrored the setbacks of other working people across Colombia, especially in Barrancabermeja. Dispossession, the production of precariousness, displacement, and insecurity formed part of a violent strategy of wealth accumulation that David Harvey (2003) calls "accumulation by dispossession." Harvey (2005) uses the concept primarily to refer to the privatization of public assets, but it can be extended to include the loss of employment, the rupture of ties to other working people, and the denial of the social wages paid by employers, such as health care, pensions, education, and vacations, that workers won through prior struggles and that shielded them from some of the ravages of capitalism. Accumulation by dispossession was key to neoliberalism, a political project that aimed to revitalize the conditions of capital accumulation worldwide and redistribute wealth upward and that, in Colombia, enhanced the wealth and power of an emergent right-wing alliance that used unrestrained violence to accomplish political and economic goals.

In Barrancabermeja, paramilitary terror substantially dismantled a "labor elite," one that had played a leading role in linking the demands of waged laborers to the democratic aspirations of peasants and unwaged workers for land, public services, and the rights of citizenship. It also created a social and political environment in which neoliberalism could develop by silencing opposition to free-market policies and underwriting the spread of insecurity and vulnerability, a process that was closely interwoven with the lives of all working people. Although the oil industry was the most dramatic example of the unraveling of a relatively privileged sector of the working class, it was not alone. Workers in other branches of the economy, such as soft drink production, telecommunications, transportation, health care, education, and palm oil manufacture, saw their unions weakened, leaders attacked and assassinated, and working conditions deteriorate.

This chapter explores how the dismantling of a "labor elite" constituted part of a corporate profit-seeking strategy that became intertwined with the political dynamics of the Middle Magdalena. It does so by examining the reconfiguration of Coca-Cola production in Barrancabermeja, as the counterinsurgent war intensified and Colombia embraced free-market policies. Unlike ECOPETROL, the Coca-Cola Company did not play an outsized role in the economic life of Barrancabermeja, and its workforce was small by comparison. Yet like the more prominent USO, its activist union—SINALTRAINAL—formed part of the infrastructure of popular solidarity, communication, and political sympathy that connected labor unions, left political movements, urban neighborhood groups, and peasant organizations in Barrancabermeja and the surrounding region. And like the USO, it was directly targeted by resurgent paramilitarism. The case of Coca-Cola demonstrates how the violent dispossession of workers operated through spatial dispersal, subcontracting, and physical attacks on trade unionists. It also illustrates how the unmaking of class remapped social relations onto new geographies of power that weakened the organizational strength of working people in Barrancabermeja, bolstered the position of a multinational corporation, and created widespread vulnerability.

After briefly discussing the intensification of antilabor violence amid the growing liberalization of the Colombian economy, the chapter first considers how corporate restructuring and political violence weakened the national power of SINALTRAINAL and disrupted its ability to coordinate member activities across the country. Paramilitary terror enabled Coca-Cola, as well as other multinational corporations in Colombia, to remap the spatial coordinates of capital accumulation in ways that would have been more difficult had the corporations acted alone (e.g., Romero and Torres 2011). The chapter then examines how the growth of insecurity, through the closure or downgrading of the bottling plants, the subcontracting of labor, and the production of fear, was lived and understood by workers themselves. The case of Coca-Cola shows how different mixes of fear and labor exploitation shape changing forms of capital accumulation and become intertwined in the lives of ordinary people. It also demonstrates how the dispossession of a relatively privileged group of laborers, who had enjoyed a brief period of relative prosperity and broadened alliances, represented less the end of "class" than a new shift in the dialectic of solidarity and fragmentation that has been at the heart of the making and unmaking of class relations.

The Most Dangerous Country in the World to Be a Trade Unionist

Beginning in the 1990s, Colombia acquired the dubious reputation of being the most violent country in the world to be a trade unionist. Some four thousand trade unionists of the CUT died between the organization's formation in 1986 and 2003, including all the CUT founders. Human rights groups held paramilitaries responsible for the vast majority of trade union deaths. Most of the rights violations were connected to specific labor conflicts, such as contract negotiations, protests, and strikes, in which selective assassinations, arbitrary arrests, detentions, unlawful raids, and anonymous threats were used to discipline labor. Yet labor issues were not the only reason that trade unions suffered such atrocious violence. Many unions were deeply involved in democratic struggles beyond the workplace, and in some cases their concerns and initiatives overlapped with those of the guerrillas, who advanced their political programs through both war and peace — known as the combination of all forms of struggle (*combinación de todas las formas de lucha*).[2] Although the presence of guerrillas in popular organizations was common in the Central American civil wars, the practice was adopted as a dogmatic theoretical proposition for all revolutionary struggle only in Colombia. And not even in El Salvador, Guatemala, or Peru, where the state security forces were always in charge, did paramilitaries achieve the autonomy that they profited from in Colombia. The result was catastrophic: unarmed activists, radicals, and communities were publicly identified as subversives and labeled enemies of the nation and then attacked by heavily armed private armies, allied with the security forces.

Targeted and discriminate violence led to the death, exile, and displacement of hundreds of Colombian workers and contributed to a climate of antiunionism. Union membership fell from 12 percent of the national workforce in the mid-1990s to 3.2 percent in 2004 (ENS 2002). To be a union leader, commented Adolfo Cardona, meant having "one foot in the street and the other in the cemetery."[3] Indeed, many people believed that affiliating with a union would only bring them threats, harassment, and charges of collaborating with the guerrillas.

Labor unions throughout the Middle Magdalena, including those in oil, cement, African palm, soft drinks, education, and transportation, fought to retain rights and benefits won in earlier periods of class struggle. They opposed economic deregulation, the privatization of state entities, especially ECOPETROL, and labor legislation that weakened unions and permitted the subcontracting of labor to so-called *cooperativas de trabajo asociados* (associated work cooperatives), which allowed employers to unburden themselves of labor unions. An increasingly radicalized right-wing alliance opposed any concessions to labor, and paramilitaries imposed a gruesome form of labor discipline on behalf of the multinationals, landlords, and entrepreneurs that they served. Nazih Richani (2005: 130) has argued that an "affinity" existed between paramilitaries and foreign corporations, especially those operating in areas of intense conflict. What this "affinity" meant was not always clear, but journalist Steven Dudley (2004: 201) noted that paramilitary commanders repeatedly told him that they protected the business interests of foreign corporations and had built bases near Coca-Cola bottling plants.

The remapping of the geography of Coca-Cola production and the dispossession of Coca-Cola workers took place amid intensifying militarization and social polarization. Anxiety about the resurgent power of popular movements and a burning anger that sought to "cleanse" society of trade unionists, human rights defenders, guerrillas, critical journalists, and left political parties and movements stoked the violence of the far right. The desire of regional elites to roll back or eliminate grassroots challenges found common cause with the agendas of multinationals, like Coca-Cola, to discipline restive labor forces and to restructure corporate operations in the aftermath of the collapse of Eastern European and Soviet communism and the freeing of markets around the world. The violent clashes of contending social forces were neither abstract nor undescribable for Coca-Cola workers and others like them: they were examples of the brute force and terror deployed by state security forces and paramilitaries who, they believed, operated in collusion with company officials to roll back their rights and create a social order in which they would enjoy fewer protections.

Coca-Cola and the Remapping of Class

In 1993, when SINALTRAINAL leader William Mendoza started his job at Coca-Cola, the Barrancabermeja local represented 115 of the 125 full-time workers who labored in the plant; there were also about 150 temporary workers, some of whom were completing a three-month trial period before signing full-time work contracts with the soft drink bottler. Everyone, whether full-time or temporary, was employed directly by the Coca-Cola franchise in Barrancabermeja. A decade later, in 2003, production operations had ceased, and the plant operated as a warehouse and distribution facility. The number of full-time, unionized workers had dropped below 30, a 74 percent decline, threatening the continued viability of the union local, and the plant operator had subcontracted hiring to a so-called worker cooperative, ridding itself of the responsibility to pay union wages and benefits to a workforce that had lost considerable control over the labor process. Nationwide, SINALTRAINAL's membership plummeted from a peak of approximately five thousand members in the 1990s to barely fourteen hundred members in 2004.[4]

The situation in Barrancabermeja reflected changes sweeping across Coca-Cola's Colombian bottling plants. In 2003, production lines closed in ten other facilities. The corporation then concentrated the manufacture of Coca-Cola products for the domestic market in "megaplants" that operated in five large cities—Bogotá, Barranquilla, Bucaramanga, Medellín, and Calí. These moves led to the firing or forced retirement of approximately three thousand workers. Combined with new antilabor laws, they fragmented Coca-Cola workforces and limited the ability of the national union to coordinate member activities across the country. All of this served to discipline a union and its membership, which had become better organized and more radical since the 1980s, and to constrict worker understandings of what was possible. To grasp how these dramatic transformations came about, and to appreciate what it meant to working people, it is useful to briefly revisit the heady days of capitalist triumphalism in the 1990s, when the Coca-Cola Company set out to restructure its worldwide operations.

The Coca-Cola corporation sold soft drinks to millions of people in some two hundred countries, where it franchised production to bottling plants owned by national elites who, in turn, hired workers to bottle and distribute Coca-Cola where the beverage was consumed. The limited autonomy of the company's bottling franchises had long frustrated Atlanta-based corporate executives who wanted uniform policies and strategies to guide the corporation's global operations. In Colombia, for example, the Coca-Cola corporation began operations after World War II, and by the late twentieth century, it had to contend with a network of twenty franchises that were managed by different operators and scattered across the country. The end of the cold war presented the company with new global possibilities for consolidation and expansion. The collapse of Soviet and Eastern European communism and the reorientation of the Chinese economy opened vast new swaths of territory for corporate expansion, while falling trade barriers and government deregulation in Latin America, Asia, and Africa permitted higher prices, reduced taxes on the imported brown syrup that forms the basis of the soft drink, and larger bottles. And in Colombia, the government's openness to foreign investment, the weak regulatory framework, and the autonomy to define security arrangements made investment attractive, despite a polarized labor environment and grave security concerns.[5]

In the 1990s, Coca-Cola launched an aggressive campaign against Colombian bottlers in an effort to create greater efficiency and boost profitability. It began by granting the Miami-based bottler PANAMCO control of the Colombian market and assigned it the task of bringing local franchises under its control. Initially, PANAMCO acquired seventeen of the twenty Colombian franchises by purchasing family-operated bottling plants or driving them out of business, and it then merged with a large Mexican bottler, FEMSA, in 2002. The new

FEMSA-PANAMCO hybrid became the Coca-Cola Company's "anchor bottler" for Latin America, where it controlled 40 percent of sales, and it moved quickly to reconfigure the geography of Coca-Cola production in Colombia, closing production lines and restructuring soft drink manufacture around a smaller number of megaplants that would theoretically churn out carbonated beverages at lower cost.[6]

The remapping of Coca-Cola production in Colombia constitutes what David Harvey (1996) calls a "spatial fix," that is, the reorganization of place around new territorial divisions of labor, concentrations of power, and physical infrastructures and transportation systems, all of which disrupt prior social arrangements and institutional forms.[7] This contentious process is closely tied to the organization and disorganization of labor. In Colombia, the reconfiguration of space and place was the outcome of intense class struggles that arose at a moment when workers were reaping the rewards of previous victories and linking their struggles in the bottling plant to wider political movements.

Coca-Cola workers from around the country, including Barrancabermeja, affiliated with SINALTRAINAL in 1993, when SINALTRAINAL merged with an older union called SINTRAINDRASCOL, which then dissolved. Although it never represented a majority of Coca-Cola workers, much less those in the industry as a whole, SINALTRAINAL exemplified the growing restlessness of one sector of the Colombia labor force. Created in 1982 by Nestlé workers, SINALTRAINAL represented an attempt to create an industry-level union in which workers from the food and beverage industry would negotiate contracts together, instead of on a plant-by-plant basis. It built ties to the peasantry and advanced workers' claims more vigorously than any other union in the food and beverage industry by promoting a working-class public linked through a network of union locals embedded in the social and political life of the cities and small towns where they operated. Early activists envisioned a union that would take an aggressive stance toward the labor politics of the state and corporations, and that would "politicize the rank-and-file about the need to build a more just society in which workers are the central actors in their own destiny" (SINALTRAINAL, n.d.). They set out to build worker power, as the Colombian labor movement unified under the umbrella of the CUT, through vigorous rank-and-file organizing, popular education, and ties to domestic social movements and international unions.

Barrancabermeja workers voted to join SINALTRAINAL after a younger and more radical generation of local labor leaders became dissatisfied with the SINTRAINDRASCOL leadership. The younger generation referred to themselves as the *clasistas*. In the opinion of the youngsters, the problem with the national leadership of SINTRAINDRASCOL was its timidity and unwillingness to fight for better wages and benefits, despite the higher pay enjoyed by workers in other cities where the cost of living was lower than in Barrancabermeja. As one explained, the union's old-guard members, who worked for the Pepsi bottler, POSTOBON, "kept the union from advancing and had no vision of the future." He recalled that these leaders "were happy to sign any contract. [They] were comfortable; they only cared about getting a good retirement deal and dying as potbellied old men."[8] He and others of his generation had grown up in Barrancabermeja's politicized northeastern neighborhoods and were not just union activists: all belonged to a variety of left-wing political parties and movements, including A Luchar and the Unión Patriotica, which were legal fronts for the insurgencies, and the Frente Amplio del Magdalena Medio, led by a former ELN militant and Barrancabermeja native, Ricardo Lara Parada. They wanted to see the union expand, as one of them put it, "beyond the four walls of the factory." Tensions between the Coca-Cola clasistas and the POSTOBON old guard intensified throughout the 1980s. The latter accused the youngsters of intransigence and feared that their radicalism would get others killed. The militant vision of social transformation held by SINALTRAINAL represented a bid to scale-up working-class power by linking workers in Coca-Cola bottling plants to each other, as well as to workers in other sectors of the food and beverage industry, and by connecting the union to political movements seeking fundamental changes in Colombian society. By building ties of solidarity beyond particular localities, SINALTRAINAL started to address the dialectic of universalism versus localism that Raymond Williams (1989) called "militant particularism." The stumbling block for working-class power is, according to Williams, the challenge of connecting the unique character of class-based organization in particular places to a more general movement for social transformation. This is because working people must demonstrate that the defense and advancement of interests that appear to be tied to a specific group are, in fact, of broader concern.

Although SINALTRAINAL made little headway in negotiations with Coca-Cola, its members were active beyond "the four walls of the bottling plants" throughout the 1980s and early 1990s. The union supported initiatives to use art as an alternative form of expression and as a means of supporting "the ideas, values and cultural concepts pertinent to the popular movement" (SINALTRAINAL, n.d.: 17). It also took steps to involve the spouses and children of workers in sporting activities and other social events as a means to both strengthen the union and convert it into the "first-line political actor and the axis of social life" in the municipalities where it operated (SINALTRAINAL, n.d.: 17). In addition, the national union committed activists and union resources to support peasant agrarian struggles in César, Antioquia, Guajíra, and Magdalena provinces. It also joined civic strikes in various cities to demand better public services and supported public school students who sought to improve their educational experiences. Finally, SINALTRAINAL sought ways to build international solidarity with other Latin American trade unions. Throughout the 1980s and 1990s, for example, national union leaders participated in a number of international meetings that brought together trade unionists from around Latin America. A 1986 gathering in Montevideo, Uruguay, supported by the Federación Sindical Mundial (World Union Federation), focused on "the unity of food workers in Latin America and of all those of other multinational corporations, as the only guarantee for the defense of their undeniable rights and the national sovereignties seriously threatened by [U.S.] imperialism" (SINALTRAINAL, n.d.: 18).[9] Two years later, another meeting convened in Caracas, Venezuela, addressed the enactment of neoliberal, antilabor policies across Latin America and called for the unification of collective bargaining initiatives.

By the early 1990s, it was not difficult for Colombian Coca-Cola workers to conclude that capitalism presented a fundamental problem, as free-market policies had already devastated working classes in Chile and Bolivia, and Coca-Cola was beginning to take advantage of antilabor laws to fire people and to erode the rights and benefits of those who remained. Backed by the national office in Bogotá, the SINALTRAINAL locals in Barrancabermeja and other Colombian cities repeatedly challenged aggressive, antilabor corporate policies with street demonstrations, hunger strikes, and legal maneuvers, which became intertwined with regional political dynamics.

They did so as the ELN waged an offensive against multinationals and state-operated companies in the process of privatization, blew up roads, bridges, and oil pipelines, and expressed its support for labor and civic strikes. Media accounts from the period fretted about the

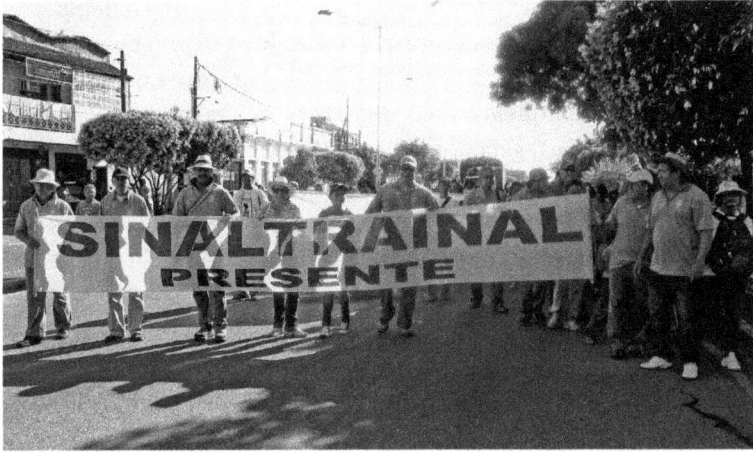

FIG. 4.1 Trade unionists defy threats and terror.

growth and spread of urban guerrilla militias and channeled the intensifying anger and frustration of businessmen and the security forces
who seemed unable to stop the insurgent advance. At a 1992 meeting
of some 130 oil company contractors and military generals in Barrancabermeja, for example, General Harold Bedoya told the assembled entrepreneurs not to give in to extortion demands. "Nowadays," he lectured
them, "we see the full pockets and coffers of the guerrillas. You should
not be their whores. We have enriched the insurgents by giving them
money to buy arms [and] dynamite." The plaintive response of the contractors was to ask who would protect them from guerrilla reprisals, if
they refused to pay (*El Tiempo* 1992). Two years later, the situation had
hardly improved. Leaders of the beer and soft drink industries complained about incessant insurgent attacks on their delivery trucks. "The
businessmen are frantic," cried *El Tiempo*, Colombia's leading conservative daily, because law enforcement's efforts to stop the assaults "have
not produced the desired results" (*El Tiempo* 1994). Not surprisingly,
entrepreneurs found hope in the rising power of paramilitarism.

The media increasingly identified labor leaders as allies of the guerrillas, while mounting insurgent attacks on police stations in heavily
populated areas of northeast Barranca served to alienate the insurgents from popular support. The SINALTRAINAL leaders endured arbitrary arrests and detentions, and they confronted an onslaught of
threats, assassination attempts, and harassment from paramilitary

groups. In Cartagena, a paramilitary called the home of a unionist and spoke to the individual's ten-year-old daughter when she answered the telephone. He told the little girl that if her father did not leave town, the paramilitaries would murder him. The labor leader estimated that the Cartagena local denounced at least eleven additional threats over the next two years. In Barrancabermeja, SINALTRAINAL leader Juan Carlos Galvis narrowly escaped death when hidden assailants shot at his car as it passed through a densely foliaged ravine, and in Bogotá, police raided SINALTRAINAL's national office on several occasions. The state security forces and the paramilitaries always operated in tandem. The complaints that SINALTRAINAL locals and the national office filed with authorities grew more numerous, but perpetrators were rarely arrested, and the security situation did not improve. The legal system deprived workers of rights that were enshrined in law, but it would not adequately address grievances related to death threats and murder, thereby facilitating the disorganization of working-class power. As impunity-fueled attacks weakened local union power, the relationships and alliances that connected union locals to each other and to wider social movements gave way.

Coca-Cola Company officials explained away the violence as a product of Colombia's intractable civil war. Although they issued vague statements that deplored the harmful effects of the violence on all Colombians, they never specifically denounced the paramilitary attacks and threats against workers in company plants and demanded that they stop. Unionists argued that murdered workers were not the product of random violence. The deaths, they said, were the result of a calculated and selective strategy carried out by sectors of the state, allied paramilitaries, and the Coca-Cola Company to weaken and eliminate trade unions. Workers in various plants described to me how, on repeated occasions, they observed supervisors talking with known paramilitaries. Like Coca-Cola, the Drummond Corporation, British Petroleum, and Occidental Petroleum were among those linked to paramilitary organizations (see Richani 2005: 130). Chiquita Brands paid a fine of $25 million in 2007, after confessing in U.S. court that it channeled $1.7 million and weapons to paramilitary forces in Colombia's northern banana zone between 1997 and 2004. When multinational criminality became public, as in the case of Chiquita, the corporation claimed that it had no other option because it was a victim caught in the crossfire of warring groups. There was, however, a difference between collud-

FIG. 4.2 Defaced Coca-Cola logo.

ing with one group or the other. When Chiquita supported right-wing mercenaries, it increased the violence and harassment directed against banana workers, peasants, and anyone labeled a "guerrilla," while channeling money to the insurgents meant more guns and firepower to harass the corporations themselves (Romero and Torres 2011). By helping multinationals like Chiquita and Coca-Cola weaken the social and organizational integument of organized labor and end relentless guerrilla extortion, paramilitaries enabled them to break the back of labor and popular struggles and reassert their power. The paramilitaries were white knights in shining armor for the corporations, which would have faced more trouble had they not been rescued by them.

The violence, and the widespread impunity that facilitated it, accomplished two things: it undermined the ability of SINALTRAINAL to build ties of solidarity beyond the bottling plants and either eroded or destroyed connections between union locals, and it fractured the social relationships, institutions, and everyday lives of workers in the places where they lived. In this way, the violent restructuring of Coca-Cola production in Colombia was contingent on the disorganization of working people's ties to each other, and on the rupture of connections between unions and working-class neighborhoods. It set in motion the dispossession of workers and the development of widespread insecurity and precariousness.

The Manufacture of Precariousness and Insecurity

As the Coca-Cola Company set out to reconfigure soft drink production in Colombia and to restructure its workforce, it jettisoned paternalist managerial practices that had once included company-organized soccer matches, Mother's Day celebrations, and waterskiing competitions on the Magdalena River. It made little effort to negotiate with its workforce and adopted the take-no-prisoners strategy of labor management already made infamous in Guatemala (Levenson-Estrada 1994). Longtime worker Gustavo Contreras described how "we [the workers] would go into contract negotiations and instead of giving things to us, all the company wanted was to take things from us."[10] Ridding the company of full-time workers, doing away with contractual obligations like health care, and redefining the labor-management relationship were fundamental to reshaping the landscape of Coca-Cola manufacture. These changes created a more vulnerable workforce and eroded the ability of workers to resist the directives of company managers.

Longtime workers who had entered the Barrancabermeja plant in the 1970s secured their jobs through the connections of fathers or other male relatives who preceded them, and after a three-month trial period, most signed indefinite term contracts (*contratos de termino indefinido*) that entitled them to health, vacation, and retirement benefits. Although several of these men recalled that, even though a job with Coca-Cola was less desirable than one with ECOPETROL, the financial stability offered by a regular wage and benefits was far superior to temporary work in the oil industry or self-employment in the growing unwaged, informal economy. Heriberto Gutiérrez, for example, started his job at Coca-Cola in 1978, when decent working-class jobs were still available for urban-born young men with a high school education. Gutiérrez explained that workers were not eager to work for Coca-Cola because of hopes for better jobs with ECOPETROL, which was expanding its refinery. Coca-Cola advertised jobs on the radio in the late 1970s because "workers were not arriving. People said, 'no, not Coca-Cola, better to work for the oil company because the money is better,'" according to

Gutiérrez.[11] Gutiérrez, like other young men in Barrancabermeja, was never able to land a full-time job with ECOPETROL, but he found Coca-Cola to be an acceptable alternative at a time when the multinational actively courted workers. William Mendoza started his job a decade after Gutiérrez, following a series of part-time jobs cleaning oil pipelines that had taken him away from home for six years. Mendoza had to grapple with episodes of financial uncertainty between contracts, and the company that employed him did not pay union wages, even though the collective bargaining agreement between ECOPETROL and its workforce stipulated that any firm that provided services to the oil industry had to do so. Discontentment over the pay disparity fueled a strike, and although workers won their demand for equivalent pay, Mendoza, one of the strike leaders, was fired. A cousin helped him get a job with Coca-Cola, where he began as a janitor and then secured a position on the bottling line. He worked a standard eight-hour shift, from 6:00 AM to 2:00 PM, and the consistent pay and the benefits were a welcome change that enabled him to have a more stable family life.

By the late 1990s, however, the Coca-Cola corporation had virtually stopped hiring full-time workers; it filled positions with subcontracted, temporary workers from so-called cooperatives. The company also started to ignore collective bargaining agreements with its unionized workforce that it had previously respected. "I would take complaints to management," recalled former union local president Efraín Zurmay, "and the company would simply deny what it had already agreed to and what was written in the contract. . . . They would say, if you don't agree, take us to court. They could say this because they knew that the justice system, the Ministry of Social Protection, and the judges all favored the multinational."[12] The ability of the corporation to ride roughshod over collective bargaining agreements highlighted the fragility and contingency of past labor victories in which workers largely succeeded in improving wages, winning benefits, and controlling the pace and organization of work.

Such arrogant corporate behavior erupted into a generalized crisis when the company decided, in 2003, to close the production line and downgrade the Barrancabermeja plant to a warehouse and distribution center. On September 8, a supervisor ordered workers to cease all bottling operations and read a statement from the national president of Coca-Cola that required everyone to attend a training seminar on "productivity and competitiveness" the following day in a hotel. By the next morning, however, workers sensed that the training seminar was a diversion; something more sinister was afoot. Ruben Muñoz knew that all was not well as he entered the hotel lobby. "I saw that the company had taken precautions against us by placing security personnel around the meeting room, that is to say, armed personnel, who didn't have any kind of identification. They observed us in a way that didn't correspond to a company calling its workers together for a so-called training seminar," he said. He then described what followed as a lockdown (*encerrona*), in which company officials coerced workers to sign buyout deals and prevented them from leaving until they complied. Human resources personnel tried to put a happy face on the occasion by offering guidance on how to set up a microenterprise. "Everything was focused around how we could supposedly earn more money if we gave up our jobs and worked independently," Muñoz explained, but the union had educated men like him well. "All of the supposed training was an effort to persuade us to renounce the labor rights that we had," he said. "The union always oriented us to never accept this type of arrangement, . . . [even though] they made us offers that frightened me when I thought about such large quantities of money, because it was really, really, really a lot of money."[13]

Yet despite the generous offers, few Coca-Cola workers signed buyout agreements voluntarily. With the exception of those already close to retirement, most were not eager to sacrifice their jobs for the risks and uncertainties of self-employment, especially at a time when public sector jobs were threatened by the specter of privatization, and private firms were going down the same path as Coca-Cola. Everyone knew of former workmates who had been fired or accepted buyout deals, and who had lost everything in bad investments. The men also understood that their reemployment prospects with another company were dim in a changing economy, and they knew that few businesses would hire people in their thirties, forties, and fifties with a history of trade union militancy.

Coca-Cola's human resource department likely appreciated that workers would balk at leaving. Because convincing them to give up good jobs and try their luck as microentrepreneurs was a hard sell, the human resource personnel targeted not just the men but also their families, using scare tactics to panic wives and children. Efraín Zurmay remembered that "the company knew that it couldn't easily pressure the workers with most seniority, so they decided to go to their homes and grab the families and tell them: 'Look, if your husband or father doesn't sign, you are all going to be left in the street with nothing, because the negotiations are ending.' So the company not only pressured the *compañeros* but their families, too. Many accepted the deals because their wives and children became frightened and convinced them to take the money."[14]

The corporate bullying enraged workers. Home visits by company personnel not only violated the privacy of their homes but also unsettled a deep-seated sense of masculinity that informed how male workers understood themselves as the protectors of wives and children. The browbeating of families came at a moment when workers were increasingly unable to shield their loved ones from harm because of threats to their own lives. All of this strained family relations. Sometimes, wives faulted their husbands and SINALTRAINAL for the harassment, murder, or kidnapping of relatives, the inability of children to enjoy normal childhoods, and the severe restrictions that the threat of violence placed on their social activities. By 2003, paramilitary threats, attacks, and the occupation of the city had substantially eroded the informal union and neighborhood networks through which women had understood and helped to sustain a capacity for collective struggle. Because wives and female companions neither worked for Coca-Cola nor participated in the daily negotiation of labor politics, they were cut off from union efforts to fight corporate policies and tended to understand the labor militancy of their husbands in individual and family-centered ways. Women worried that their husbands and companions would be killed or forced out of work, leaving them to fend alone for the children. There were, of course, women who maintained a broader sense of what was happening to their families, but the unrelenting corporate and paramilitary pressure isolated union families, who increasingly found themselves dealing with the constant fear, uncertainty, and corporate strong-arm tactics alone.

Most workers eventually signed the buyout agreements and retired. In some cases, they were in debt and viewed a seemingly large payout as a windfall, but in most cases, as a former union official explained, "they were tired of the corporate pressure. They said that they couldn't take the stress anymore; that their lives had become chaotic; and that they didn't want to end their days in jail or worse. That's why they accepted the company's proposals."[15] A small group of six trade unionists in Barrancabermeja, however, refused to leave and insisted that Coca-

Cola respect their contracts and relocate them to other bottling plants; one of them was SINALTRAINAL leader William Mendoza. Coca-Cola, he said, presented him with an especially attractive buyout plan, but it depended upon his willingness to convince rank-and-file members to leave the company along with him. After greeting the offer with a series of expletives, Mendoza claimed that the company, which had profiled him as a womanizer, enlisted an attractive woman to convince him to change his mind, but he never did. The trade unionists' case wound up in court, and while lawyers for both sides argued back and forth, the company obliged the six dissidents to present themselves at the bottling plant every day. It did not, however, let them work. For six months, the men sat in a kiosk for the duration of their eight-hour shifts with little to do except read the newspaper and talk with each other under the watchful eyes of the security guards. They eventually prevailed in court and kept their jobs, but their case was unusual. Moreover, workers' reliance on a judicial system that typically upheld the claims of Coca-Cola and other multinationals pointed to the general weakness of the Colombian labor movement. Most workers had to face a stark new reality in which deepening insecurity and economic instability created new imperatives.

Forced retirements and firings obliged former Coca-Cola workers to devise alternative economic arrangements to support themselves and their families. Becoming so-called microentrepreneurs was not the first choice of most of the men; indeed, entrepreneurialism was forced upon them because stable working-class jobs, like the ones they lost at Coca-Cola, did not exist. The transformation from Coca-Cola workers to microentrepreneurs, or what Jan Breman (1994) has more accurately called "wage hunters and gatherers," typically severed their ties to each other. Downsized Coca-Cola workers ended up laboring as taxi drivers, vendors, and part-time contractors and in a myriad of other activities in which rights, regulations, and bargaining power did not exist and where invisible, exploitative networks shaped relationships of inequality (see chapter 5). Together with cast-off public sector employees, they formed a generation of newly dispossessed workers who expanded the ranks of the so-called informal economy that was already bursting with displaced peasants from the countryside. They typically worked alone in an ever more competitive environment in which existing work was fragmented, incomes grew more precarious, and their identities were reworked around autonomous individuality.

For many years, Javier Garcia, for example, drove a truck for Coca-Cola, delivering crates of soft drinks to merchants in Barrancabermeja and the Middle Magdalena region. The job was not easy; it required loading and unloading heavy crates of bottled soda, and it came with considerable perils. As the Coca-Cola Company and its workers became enmeshed in an ever more polarized civil war, the multinational—a global icon of U.S.-led corporate capitalism and Americanization—became an obvious target for guerrilla groups who opposed the presence of foreign multinationals and the loss of national sovereignty that they represented. Traveling the Middle Magdalena's back roads posed considerable risk for any driver of a big red truck with the Coca-Cola logo splashed across the side. Garcia had to contend with assailants—sometimes guerrillas, sometimes common criminals—who stole the soft drinks and made off with the money that he had collected from merchants along the route. "Once," he recalled, "we were traveling to Antioquia when a group of guerrillas appeared on the road and made us stop and get out of the truck. Then they dumped all the soft drinks and burned the truck. . . . The same thing happened when drivers went to the northeastern neighborhoods. They [the guerrillas] told them to get lost, . . . and then they gave away the soft drinks to the people and burned the trucks." Back at the plant, however, Garcia and his fellow drivers faced distrustful supervisors who suspected that they participated in the robberies and offered little in the way of protection. This was the dilemma that the insurgencies and the *combinación* strategy created for organized labor.

In 2002, Garcia was forced to sign a buyout agreement, which he still referred to years later as the "kick out" (*la echada*), and purchased a taxicab to support his family. Yet despite the dangers and the suspicious supervisors, Garcia missed his job and the social life that he had once enjoyed with his workmates and their families, which was one casualty of the broader process of dispossession that Coca-Cola workers endured. Economic restructuring dispersed workers and cast them adrift in family and kin networks that could not fill the void of cooperative labor and collective action. "Back in the 1980s," he recollected in 2007, "the compañeros shared a lot together. It's not the same today. Nowadays, the company is doing away with everything."[16] Moreover, driving a taxicab in the already taxi-saturated city simply could not compare to a steady job at Coca-Cola. Erratic and unpredictable daily earnings replaced a regular wage, forcing Garcia to work as many as sixteen hours a day to cover his household's basic expenses, while the proliferation of illegal motorcycle taxis undercut the rates charged by registered cabbies and made work more stressful and difficult. Sometimes even sixteen-hour workdays were not enough, and the economic pressure obliged his family to make difficult decisions: an elder daughter, for example, opted out of attending the local university so that she could help support her younger siblings. His wife tried and failed to augment the household income through the sale of vitamin supplements to neighbors, friends, and relatives and then decided to rent out a bedroom, making it necessary for other family members to share less space.

The Garcia family was not only economically vulnerable; the loss of the Coca-Cola Company's relatively generous health insurance plan was a particularly worrisome development, Garcia explained, because of the threat posed by what he referred to as the *delincuencia*, a gloss for common crime and the continuing menace of paramilitaries, to people like himself. "There is a lot of common crime [in the city]," he told me, "and you never know when they are going to use you or when they might see you [with the wrong person] and think that you are collaborating with the guerrillas."[17] Garcia had good reason to be worried, as paramilitaries were known to use taxi drivers to supply them with intelligence. The crisis provoked by corporate downsizing, which entailed the loss of both steady waged work and the social wage, amid the violent turbulence of Barrancabermeja, provoked a breakdown in what social scientists call "social reproduction," that is, the material and emotional possibilities of organizing viable livelihood strategies in the present and projecting them into the future (Narotzky and Besnier 2014; Sider 2008). It signaled a rupture between older forms of work, cooperation, and the expectations associated with them and a new configuration of possibilities and pitfalls that was more unstable, individualistic, and uncertain, one that Garcia had not chosen but to which he had to accommodate.

With the departure of Garcia and unionized workers like him, newly hired, subcontracted employees represented a generation of younger laborers, as well as previously downsized workers obliged by economic circumstances to return to the Coca-Cola workforce under new conditions. Garcia's younger brother became a temporary worker in the Coca-Cola plant. "One day he works, the next day he doesn't," Garcia explained. "When they want him, they call him."[18] The new labor regime was not unique to Barrancabermeja. Alejandro Nieto, a temporary worker in the Bucaramanga megaplant, described an exploitative regime in which workers like himself had no control over working conditions and in which waiting signified a new form of domination and relationship to power:

> When I started work at Coca-Cola, the human resources head explained the system of pay. I was going to earn 706,000 pesos a month, but this amount depended on the number of hours I worked every month. So, I worked Monday for fourteen hours, but then I went home and waited, glued to the telephone on Tuesday, for the boss to call me at six, seven, eight, nine, ten—at any time. It's really demoralizing. I worked for fourteen hours on Monday; I didn't work on Tuesday, just sat in the house all day. Then, they called me on Wednesday, and I worked from 9:00 AM to 11:00 AM and then went home, after spending money on lunch and transportation. . . . Sometimes you get to the plant and change into your uniform and then wait in the temporary workers' locker room, which is grimy and damp. That's where they keep you. You can wait all morning until the boss sends someone to get you. They give you a couple of hours of work, after you spend the entire day sitting around, waiting for the boss to call you.[19]

Nieto's account of the hopes and frustrations associated with waiting expresses in poignant detail the new terms that structure labor-management relations in the Coca-Cola bottling plants. The connection between time and domination has been noted by Javier Auyero (2009: 109–29; see also Auyero 2012), who has documented how endless waiting shapes forms of submission in an Argentine shantytown, where impoverished residents with little sense of personal agency must constantly wait for more powerful people—lawyers, corporate officials, politicians—to make decisions about their lives. In the case of Alejandro Nieto and other temporary Coca-Cola workers like him, waiting for bosses to call or to assign them to a shift signals the loss of worker power in neoliberal Colombia, as the decline of trade unions and the rise of subcontracting and temporary work have undercut the eight-hour shift, the assignment of tasks, and the pace of labor on the shop floor. The hopes and the frustrations that waiting elicits in temporary workers constitute part of the more generalized uncertainty of their lives and the difficulty that they, as individuals, face in exercising a modicum of control over working conditions.

Not surprisingly, the two-tiered structure of the workforce has eroded ties of familiarity that once bound workers to each other. New divisions have emerged between an emergent majority of "flexible" workers with no union representation or benefits and a dwindling number of older, unionized workers who have managed to hold onto their jobs. Indeed, for temporary hires, the possibility of acquiring a short-term assignment often depends on the absence of full-time employees. As Nieto explains:

> When a person who is full-time [*termino indefinido*] has a dentist or a doctor appointment at, say, 8:00 AM, temporary personnel are allowed to replace him. As long as the person is gone—and we say, "Oooh take your time"—then we get a few more little hours. But then, [the boss says] OK, brother, the person has returned. Change your clothes and wait until we call you again. . . . So, you see, we work for miserable wages, for the leftovers of the full-time personnel. That's what it is: the hours that they leave us because they have medical appointments or vacations. That's what temporary people pick up for their salary.[20]

The downward pressure on working-class livelihoods extends well beyond the Coca-Cola plant, and as the income of a large cross section of working people has eroded, those who still have full-time positions with a multinational like Coca-Cola experience more requests from family members for assistance. Efraín Zurmay, for example, still worked for Coca-Cola in 2006, after more than twenty years of service to the corporation, and he had become the economic pillar of his family. He explained, "I pay all of my mother's expenses—food, medications, everything—because my brothers and sister do not have steady work. I am like the rich person of the family [laughs], the family potentate, because I have a stable job, because I have an income. The others live from hand to mouth. They go out to work for a while, but then they are unemployed. That's how it is."[21]

The dispossession of workers and the emergence of a two-tiered labor force have diminished the familiarity and common routines that once shaped workers' ties to each other and have intensified the worries of longtime workers like Zurmay that paramilitaries operate in their midst. These fears were well-founded. Despite tight security and an extensive surveillance system in the bottling plants, paramilitary graffiti frequently appeared on plant walls after the BCB takeover, and signed death threats materialized in workers' lockers, but verifying fears about suspicious workmates was extremely difficult. Unionists had no way of resolving gnawing doubts and anxieties, which limited their ability to organize opposition to company policies. Trade union leaders found themselves caught in a social "order" that had come unhinged, and there were few workers who had any desire to replace them. "Today, nobody in Colombia wants to be a union leader," explained Zurmay in 2007. "I've spent over twenty years in the union and am fifty-one years old. I should be in the reserves by now. There should be younger people replacing me, but they are too afraid. . . . Nobody wants to expose themselves to the possibility of being killed and put in jail. They understand the power that the government and the multinationals have to commit any kind of abuse."[22]

The violence against trade unionists has undermined the ability of working people to reproduce a class culture. It has severed the relationships in the workplace and in the neighborhoods where people live that once made it possible to develop collective struggles and act together. It has also limited the ability of labor leaders to reach out to temporary workers and the unemployed. William Mendoza's life, before and after the BCB forced him out of his home (see chapter 3), illustrates how a new, more constricted sense of what was possible, personally and politically, arose from the social ruptures and betrayals that disorganized working-class power. Terror cheapened labor and narrowed the political horizons of working people, as it opened the floodgates for a new wave of capital accumulation to sweep into the city.

Betrayal and the Erosion of Trust

Mendoza had been at the center of the gathering storm in Barrancabermeja for many years, because of his work as a human rights defender and as an outspoken union leader, but before the BCB assault, he had still managed to enjoy time with friends when he was not working in the Coca-Cola bottling plant, and he moved about the city freely. Yet his life started to change in 2000, amid mounting disquietude about the accumulating strength of paramilitarism in the Middle Magdalena. Sometime at the beginning of the year, his close friend Edilberto

FIG. 4.3 SINALTRAINAL leader William Mendoza.

Araújo, a fellow trade unionist who worked for the Pepsi bottler, purchased a beat-up, red Renault.²³ The car was somewhat of a novelty for Mendoza and his circle of friends, who were accustomed to getting about on motorcycles or bicycles, and it soon became the preferred means of weekend transportation for Mendoza, Araújo, and two other workers, who spent time together on their days off. "Because we were such good friends," Mendoza said, "[the other guys] called us 'the Red Car Band' [and] as we barhopped and went from party to party, we met up with other friends. Life seemed really good from our perspective."²⁴

As the paramilitary noose tightened, Mendoza began to notice that when they arrived at a bar or restaurant, friends who used to join them at their table began to leave. And it was not long before the so-called Red Car Band itself dissolved. One of the four men decided to stop participating on the weekend outings, and then another broke off ties with Mendoza. According to Mendoza, he "told me without blushing and with all possible crudeness that 'you know old man, I am not going to hang out with you anymore. They are going to kill you and hanging out with you is like having a gravestone overhead. I'm sorry, but don't even come to my house anymore.'" Mendoza was devastated. "I was really hurt," he said. "That guy was more than a friend. We were buddies [*com-pinches*], companions [*compañeros*]. He was my best friend. I felt really alone and distressed that day. And then compañeros from the union started distancing themselves from me. To them, it was as if a plague had arrived. . . . Luckily, there were compañeros who continued with me and gave me hope, but the Red Car Band ended forever."

Mendoza's troubles worsened after the BCB takeover. Not only was he forced from his home, but a fellow worker at the Coca-Cola plant named Saul Ramírez exposed him to paramilitary retribution.[25] During the late 1980s and 1990s, Ramírez belonged to SINALTRAINAL and worked as a night watchman. Mendoza was the president of SINALTRAINAL in Barrancabermeja and had long served on the union's national board of directors. When corporate restructuring threatened Ramírez's job in the mid-1990s, the union placed him on its local directorate to give him more job security, but Ramírez eventually accepted a buyout offer and quit. He then purchased a taxicab, which he drove to support himself and his family. Mendoza recalled that Ramírez "wasn't the kind of compañero who could lead the union, [but] he was very good when it came to protests, even though you couldn't assign him a task or expect him to propose anything." Ramírez lived in La Esperanza neighborhood, close to Mendoza, whose wife often assisted him with injections for a back problem and sometimes even bought groceries for his family. According to Mendoza, Ramírez liked to brag to his workmates that he collaborated with the guerrillas who controlled the neighborhood in the 1990s. He also boasted that he allowed them to store guns in his home and that he transported commanders around the city in his taxicab. In 1998, he availed himself as a courier to the EPL insurgents after they burned four Coca-Cola trucks and detonated a bomb in the company's bottling plant that temporarily shut it down. Ramírez purportedly carried messages from the guerrillas to company representatives, as the two sides sought to renegotiate a relationship that both could accept.

When the BCB moved into his neighborhood, Ramírez knew that he was in trouble. Like Mendoza, the paramilitaries allegedly had his name on a hit list, and Ramírez was desperate to get out of the city. He contacted Mendoza in the hope that his neighbor and former workmate would use his ties to human rights organizations to clear a path for him to leave and resettle, at least for a time, in Bogotá. Mendoza, who was living his own nightmare, managed to raise money to cover a plane ticket for Ramírez, and SINALTRAINAL contributed money for living expenses in the capital. Mendoza and a team of human rights defenders then accompanied him to the airport and saw him off to Bogotá. Over the next several months, both the Barrancabermeja local and the Bogotá-based national office of SINALTRAINAL maintained contact with Ramírez, and when Mendoza traveled to the capital, he shared his per diem travel allowance with him. Yet Ramírez's money eventually ran low, and his family was struggling to make ends meet in Barrancabermeja without him. Ramírez began to consider going back. Perhaps he did not want to live apart from his family, or perhaps the cold, dreary mountain capital was too inhospitable for a man used to the tropical heat of the Magdalena River valley. Whatever the reason, Ramírez contacted the paramilitaries to negotiate his return to Barrancabermeja, and as he later told Mendoza, he received assurances that he could go back. But there was one condition: he had to work for them.

Ramírez subsequently resurfaced in Barrancabermeja, driving a white Mazda and carrying out low-level tasks for the BCB, who identified him as "Coca-Cola." The BCB considered Mendoza a "military target" because of his outspoken leadership of SINALTRAINAL during a period of corporate restructuring, job loss, and outsourcing, and his recent charges that the Coca-Cola corporation colluded with the paramilitaries to terrorize trade unionists. Ramírez contacted Mendoza and urged him to meet with the BCB to discuss the situation. Believing that he stood no chance with the mercenaries, and citing official union policy that prohibited communication with any of the so-called armed actors, Mendoza refused. The pressure then intensified, when the paramilitaries tried, and failed, to kidnap Mendoza's four-year-old daughter in a public park. As Mendoza recounted, "He [Ramírez] started to pressure me really hard, saying that the paramilitaries had sent him to tell me that I had to talk with them because I was speaking out against Coca-Cola and the alliance between Coca-Cola and the paramilitaries in Barrancabermeja." Mendoza flew into a rage and told Ramírez that he would denounce him as a paramilitary if the harassment continued. "From then on," Mendoza said, "he swore that he was going to split my head open, that's the expression that he used. He accused me of belonging to the FARC and claimed that the union didn't do anything, nothing moved, without my authorization." Such accusations further deepened Mendoza's troubles.

Mendoza was not the only Coca-Cola worker to run afoul of Ramírez. As word circulated among SINALTRAINAL members that Ramírez was aiding the BCB, Juan Carlos Galvis, another SINALTRAINAL leader, saw him at the Coca-Cola plant with a policeman. He observed the two men conversing with a plant supervisor whom he then confronted, demanding to know how the company could claim to have no dealings with the paramilitaries when, in fact, the man had just spoken to one of them. Soon thereafter, Galvis also began to receive death threats, confirming for SINALTRAINAL leaders what they had long suspected about the corporation's involvement with the paramilitaries. Although neither Galvis nor Mendoza would see Ramírez again, their difficulties with him would continue.[26]

Ramírez's betrayal exposed the private recesses of two trade unionists' lives to the calculated brutality of the BCB and created new vulnerabilities that they had not previously experienced. The betrayal imperiled Mendoza's life to a degree that would have been nearly impossible for a stranger, because Ramírez was familiar with Mendoza's daily routine, and he knew, or could identify, many of Mendoza's friends, family members, and trade union confidants. This knowledge undercut Mendoza's feelings of safety, jeopardized the security of those around him, and challenged his capacity to protect and care for his family. In addition, Ramírez could unveil the inner workings of SINALTRAINAL and make the activities of its members available for paramilitary scrutiny. Ramírez's behavior also revealed to Mendoza that his basic assumptions about their relationship were false, and it raised questions about his ability to judge people at a time when the city was in turmoil and the balance of power was rapidly shifting. As Mendoza explained years later, "Saul Ramírez wasn't alone. A lot of people that we managed to get out and save their lives returned; some of them started working for the paramilitaries. Of course, now we are very mistrustful about extending solidarity to anyone. . . . You first have to figure out who you are dealing with, and we check people out in depth so that there are no surprises."[27]

We can appreciate from Mendoza's experiences how the political crisis placed him in new danger and forced him to deal with radical uncertainty. As the betrayal of a fellow worker plunged his life and the union into turmoil, Mendoza became more vulnerable to the full force of BCB terror. The paramilitary threat also opened a cleavage between him and some of the rank and file, who feared that associating too closely with a marked leader put their own lives at risk. All of this aggravated mistrust and fueled suspicions about workmates, friends, and associates, dividing them from each other and isolating union leaders from the rank and file.

Meetings in public places became more difficult because of the constant fear of attack, which transformed the spaces where workers could gather. Unrelenting threats and harassment against Mendoza and other union leaders cast a halo of danger around the SINALTRAINAL union hall, which is located behind a thick, bulletproof glass window and entered through a steel door with multiple locks and reinforcements that give it the appearance of a bunker. Although it sits across the street from the Coca-Cola plant, the union headquarters was not a place that most workers chose to congregate after work. Even arriving at SINALTRAINAL headquarters was a fraught experience for union leaders.

For Juan Carlos Galvis, the enduring paramilitary menace structured every aspect of his waking life, in which security was organized down to the smallest detail. En route to the office one day in 2007, Galvis telephoned from his SUV that he was about to arrive. The bodyguard at the wheel pulled up to the building, bounced the heavy vehicle over the curb, and stopped under a small tree that shaded the union's headquarters. Both guards then drew their guns, jumped out of the car, and scanned the street in each direction, before opening the back door next to Galvis, who got out and quickly walked a few paces into the building through the door that someone had already opened. The entire ritual, repeated every time he came to the office, took only a few seconds. Even more disturbing, it was not unusual for Galvis and other local leaders to receive threatening telephone calls immediately after their arrival, suggesting the building was under surveillance. The sense of peril that enveloped the union hall was indicative of how the elimination or the constriction of the spaces for sociality undermined the vitality of working-class culture.

The creation of vulnerability and insecurity has been key to the unmaking of a privileged sector of the working class and the weakening of working-class power more generally. This process has not happened all at once, and even though now far advanced, it is still not complete, as the continued existence of SINALTRAINAL attests. The dispossession, disorganization, and terror that shaped the erosion of privilege began with the spatial fix that reconfigured the geography of Coca-Cola production in Colombia and was closely intertwined with the lives of Coca-Cola workers in Barrancabermeja. The Colombian state facilitated the process through the enactment of antilabor laws and lower tariff barriers, and it promoted a favorable investment climate for multinationals, which facilitated the conversion of the Barranca-bermeja plant into a warehouse and distribution center, the firing or forced retirement of longtime workers, and the subcontracting of temporary personnel. These moves were enforced by paramilitary violence, which provided the solvent that eroded social solidarity and created the grounding for neoliberalism to flourish. What the dispossession of a relatively privileged group of Coca-Cola workers and the disorganization of their lives meant was that the contours of class were changing. More and more people were forced to compete with each other for unstable, low-paid work over which they had less control, and the political space for opposing these transformations was closing. Working people had to take stock of their situation once again and create new relationships and institutions that allowed them to act together and press their claims on the powerful, which they had done at different times in the past. The homicidal forces allied against them were more capricious and unrestrained than anything they had previously confronted. How they negotiated their way across the changing political landscape shaped, and was shaped by, the emergence of a new geography of power in the Middle Magdalena, which we turn to in the next chapter.

FIVE

FRAGMENTED

SOVEREIGNTY

. . .

By the early twenty-first century, the counterinsurgent war and the advent of neoliberalism had ignited a highly combustible process of state formation in Colombia, especially in regions deemed "ungovernable" because of the presence of the guerrillas. The war aimed to extend the power of the institutional state more deeply into contested regions via the expulsion of the insurgencies, the repression of labor, and the imposition of the rule of law, a strategy referred to as "clear, hold, and build" that dated to the 1960s and aimed to open "pacified" regions to capitalist investment (Hylton 2010). It depended upon the formation and support of paramilitary organizations, which had initially operated as adjuncts to the security forces but subsequently formed regionally based "armed authoritarian enclaves" that acquired their own violent dynamics (Bonilla 2007). Paramilitarism and counterinsurgency fused with politics to reconfigure the geography of power across scales, enabling the mercenaries and those they served to reorganize their ties to the institutional state at the local, regional, and national levels.

In the Middle Magdalena and elsewhere, the intertwining of paramilitarism and counterinsurgency destabilized and then reconfigured relationships and alliances within places and across space. The private violence of paramilitarism was key to the control of territory, the capture of elected political office, and the privatization of state functions as they were being decentralized to municipal and provincial authorities (Ballvé 2012). It undergirded a new public order based on corruption, intimidation, and dispossession in which the distinction between paramilitarism and the institutional state blurred. The convergence of political violence and the economic and administrative reforms mandated by neoliberal economic policies within the context of a counterinsurgent war reconfigured the geography of political power in the Middle Magdalena. They did so by strengthening a violent, right-wing power bloc that achieved a high level of interregional connection, control of electoral processes, and representation in national political office (Ávila 2010; López 2010) and that used elected office to siphon public funds toward private coffers and legitimize ill-gotten wealth. Private terror and economic reform simultaneously disorganized, destroyed, or vastly weakened the capacity of the insurgencies and unions, peasant organizations, and neighborhood associations to build scale-spanning solidarities and create spaces of power through the development of alliances and common political projects. My analysis demonstrates how neoliberal restructuring, state formation, and the unmaking of class were shaped by paramilitarism and counterinsurgent war.

The emergence of armed authoritarian enclaves that carried out some of the functions assigned to the institutional state diminished a vision of the state as the guardian of the public interest, deepened a particularly pernicious form of armed neoliberalism, and forced working people to reconsider how to advance their claims on the powerful. Yet the violent push by a far-right power bloc to secure property rights, undermine the power of labor, subvert democracy, accumulate wealth, and suffer no consequences for massive human rights violations and drug trafficking created a weak basis for legitimizing the new order in the Middle Magdalena.[1] The BCB faced the difficult task of establishing legitimacy among people whom it had terrorized. Several years after the BCB takeover of Barrancabermeja, *barranqueños* who initially either welcomed or were indifferent to the paramilitary incursion told me on numerous occasions that "they were worse than the guerrillas."

This chapter examines the formation of a violent, new power-laden geography of capitalist power in Barrancabermeja, beginning with BCB seizure of the city in 2000 and ending with the paramilitary demobilization of 2006. It does so by exploring how one mercenary army — the BCB — remapped the geography of power through the violent suppression of democratic alternatives, the control of electoral office, and the incorporation of working people into new relations of inequality. The BCB operated alongside or in place of the institutional state. For a period of four years, it blurred the boundaries between public/private and legal/illegal, as it created strategic networks, exercised the power to regulate social, political, and economic life, and killed with impunity.[2] The cumulative result of these strategies and actions was the reterritorialization of power and the creation of manageable spaces for the attraction of foreign capital. Like other Colombian regions where inhabitants were confronted with competing political projects (Ballvé 2012; Ramírez 2011; Tate 2015), the BCB occupation raises questions about what the state is, where it is located, and who has the legitimate right to act in its name.[3] The chapter argues that the BCB was one of several groups contending for power in the Middle Magdalena that sought to normalize different configurations of social relations and legitimize them as the state. My analysis builds on research that envisions the state less as a thing or container for political, social, and economic activities than as a contradictory and conflicted process in which actors and entities not understood as "the state" play a central part in shaping how "it" is organized, understood, and legitimized.[4]

For six years (2000–2006), the BCB ruled in alliance with sectors of the institutional state, which itself was not a unitary phenomenon, and stifled the language of class as a form of claims making. Yet after pacifying the region with "blood and fire" and securing the rights of capital, the BCB and the violent "gangster capitalism" associated with it became a liability for the institutional state, which initiated a "peace process" with the mercenaries in 2003 that led to their demobilization three years later. The institutional state then reasserted its legitimacy by locating paramilitarism in the past, even as neoparamilitaries regrouped in the same territory once occupied by the BCB. The organization, decomposition, and reassembly of claims to legitimate rule were central to the violent process of state formation.

The chapter first describes how the BCB created a realm of de facto sovereignty in Barrancabermeja, where it incorporated working people into new forms of labor discipline, rent extraction, and political subjugation through intimidation, predation, and the erection of armed, clientelistic relationships. It then considers how conflicting claims to legitimate rule shaped the efforts of paramilitary avengers to regulate social life and how barranqueños negotiated a vast gray area in which it was difficult to understand where the paramilitaries and the institutional state began and ended. Finally, the chapter explores how the paramilitary demobilization, which culminated in 2006, and the so-called parapolitics (*parapolítica*) scandal, which exposed the connections between paramilitaries and political leaders, allowed the institutional state to reaffirm its lawfulness and legitimacy. "The state" reemerges less as an object "akin to a human ear" than as a claim to the legitimate right to rule (Abrams 1988: 76), a right that was grounded in the separation of the violent, paramilitary past from the still unsettled present in which, government officials asserted, illegal armed groups no longer used ties to politicians and the security forces to amass wealth illegally and kill with impunity. The long-term durability of the resurgent state's legitimacy, however, remains uncertain, as the current neoliberal order rests on a foundation of disorder, displacement, exclusion, and economic distress created by decades of war and economic restructuring.

A New Node of Power: The BCB

Like counterinsurgent Colombian paramilitaries, numerous semiclandestine groups operated during the cold war to annihilate leftleaning political movements and suppress democratic politics, and they effectively muddied the distinction between institutional states and criminal networks. The Sicilian Mafia, for example, assisted in the suppression of peasant insurgencies and supported the expansion of anticommunist political parties after World War II. It then took control of urban construction and drug trafficking networks and utilized money-laundering channels created by the cold war to amass wealth and reestablish control of politics (J. Schneider and Schneider 2003). In addition, some Islamic terrorist organizations, such as al-Qaeda, were either cultivated by the United States during the cold war or tolerated as alternative poles of legitimacy to secular nationalist and communist movements (Saull 2006), and Salvadoran and Guatemalan death squads that fought counterinsurgency wars backed by the United States in the 1970s and 1980s operated as extensions of state security forces. Yet unlike Central American death squads, which remained under the control of the Salvadoran and Guatemalan armies, or the Nicaraguan contras who received support from the United States, Colombian paramilitaries became standing armies that conquered and held territory and financed their own expansion through drug trafficking and a variety of legal and illegal activities. They did so within the broader context of a counterinsurgent war in which the United States channeled millions of dollars to the state security forces to wage a "war on drugs" in which coca eradication programs targeted the peasant support base of the guerrillas.

The Colombian state facilitated the large-scale expansion of paramilitarism when, in 1994, the administration of César Gaviria authorized the creation of legal self-defense groups, known as the Cooperativas de Vigilancia y Seguridad Privada (Cooperatives for Vigilance and Private Security, CONVIVIRs), that provided legal cover for paramilitary organizations and guaranteed impunity. The CONVIVIRs maintained close connections to the police and military commanders and received financial backing from wealthy cattle ranchers and other sectors of the elite in the regions where they operated. During their four-year existence, the CONVIVIRs grew to include more than 120,000 members and spread throughout Colombia. They became particularly well established in Antioquia province, where then governor and future president Álvaro Uríbe Vélez vigorously promoted them. When the Colombian court declared the CONVIVIRs unconstitutional in 1998, the paramilitaries lost their façade of legitimacy, but they had already begun to expand clandestinely with the creation of the AUC in 1997. Former CONVIVIR operatives who had roots in the Medellín and Calí drug cartels passed into the leadership of the AUC (Ávila 2010: 113–18), which attempted, but ultimately failed, to unite disparate regional paramilitary entities under one umbrella.

By the mid-1990s, the paramilitaries had outgrown their role as so-called self-defense forces, even though ties to state agents—politicians and military officers—remained a crucial factor in their rapid expansion. They had become armies complete with uniforms, insignia, hymns, and doctrine, and they bristled with sophisticated weapons (Duncan 2006). According to Colombian analysts León Valencia and Juan Carlos Celis, "By 1999, these forces configured themselves as a veritable irregular army with a particularly offensive quality. . . . The war acquired a new face: the occupation of territory with blood and fire, the massive connection of drug traffickers to the paramilitary business and a strategy to capture local power and influence national power" (2012: 15). A number of factors accounted for the rapid paramilitary expansion, including well-developed networks of local, regional, and national political support, a strong military structure, the support of a significant number of military officers, and control of the enormous profits of the illegal cocaine traffic, which allowed them to operate autonomously from the institutional state. Moreover, their counterinsurgent discourse drew sectors of the middle class to the paramilitary project who might have otherwise been repelled by the extreme violence and criminality (Ávila 2010).

Paramilitary commanders amassed wealth and power at the head of regional armies, or blocs. The mercenaries conquered territory by forcing guerrillas and other paramilitary competitors to either join forces with them and abandon areas that they claimed or face annihilation, and by expelling or massacring civilians perceived to belong to the support base of the insurgencies. They not only used threats and bribes to force their way into the political system; they were also sought out by right-wing politicians who approached them about forming electoral alliances as the power of paramilitarism grew (López 2010). Access to the institutional state enabled them to legalize stolen assets and guarantee immunity from prosecution for human rights violations and extradition to the United States on drug trafficking charges.

Paramilitary expansion turned on the ability to extract resources in areas under the mercenaries' control, and those who dominated the cocaine economy became the most powerful within the loosely organized AUC federation. After the collapse of the Medellín cartel in the early 1990s, the AUC's public spokesperson and former cartel hit man Carlos Castaño dedicated himself to the formation of the Autodefensas Campesinas de Córdoba y Urabá (Peasant Self-Defense Forces of Córdoba and Urabá), which was basically coterminous with a CONVIVIR and drew on the experiences of the Middle Magdalena prototype—Muerte a Secuestradores—of the 1980s. He then built alliances to other regional paramilitaries to create the AUC.[5] Castaño, his brothers, and workers from his estate received military training from the army in Puerto Berrío, upriver from Barrancabermeja. Like the Middle Magdalena, trade unions were strong in Urabá, where the banana worker unions had won the right to represent laborers on an industry-wide basis, rather than on individual plantations. In addition, land takeovers on the outskirts of towns and on the plantations expressed the desire of banana workers for housing, land, and public services and gave rise to a high level of social organization through cooperatives, producer associations, and community groups, as well as support from the guerrillas. In a preview of what would unfold in Barrancabermeja, Castaño's forces devastated popular organizations in Urabá or reconfigured them in accord with neoliberal principles (Chomsky 2008; Romero 2003: 159–220).

Despite Castaño's efforts to organize diverse paramilitary blocs under the banner of the AUC and present a unified public front, the AUC never articulated a national political vision nor did it manage to solidify alliances among all regional commanders, who were divided by personal rivalries, suspicion, and competition over control of the drug economy. The BCB grew out of the dissolution and consolidation of other paramilitary entities, in 2002, with the vision of capturing Barrancabermeja and in reaction to President Andrés Pastrana's proposal to create a demilitarized zone in the Middle Magdalena for the ELN in order to negotiate peace. Carlos Castaño created it from the remnants of the Self-Defense Forces of Santander and South Cesar, whose leader, Camilo Morantes, was murdered on Castaño's orders, after orchestrating the infamous May 16, 1998, massacre of thirty-five people in Barrancabermeja, and from the amalgamation of other groups, including the South Bolívar front, which Castaño "franchised" to Carlos Mario Jiménez, alias Macaco, a drug trafficker associated with the defunct North Valle cartel. The sale of "franchises" to drug traffickers turbocharged the growth of the BCB in other parts of the country, including key coca-producing regions such as Putumayo province (Ávila 2010). As Vicente Castaño, an AUC leader and brother of Carlos Castaño, explained: "In the last phase of the expansion, some very difficult zones remained that the self-defense forces could not reach. So a national discussion was opened to figure out who could take charge of these regions" (qtd. in Ávila 2010: 134). The distinction between paramilitaries who waged counterinsurgent warfare and drug traffickers who used violence to protect their illegal operations became largely meaningless within the AUC. Proceeds from the drug traffic enabled the paramilitaries to buy the weapons, vehicles, and even helicopters that facilitated their military buildup in former guerrilla strongholds rich in natural resources and stoked the repression and subjugation of the people who fell under their long shadow.

With its close ties to the cocaine traffic, the BCB became the largest and most powerful paramilitary bloc in the country. It amassed a fighting force of more than seven thousand men, operated in eight provinces that spanned the length and breadth of Colombia, and maintained several fronts, one of which, the Fidel Castaño front, took over Barrancabermeja. Like most paramilitary strongmen, the three major leaders of the BCB came from modest social and economic backgrounds (Richani 2007). Ironically, Supreme Commander Carlos Mario Jiménez was the son of a butcher. Military strategist Rodrigo Pérez Alzáte, alias Julián Bolívar, had tried his hand at the sale of fast food and ice cream, but when these failed, he became a cattle trader in Antioquia province and teamed up with ranchers to form the Grupo Pérez, a "self-defense" organization dedicated to ending guerrilla extortion. Iván Roberto Duque Gaviria, alias Ernesto Báez, the BCB political boss, was a lawyer who began his career as a Liberal Party member and who, in 1982, was a founder of ACEDEGAM, which had acted as a shield for the formation of paramilitary groups in the Puerto Boyacá region. As the BCB consolidated its grip over more territory, it organized new fields of power that sprang from the connection of preexisting regional social relations and structures of criminality and counterinsurgency with new national and international networks of capital accumulation and political domination. These connections are what Don Kalb and Herman Tak (2005: 2) call "critical junctures," power-laden sets of interconnected social relations that extend across space and through time and connect nominally different spheres of activity, such as legal, illegal, political, and economic. They help us to understand the contested politics through which landscapes of organized power emerge and shape the actions, visions, resources, and territory-making capabilities of different people.

Paramilitaries supported a particular kind of undemocratic state and a form of capital accumulation without limits, and their ability to build ties to regional elites, politicians, and the security forces enabled them to control the electoral process in many parts of the country, place individuals sympathetic to their agenda in municipal, departmental, and national office, and manipulate political institutions to further their particular agendas. These relationships and practices were instrumental to the national extension of an emergent right-wing alliance that used unrestrained violence to break the power of popular organizations and drive the guerrillas from resource-rich areas under their control. Such connections set the paramilitaries apart from the insurgents, whose political base was rooted in the peasantry and the working class. The guerrillas were critical of capitalism and, for many years, sought to replace it, but their power never transcended the municipal level, where they controlled neighborhood committees, extorted mayors, cut deals with corrupt ECOPETROL officials, and threatened politicians.[6] As Winifred Tate (2011: 193) notes, one of the most controversial issues raised by the expansion of paramilitarism for social science analysts was the extent to which they were able to assume the regulatory power of a state and control social life in areas under their control, especially given the volatile and dynamic nature of the new configurations of paramilitary, guerrilla, and popular power that existed across Colombia. A closer examination of the forms of political subjugation, labor exploitation, and rent extraction that emerged in Barrancabermeja between 2000 and 2006 can begin to address this concern.

"Who Has the Arms Has Power": Narco-paramilitarism and Political Power

The BCB crushed reformist and revolutionary projects of political change, and it mobilized private power to create a new political order, based in the repression of labor, the suppression of democracy, and unrestricted capital accumulation. It also reorganized the geography of power and deepened an extreme form of armed neoliberalism, as decentralization enabled paramilitaries and individuals associated with them to secure public contracts and develop ties to the state sector that facilitated the theft of public resources. At the same time, the retrenchment of social welfare services, the weakening of labor laws, and growing immiseration were already heightening the importance of clientelism for working people as a means of acquiring housing, jobs, medicine, food, and solutions to problems. The BCB took advantage of these vulnerabilities, which it had helped to create, and incorporated working people who sympathized and collaborated with it into new forms of authoritarian clientelism, while excluding others because of presumed political sympathies and associations.[7] Such a strategy was instrumental in fracturing the remaining power of the left in Barrancabermeja and dismantling networks of popular solidarity.

The ability of the paramilitaries to capture state institutions began, in the 1990s, with the emergence of new political parties and movements, such as Convergencia Ciudadana, Colombia Viva, Cambio Radical, and Alas, and the decline of the traditional Liberal and Conservative Parties. The alignment of these new parties with regional paramilitary groups during key electoral competitions, especially those in the first decade of the 2000s, redrew Colombia's national political map (López 2010). Regional-based paramilitary blocs used violence and threats to force candidates out of races and create a single electoral option, as well as to pressure voters to cast their ballots for politicians approved by the mercenaries. When I asked residents of northeast Barranca about the experiences of their neighborhoods, I repeatedly heard the same refrain: "Whoever has the arms has power" (*Quien tiene las armas tiene poder*). As power flowed from the barrel of a gun, candidates associated with the paramilitary blocs won municipal, departmental, and national political office, especially in northern and northeastern Colombia, where paramilitarism was strongest. These developments moved paramilitary commander Salvatore Mancuso to boast, after the 2002 elections, that the AUC controlled 35 percent of the Colombian Congress.

In Santander province, where Barrancabermeja is located, the backing of the BCB was crucial to the rise and expansion of Convergencia Ciudadana. Luis Alberto Gil founded Convergencia in 1997 and then crafted an alliance with the BCB during the 2002 parliamentary elections and the 2003 departmental elections, exchanging the promise of political favors, if elected, for paramilitary support. The BCB, in turn, pressured voters to support Convergencia candidates, leading to Gil's election to the Colombian Senate. Two other Convergencia candidates won seats in the House of Representatives in 2002. In 2003, the party capitalized on these national gains to expand in Santander province, where it captured the governor's office and elected fourteen deputies, fourteen mayors, and numerous city council members, including four in Barrancabermeja. A few years later, in 2006 and 2007, respectively, the party won additional victories in electoral races across the country. The consolidation of Convergencia in Santander took place at the expense of the Liberal Party, whose networks of clients collapsed, and whose key figures joined Convergencia. In addition, a left-wing faction of the Liberal Party, known as "El Sindicato," which had been strong in the municipality of Barrancabermeja, was debilitated and marginalized, as a new configuration of alliances that included former Liberals and Conservatives, well-known political bosses, some independent groups, and the armed right rose to prominence within Convergencia (Ávila and Acevedo 2010).

The control of political office was key to acquiring access to public funds and contracts, as the decentralization of fiscal and administrative activities opened the door for private entrepreneurs to compete in the provision of a wide range of services and for public officials to steer contracts to front companies controlled by the paramilitaries or those associated with them. With the reorganization of the health care sector, in 1993, and the weakening of labor legislation, for example, hospitals and clinics no longer hired workers directly. They utilized so-called job agencies (*bolsas de empleo*) that negotiated temporary contracts between people seeking employment and prospective employers. Provisioning workers to the health services sector created the possibility for regional political leaders, who often controlled these agencies, to receive the constitutionally mandated budgetary transfers assigned to municipalities for the provision of health care. It also enabled them to offer jobs to supporters—jobs that came with wage deductions charged by the agencies and without significant benefits or union representation—and to charge the health service providers a fee for the employees. Gil was one such health care entrepreneur who used his businesses to acquire public contracts and to build clientelistic networks by rewarding supporters with jobs. Rather than contributing to a more efficient, effective health care system, however, these practices strengthened paramilitary front businesses and the enterprises of the politicians or families allied with the mercenaries, weakened the power of organized labor, and created troubling, new public-private business ventures in which the paramilitaries acted as handmaidens for the configuration of a new geography of power that extended from the towns of Santander to the halls of state power in Bogotá.[8] This new organization of social, political, and economic relations was undergirded by the coercive power of the BCB.

Predation, Intimidation, and Authoritarian Clientelism in the Barrios of Barranca

Although residents in Barranca's working-class neighborhoods were pressured by paramilitaries to vote for particular candidates, including those of Convergencia Ciudadana, the city's strong leftist tradition presented the BCB with a more complicated challenge than other regional towns that were more easily subdued. The left-wing Democratic Alternative Pole enjoyed strong support in Barrancabermeja, and in the 2004 mayoral election, its candidate, Edgar Cote, ran for office and won the election without any identifiable links to the BCB. Only a week after winning office, however, Cote began to fill municipal positions with individuals tied to the paramilitaries, and it was later revealed that he was taking orders from Ivan Roberto Duque, who demanded the submission of municipal budgets for his approval. Duque, it turned out, was related to Cote, and he played a major role in orchestrating the BCB's political project in Barrancabermeja.[9]

While the BCB made pacts with politicians and supported the expansion of new political parties, it also developed a system of control and exploitation in Barrancabermeja's poor neighborhoods based on predation, intimidation, and authoritarian clientelism. Clientelistic relationships had long been a source of political power and jobs in a city with a chronically high unemployment rate. The creation of JACs by the National Front in 1958, for example, was one way in which the government tried to co-opt the urban poor through the creation of new clientelist networks and to avoid the emergence of alternative organizational forms. The JACs had a dual character: they were simultaneously community organizations in which ordinary citizens were empowered to resolve neighborhood problems, and they depended on the government for legal recognition and financial support. Clientelism operated primarily at election time when state officials channeled public resources and the promise of services to poor urban residents in exchange for votes (Leal and Dávila 1990). Under the paramilitaries, however, threats and intimidation played a more important role in getting out the vote, and clientelistic relations tied people less to public officials than to predatory mercenaries who controlled a broad swath of the popular economy. By the twenty-first century, the privatization of public entities and resources, the restructuring of labor relations, and the violent displacement of peasants to the urban periphery created new vulnerabilities in the lives of many barranqueños and provided fertile soil for the flowering of authoritarian clientelism under the BCB.

Although guerrilla groups had also erected clientelistic networks in Barrancabermeja's poor neighborhoods, significant differences distinguished the ability of the insurgencies and the paramilitaries to harness clientelism to the advancement of political and economic projects. Although the ELN was the dominant insurgency, no single guerrilla group had ever controlled the entire city, or even all of the northeastern district, where three guerrilla organizations—the FARC, ELN, and EPL—had alternately cooperated and competed with each other. In contrast, the BCB took over the entire city and laid claim to a broad swath of economic activities through the control of subcontracting, the provision of credit, and a variety of illegal activities, while the security forces either turned a blind eye to what was happening or received a cut of the action. By eliminating the competition and developing more pervasive, brutal forms of social control, the paramilitaries were in a commanding position to distribute favors and accumulate wealth. To gain access to vital goods and services, working people had to surrender the right to associate with their equals in unions, political parties, and neighborhood associations that retained enough autonomy to allow them to pursue common class interests, while the language of class as a form of claims making was suppressed. This was the biggest difference between the periods of guerrilla and paramilitary rule. Those who refused to give in to the paramilitaries, or who were stigmatized because of their place of residence or perceived affiliations, were violently excluded from the new clientelistic relations that sprouted like mushrooms under neoliberalism.

The job agencies that multiplied with the passage of Law 100, which weakened labor regulations, provide a case in point. These legal entities provided workers to state agencies and private firms that no longer hired directly, and as we saw earlier with the experience of Luis Alberto Gil, they enabled the paramilitaries and those tied to the paramilitaries to manipulate the labor force and build ties to both the state and the private sector. A former oil worker whom I shall call Luis watched the development of job agencies in Barrancabermeja and described their impact on workers:

> After the paramilitary incursion, [the paramilitaries] created their job agencies. They opened an office and recruited individuals who had once been involved with associations of the unemployed and who did not support the union. Those people started saying that they were going to interface with the employers in order to give opportunities to the workers, and leaders like us were not recognized. And at the same time, the paramilitary goes and "dialogues," between quotation marks, with the manager or the administrator of the business, and lays out the rules of the game: any person that agrees to work for the business has to first pass through the job agency. The manager can't hire anyone that [the paramilitary] doesn't approve. Everyone who gets a job is on the paramilitary's list. And the paramilitary gathers information about you and your family from your vita. . . . That's how it worked and continues to work.[10]

Although Luis was unemployed at the time of our interview, he had never sought work through a job agency. "I am afraid," he said. "It is better to prevent than to cure." People with a trade union background, a prior history of collaboration with the guerrillas, or residence in a neighborhood stigmatized for its guerrilla sympathies were forced to either keep their distance from the job agencies that operated as fronts for paramilitaries and their supporters or remain silent and risk physical harm, if their personal histories were revealed. Luis explained, "The victimization of many people [by the paramilitaries] has been because of the information that [they] have obtained about people in the job agencies, often through rumors and innuendo, like the unguarded comments of someone who says unknowingly in the presence of a paramilitary informant that 'ah, that guy was a guerrilla, or a guerrilla supporter.' So, you see, there is this kind of indicating [señalamiento], even though indirect, and the information gets back to them."[11] The threat posed by rumor and gossip aggravated fear, and like Luis, many other people found that their employment opportunities narrowed, which intensified the imperative to find work. Access to jobs and benefits became gifts or favors instead of social rights, which Barranca's popular organizations had long demanded; as Luis noted, "At some point, they [the paramilitaries] are going to come to you and say, 'Do me this favor.' That is what you fear."[12] The rigid patterns of inclusion and exclusion that characterized paramilitary clientelism were a central part of the BCB's effort to break the back of the left in Barrancabermeja.

Yet the job agencies were more than a tool to marginalize the left. They provided an opportunity to extract exorbitant discounts from workers' wages—10 percent for the privilege to associate with the job agency, 10 percent for each wage payment, 10 percent of any bonuses, and 10 percent of settlement payments at the end of a contract—as well as the fees (or the extortion) charged to the firms. As Luis explained, "All the money that they amassed through the job agencies and the drug traffic was used to create loan offices in which people could borrow money. But unfortunately, because of the difficult employment situation, people can't always repay the loans. The paramilitaries then take their possessions, and if they have nothing to take, the paramilitaries kill them."[13] Under the control of the paramilitaries, the job agencies operated as a tool for controlling and dispossessing workers and accumulating wealth. They arose from the Colombian government's neoliberal labor reforms, which paramilitarism then deepened by eliminating opposition to them and incorporating working people into new forms of inclusion and exclusion that weakened the power of organized labor.

The job agencies represented one of a variety of businesses and front organizations operated by the paramilitaries, such as the lottery, transportation enterprises, private security firms, discos, brothels, gas stations, hotels, and clothing stores, through which the mercenaries distributed jobs and other rewards to supporters, laundered drug money, extended their political domination, and redistributed wealth upward. Avoiding their clutch was not easy. Juan Sebastián Sánchez recalled his family's trauma when the BCB moved against independent subcontractors who provided services to ECOPETROL.[14] Sánchez had operated a small business that performed maintenance functions for ECOPETROL. Even though he had been losing contracts to larger firms, the BCB kidnapped him and his entire family, in 2005, because he had not acceded to its extortion demands. He was shocked when an individual, seated before a local commander, pulled up his past contract information on a computer screen, cited his earnings, and quoted an amount that he had to pay in order to leave alive. Such predation and extortion victimized individuals, like Sánchez, who competed with the paramilitary front companies that also provided services to the oil industry.

The brutal labor discipline developed at the same time as the privatization of public enterprises limited poor residents' access to basic services and forced them to pay higher fees. For example, telephone and electricity rates became more expensive in the aftermath of privatization, which cost additional jobs, and water rates shot through the roof, spiking to 60 percent in 2007. Yet when hundreds of residents protested usurious electricity rates after newly installed meters malfunctioned in their homes, the paramilitaries threatened them and the president of a consumer protection group that oversaw the cost of public services. The erosion of well-being pushed some people into coercive debt relationships with the paramilitaries, after a health crisis or a financial emergency overwhelmed their ability to cope. Many residents told how flyers offering generous credit started to appear in their neighborhoods after the arrival of the BCB. To access the money, one had only to call a cell phone number, and a young man would appear on a motorcycle to negotiate the deal and provide the funds, which usually required payment at 20 percent interest. The arrangement built on older forms of quasi-legal credit known as drip by drip (*gota a gota*), but it required no guarantors, collateral, or signed documents, and it turned on fear.

One woman explained that after surviving a traffic accident with a bus, she faced the task of paying for expensive repairs to the vehicle because the owner—a suspected paramilitary—insisted that she bore responsibility for the accident. Her husband had lost his job with ECOPETROL, and the family of five depended on her wages as a nurse for basic necessities. Fearing what might happen if they neglected the damaged bus, husband and wife borrowed money from a local lender whom they suspected of paramilitary ties and then began to repay the funds immediately. When they fell into arrears, two men came to their home and threatened them with harm if the payments did not continue on schedule. As the woman later explained, "I didn't know what to do. I could borrow from another paramilitary to pay off the first one, or I could plead with my relatives to lend me the money which they don't have."[15] The paramilitaries used intimidation to weave exploitative relationships of credit and debt out of the vulnerabilities of residents. Debtors faced the impossible situation of living with the imminent threat of violence or squeezing their social networks to the breaking point.

Although using personalistic relations to make a living, advance political claims, or weather a personal setback was not new, the intimidation, predation, and authoritarian clientelism that emerged under the BCB created a sense of radical uncertainty for many working people that structured fear into the fabric of their lives. Such unpredictability meant that people were always physically, emotionally, and economically vulnerable. By incorporating working people into autocratic, hierarchical relationships, and excluding or murdering those they defined as "enemies," the paramilitaries used menace and threats, rather than the law or notions of legality, to regulate social life in a context in which the despotic power of the BCB was premised on the ability and the willingness to unleash horrific violence, and to do so with impunity.[16]

Yet as the BCB consolidated its military control of Barrancabermeja, the use of exemplary, spectacular violence was increasingly unnecessary to control a population that had been traumatized and disorganized, and BCB commanders set out to legitimize their rule over a social landscape that they had largely destroyed. As one mercenary asserted, "We realized that arbitrary murders and terrorist-like collective assassinations generated rejection among the civilian population" (qtd. in González and Jiménez 2008: 160). His recognition that a system of rule based on terror was unsustainable constituted the first step in paramilitary attempts to reconstruct the social order "from the bottom up," a process that would unfold through "social and political work." To legitimate their domination, the paramilitaries had to contend with the tensions at the heart of their relationships with local residents: either win followers by improving the lives of residents or maintain control through the naked exercise of force. It was a tall order, given the drive to amass wealth and the volatility of the BCB project in which violence was the primary form of conflict resolution among paramilitaries and between them and others.

Paramilitary Social Work: Discipline and Manipulation

Shortly after the takeover of Barrancabermeja's northeast neighborhoods, the BCB circulated manuals that spelled out the new rules of coexistence (*normas de convivencia*) between the BCB and the civilian population. These regulations sought to discipline working people through the reaffirmation of rigid gender, generational, and sexual hierarchies disrupted by years of violence and economic restructuring, and to regulate the use of space. They included a Monday through Friday evening curfew for young people that was extended slightly on Saturdays and Sundays. Youth caught out beyond the curfew faced a twelve-hour detention, during which time the paramilitaries forced them to work. In addition, the BCB prohibited young men from wearing long hair and earrings and forbade women from dressing in miniskirts; those caught violating the dress code risked apprehension, confiscation of the offending articles, and expulsion from the city. Moreover, "public scandals" were resolved by the paramilitaries, who humiliated those accused of "scandalous behavior" (e.g., prostitutes) by forcing them to wear signs around their necks and engage in public work projects, such as picking up trash or sweeping parks.[17]

The code of conduct envisioned a fortified patriarchal order in which the BCB itself would regulate women and youth whose dependence on husbands, partners, and fathers had increased during the long years of political violence and neoliberal reform, even as men were less able to care for their families. The death, disappearance, and flight of men, who were the primary targets of paramilitary violence, had left more women to head households and raise children alone. And the erosion of full-time, waged employment—a domain of the economy dominated by men—weighed heavily on women and children who had always depended on male wages. Shoring up patriarchy was a bid to control some of the social chaos created to a considerable degree by the paramilitaries themselves and to incorporate gender and generational hierarchies into class rule.

The paramilitaries also claimed to provide "protection" to local residents. They set up rackets in which payments were extorted from residents in exchange for "security." One resident described how a local commander called his neighborhood to a meeting in a public school, where the individual explained that the BCB had entered the city at the request of local citizens to deal with the "security problem" caused by the guerrillas. He then offered the services of his men to the community. Shortly thereafter, young enforcers began to visit residents on Saturday afternoons, requesting weekly payments of two thousand pesos for the protection of their homes.[18] Such demands did not endear the paramilitaries to local residents, however. They were widely resented and did little more than guarantee protection—for a time—from the paramilitaries themselves. Other paramilitary practices, however, were quietly welcomed by many urban residents.

The BCB aimed to purge the urban environment of drug users, prostitutes, homosexuals, trade unionists, and alleged "subversives," whom it defined as dangerous, dirty, and immoral. It did so through periodic, selective assassinations that sent a message to everyone about what awaited nonconformists. The quiet assent of some residents to extrajudicial executions expressed wider anxieties about the spread of HIV/AIDS, the presence of unknown men on the streets, and the crime and score settling associated with the drug traffic in some neighborhoods. A young man from the northeast recounted how he and a group of friends used to congregate on a street corner in the evening to talk and smoke marijuana, until a paramilitary threatened them and then shot one of his friends in the face. After noting the hypocrisy of drug traffickers enforcing a ban on marijuana consumption, he lamented that some residents did not object to what was widely referred to as "social cleansing," because "seeing young men on the corner [smoking pot] makes them uncomfortable."[19] Because the paramilitaries represented the de facto urban power, residents increasingly had to turn to them to resolve problems, including domestic disputes, conflicts with neighbors, and problems with teenagers. By so doing, they inadvertently legitimized the power of the mercenaries and the social order that the latter sought to create and, at the same time, abetted the unraveling of working-class culture.

Barrancabermeja's neighborhood councils—the JACs—were key institutions through which the paramilitaries tried to naturalize their power, much like the guerrillas before them, and they illustrated the tensions between problem solving and violence that shaped the BCB's bid for legitimation. They carried out neighborhood development projects with municipal funds and sometimes grants from NGOs, such as the construction of schools and health centers, paving roads, and the creation of soccer fields, designed to improve the quality of life in urban neighborhoods. The BCB saw the JACs as local-level structures that would act as echo chambers for their views and allow them to reach out to and connect with the concerns of urban residents.

Unlike the paramilitary Bloque Norte, which imposed new leaders on the councils in the areas under its control, the BCB tended to work through preexisting leadership structures, while making it clear that council leaders were subjected to its rules (Ávila 2010: 131–32). As one resident explained, "The council leaders were subdued with money, and others with force. Some of them just looked the other way when the paras did something. Others sympathized with the paras."[20] His statements suggest that both support for the BCB project and fear-induced corruption moved council presidents to work with the mercenaries. Through these individuals, the BCB then appealed to neighborhood residents with acts of benevolence, such as the sponsorship of bingo events, Mother's Day celebrations, fiestas, the creation of parks and holiday gift handouts, or in some cases, the initiation of development projects.[21] The largesse was often appreciated, but crafting legitimacy meant building a safety net for urban residents that would protect them from the erosion of social well-being that was taking place all around them and help them resolve daily problems. It depended on enduring, daily personal interactions that required constant cultivation and updating and the trust that flowed from them.[22] The case of Leonardo Páez illustrates some of the conflicts and tensions that shaped the BCB's efforts to normalize its rule and build a supportive political base in the barrios of northeast Barranca.[23]

Páez had been the president of a large, northeastern neighborhood council under guerrilla rule, and he continued to serve after the BCB arrived. Páez had lived in the community since the 1970s, when his family migrated to Barrancabermeja from Bolívar province, and after the departure of his siblings, he continued to reside with his mother in the family home, an unpretentious green house on a shady street corner. Residents constantly sought him out for advice, information, and assistance. His disarming sense of humor put them at ease, and his tips, suggestions, and occasional material support, such as access to a subsidized lunch program for young children, communicated to people that he cared about them and could help them contend with some of their problems. It was impossible to sit in his living room, visit him at the community center, or walk down the street with him alone. Someone was always asking for a moment of his time, and his cell phone never seemed to stop ringing.

One day in a private room of the community center with his phone turned off, Páez explained to me the difference between guerrilla and paramilitary domination of the neighborhood. "The neighborhood councils," he began, "had operated in alignment with the guerrillas, but the guerrillas didn't interfere with their decisions; they monitored them, but they did not oblige them to do anything." Despite underlying friction with the insurgents over the question of council autonomy, Páez and other elected officials had "more political space to move in" than would subsequently be the case under the BCB. Indeed, Páez recounted how, in 1999, he stood for his first election at a time when the FARC garnered little legitimacy in the northeast. The insurgency fielded its own list of candidates, which lost to Páez and his electoral slate, but then permitted Páez to assume the presidency of the neighborhood body. With the expulsion of the FARC two years later, Páez's relations with the new overlords grew much more fraught.

Almost immediately after the BCB seized control of his neighborhood, a guerrilla-turned-paramilitary named Eduardo began to investigate Páez. He first went to the home of the council treasurer to demand that she open the books for his review and asked her a series of menacing questions about Páez, whom he referred to as a "faggot." Was he embezzling money? Was he collaborating with guerrillas? And who were his friends? The treasurer, who was Páez's close confidante, feared that Eduardo planned to murder him. She had known Eduardo since he was a child and drew on their relationship to insist that Páez was an honorable person who had always carried out his duties in an upright and honest fashion. Her intervention may have saved Páez's life, but he was then left in the unenviable position of negotiating paramilitary claims, on the one hand, and responding to the needs of his constituents, on the other hand, within a lopsided balance of power.

Páez explained how, in the immediate aftermath of the BCB takeover, rank-and-file troops went door-to-door summoning residents to an assembly in a local park, where men dressed in civilian clothing introduced themselves as members of the BCB of the AUC. The men spoke with *paisa* accents that identified Colombians from Antioquia province. They announced that they had come to clean out the neighborhood and provide jobs for local residents and instructed those people in need of employment to provide the junta president with their vitae so that he could find work for them. Páez, who stood in the middle of the gathering, was mortified. He understood the announcement as an opening gambit to involve and compromise key neighborhood leaders in the BCB move to establish a social base and to use it as a source of social, economic, and political power. It was also, he believed, a gesture to him and other council presidents to indicate that they operated under paramilitary supervision. Páez knew that he could not provide jobs for everyone who needed them; the mercenaries were, he felt, placing the onus of job creation on him and directing any blame for future economic hardship away from themselves. He thus found himself in an untenable situation in which failure to accommodate to the paramilitaries posed risks to his safety, but appeasing them exposed him to the wrath and rejection of his constituents, who would remain unemployed. At great personal risk, Páez spoke up. He identified himself as the neighborhood council president, told the men that he did not know who they were, and informed residents that he was not in a position to locate employment for them.

On another occasion, as the end-of-the-year holidays approached, the paramilitaries assembled a number of council presidents, including Páez, and instructed them to hand over lists of the children in their jurisdictions, allegedly so the BCB could distribute Christmas gifts to the youngsters. Páez informed the paramilitary commander that he did not have such a list, nor did he know the names of all the children who lived in his populous neighborhood. He understood the implications of handing a list of names to the mercenaries and doubted their sincerity. The offer of gifts was, he believed, a move to soften the brutal image of the BCB by demonstrating its concern for children. The next day, a local radio station announced that the BCB would hand out presents to neighborhood youngsters on Christmas Eve, and it broadcast a schedule of the times and locations where the gifts would be distributed. Shaking his head, Páez described how groups of parents and children moved en masse from one distribution site to another, only to be disappointed at every turn. Finally, he said, the radio announced that the truck bearing the presents had been turned back, but there was no mention of who had interfered with its journey. Even though there would be no Christmas presents for the children, the paramilitaries had demonstrated their good intentions and placed the failure of their plan on forces operating outside the city. Given the total impunity that undergirded paramilitary rule, Páez's timorous refusal to collude with the BCB was notable, but it was not widely imitated. One resident insisted that Páez was unique: "He is very loyal to the principle of nonviolence. He was one of the few [council presidents] with the balls to take on the guerrillas and the paras equally."[24] Although it is likely that Páez made accommodations with the mercenaries that he was not comfortable talking about with me, the resident's sentiment was widely shared by others. For Páez and other council presidents like him, clientelism had grown much more unpredictable in northeast Barranca, where raw intimidation frequently displaced the more benign exchange of public resources for votes.

In the case of the neighborhood council, the BCB drive to win broad popular acceptance ran up against a local leader who had been enmeshed in long-term, regular interactions with neighborhood people. Páez's close personal bonds with many people underwrote his authority as council president and moved those most closely tied to his personal networks to understand that he cared about their welfare. To the extent that such individuals and their networks represented an alternative way to access resources and a legitimate claim to look out for the well-being of the community, they posed a threat to paramilitary power; Páez was therefore exceptional in his ability to negotiate paramilitary demands and remain alive. What his case suggests is that after the violent conquest of Barrancabermeja, the BCB attempted to co-opt council presidents like Páez and then use their dense social ties as a basis for sanctioning paramilitary authority. This was an important move because in Páez's neighborhood, residents viewed the BCB's paisa commanders as outsiders, and young foot soldiers like Eduardo did not inspire confidence. In addition, the BCB was itself a volatile organization riven by competing interests and personal rivalries. Even though paramilitary bosses could distribute jobs and favors to a web of clients and sympathizers, those incorporated into the BCB's authoritarian networks had to deal with the constant threat of violence for perceived missteps, the inability to repay a debt, or the refusal to respond to the request for a favor. None of this constituted fertile ground for the construction of legitimacy, and it further shredded the tattered fabric of working-class Barranca.

The BCB's efforts to sanitize its sanguinary image met with uneven results elsewhere in the city as well. The creation of a social fund with proceeds from the massive theft of gasoline from ECOPETROL's pipelines enabled it to finance a range of good works, including the completion of a park in the Ninth of April neighborhood that had begun under the guerrillas. Council leaders remained silent about the project as it unfolded, but when the park was named the Fidel Castaño Gil Park—after the BCB front that took control of the city—amid a public ceremony replete with firecrackers and a speech by "Jhony," the paramilitary commander, word of the "para park" spread, and a tenacious group of human rights activists raised an outcry.[25] One activist explained how, after the inauguration, "we found out about it and began the most ferocious denouncement and pressure so that the municipal authorities, who were complicit in the project, would have to tear it down. The protest was so great that they had to take down the bust and the plaque that had been installed in honor of that sociopath called Fidel."[26] By sounding the alarm with the mayor's office, the activists called attention to the clandestine connections that linked the municipal officials and neighborhood council to the paramilitaries. They also signaled that legitimizing the paramilitary project would be much more difficult in Barrancabermeja than in surrounding towns and hamlets because the remnants of a shattered opposition remained a significant, albeit vastly reduced, counterweight to the emergent status quo.

Unlike victorious revolutionary armies that face the task of addressing popular demands and incorporating them into new state structures, the BCB never sought to replace the institutional state; rather, it worked with and through the JACs, the mayor's office, and state institutions at the local, provincial, and national levels by corrupting and coercing state personnel, placing sympathizers in positions of power, and murdering competitors. By using the juntas as vehicles to naturalize their power, the paramilitaries aggravated enduring concerns about the stated autonomy of these bodies and raised questions about whether they protected the well-being of residents or undermined their security. Such worries pointed to the ongoing struggle over the right to rule that was woven into the fabric of daily life and continued after the paramilitary takeover. They reflected both the hopes and the fears that embodied popular perceptions of the state, whose institutions themselves were rife with conflicting logics of rule.

An Undeclared Death Penalty

Hopes and fears about the state emerged in a conversation that I had with Pedro Lozada, as we chatted one day on the patio behind his home. "Do you know that in Colombia they use the death penalty?" he asked. Lozada straddled a hammock and paused for a moment to judge my reaction before continuing: "I don't believe that I have ever heard anyone use that expression. It is not a death penalty written in the constitution. . . . [It's] an undeclared death penalty; the government can kill anyone. That's what has happened in Colombia."[27] His notion of an undeclared death penalty evinced an understanding of an outlaw state—violent, predatory, unpredictable, and criminal—that acted outside the constitutional bounds of legality. Such fears were amplified in Barrancabermeja, where the webs of power that connected the institutional state to the "parastate" were not only unclear; their very ambiguity expressed how powerful actors were reconfiguring the state and the ways it was understood. Fears were further aggravated by a strong belief that powerful individuals manipulated violent events behind the scenes and escaped responsibility for their actions. The struggle between fear and hope emerged in sharpest relief among those men and women who participated in a state-sponsored protection program that placed their physical security in the hands of the Ministry of Interior and the highly suspect DAS. Their worries that the institutional state left them unprotected—even targeted them for death—and their insistence that it operate within the law, provide for their needs, and protect them influenced how they negotiated a relationship with it and illustrated how few options were available.

Since 1997, the Colombian Ministry of Interior has operated a protection program called the Program for the Protection of Human Rights Defenders, Members of Social Organizations and Witnesses of Human Rights Violations and Breaches of International Humanitarian Law, which is implemented by the state security forces. The program arose at a moment when the Colombian government was under intense pressure from other governments, primarily the United States, Canada, and the European Union, and international organizations, such as the International Labor Organization, to address the abysmal human rights record of its security forces. Shaped by the training, finance, and advice of transnational NGOs and Western governments, it was part of a much broader initiative that began in the 1990s to create new state human rights agencies to monitor other Colombian state institutions, primarily the military and the judiciary, and to fund new human rights programs within preexisting state bureaucracies.[28] It purported to safeguard the lives of threatened activists from union, civic, human rights, and peasant organizations, and, between 2001 and 2006, the initiative received financial support from the United States.

More than six thousand Colombians participated in the program in 2006; more than a third of these individuals were either trade union leaders or members of human rights organizations. The program provided them with a series of "hard" and "soft" forms of support, depending on the level of risk established by either the police or, prior to 2011, the DAS.[29] The hard support for the most gravely threatened individuals included armored vehicles, bodyguards, bulletproof vests, and weapons, while the soft support consisted of communication devices that linked activists to an early warning system and financial assistance to move to safer locations. In Barrancabermeja, a number of trade unionists and other activists received a full range of hard security measures from the DAS, but the protection program was a constant source of tension, mistrust, and suspicion, as DAS officials and program beneficiaries became enmeshed in a series of conflicting demands.

Trade unionists and human rights leaders insisted that state officials do their duty and protect citizens from paramilitary violence, and they embraced the security measures provided by the state. Yet by participating in the protection program, they placed themselves in the difficult position of turning to the security forces, whom they had long regarded as paramilitary collaborators, and asking them to safeguard the very people whom the security forces regarded as "subversives," a label that legitimized the use of lethal violence against them. Their dilemma highlighted both the grave threats to which they were exposed and the absence of alternatives for dealing with them. Much of the conflict turned on the issue of bodyguards. The DAS oversaw the hiring and performance of all bodyguards in the Colombian state's protection program, but the agency was profoundly mistrusted because of widespread belief that it maintained close ties to paramilitary organizations. The respected Colombian newsweekly *Semana* confirmed these fears in 2006, when it revealed that the DAS had drawn up a list of trade union leaders, academics, and government opponents and given it to a paramilitary bloc that operated on the north coast. The individuals on the list were then threatened, and several were either murdered or disappeared.

The tussle between endangered social movement leaders and the security forces began with a risk evaluation that either the DAS or the police conducted before assigning protective security measures. Those under evaluation complained that the risk assessment routinely underestimated the threat level and resulted in the provision of inadequate security or none at all. According to one trade unionist, "Over the years, there are people who died in the protection program. There are also people who have been shot at and who have had to leave town on the run. Then the DAS or the police do a study of the risk level, and they assign an average level that doesn't come with bodyguards. And what is really idiotic is that sometimes they will give you a bulletproof vest, but the city is full of paramilitaries who shoot at your head."[30] Yet a government official who oversaw the protection program insisted that because of the widespread mistrust of the DAS, individuals did not always provide enough information to complete an accurate evaluation.[31] The program director dismissed the complaints and argued that "everyone wants to have an armored car because [the cars] are status symbols." He claimed that this was especially true for men who were accustomed to riding motorcycles and bicycles.[32] And like other officials in the Uribe administration, he harbored suspicions that trade unionists and human rights workers were linked to the insurgencies.

Even when the DAS assigned a bodyguard to protect a vulnerable individual, many trade union leaders did not accept personnel from the DAS because they believed that the agency ordered the guards to collect intelligence and then used the information to murder them or their family members. The protection program, however, permitted participants to nominate their own bodyguards, and if the nominees passed muster with the DAS, the agency extended them a contract that lasted approximately six to eight months. Nevertheless, there were constant complaints that the DAS canceled these contracts without due cause, that it periodically refused to provide airline tickets for bodyguards to travel on official business with their charges, and that it left endangered individuals without protection. Indeed, when the DAS refused to provide transportation for a bodyguard, threatened activists were placed in the uncomfortable position of accepting an unknown and untrusted guard from the DAS or traveling alone. A trade union leader who had been in the DAS protection program for several years expressed his frustration:

> Our guards are fired on the slightest pretext. The DAS kicked out my two bodyguards in 2006, even though I complained. It maintained the position that I had to accept the guards that the agency sent me, but the union has a very clear policy that we do not take any bodyguard that we do not know, because the DAS tries to use the guards to gather intelligence on us. Many times, but really very often, we have to travel alone because the DAS will not give the boys tickets. It says that there is no money for the tickets. You call up the Ministry of Interior, and they tell you, "Oh, what a pity, we've run out of money. We can't. But if you want, we'll send you a man from the DAS as soon as you arrive in the airport." Obviously, we say no. . . . So we have to travel alone, and we have to stay in other cities without protection because the DAS says that there isn't money for the tickets.[33]

The struggle over bodyguards points to the uncertainty and the chaos that arise from the violent social order that the private power of paramilitarism has created, a social order in which the Ministry of Interior emerges as a contradictory site of both arbitrary, ruthless force and citizen protection. Such contradictions arise from the competing social forces, both foreign and domestic, that shape state institutions and their programs within wider fields of force and mold how contradictory claims to rule emerge within government institutions, as well as outside of them, and shape how people understand their encounters with "the state."[34] The contest over security also underscores how the institutional state acts in ways that, by its own definition, are illegal, and demonstrates how impunity massages the tensions between legality and illegality, which shape the process of governance; indeed, as Philip Abrams (1988) reminds us, "legitimizing the illegitimate" is one of the central features of state formation. This view of the state forces us to move beyond the institutions of the state and grasp how the aggregation of power-laden social relationships, both public and private, coalesce around conflicting political projects that seek to naturalize relationships of inequality into a concept of the state and translate them into a common understanding of citizenship.

The Resurgence of the Institutional State:
Legitimizing the Illegitimate

Although the BCB managed to subdue Barrancabermeja and pump wealth out of the city through the incorporation of working people into new, militarized relationships of exploitation, its attempts to legitimate paramilitary rule were uneven and incomplete, and it eventually became a threat to the domestic and international legitimacy of the official state. Once the BCB and other paramilitary armies had converted vast extensions of rural Colombia—including the Middle Magdalena region—into zones of resource extraction, megaprojects, and export agriculture for themselves and those they served, they became a liability and an embarrassment for a government that claimed to represent South America's oldest democracy. The presence of mercenary armies that massacred civilians, destroyed reformist political projects, trafficked cocaine, and amassed private fortunes after seizing control of huge extensions of land, portions of the state apparatus, and an array of legal businesses finally became untenable. Forced to contain the violence that it unleashed to defeat the insurgencies and no longer able to deny the existence of paramilitaries, the right-wing government of Álvaro Uríbe announced a "peace process" in 2003. Negotiations between the Uribe administration and paramilitary chieftains lasted until 2006, when some seven thousand BCB troops officially demobilized in media-saturated demobilization ceremonies that featured news footage of young fighters surrendering weapons and speeches by commanders and government officials extolling the end of hostilities.

Because the government had never been at war with armed, right-wing groups, however, the so-called peace process was a negotiation between two sectors of the Colombian state: the official state and its illegal, regional counterparts (Hristov 2010); the guerrillas of the FARC and the ELN did not participate. The result was a government-brokered amnesty program, condemned by human rights groups for institutionalizing impunity, that sought to incorporate the paramilitaries into politics and society, while dismantling their armies. A new 2005 law—the Justice and Peace Law—made no effort to expose the official state's responsibility for creating, consolidating, and expanding paramilitary organizations, nor did it provide mechanisms for seizing paramilitary assets and dismantling the political and economic foundations of their power. In exchange for demobilizing their troops, confessing their crimes, and dismantling their criminal operations, the law granted minimal prison sentences of five to eight years to commanders who had committed crimes against humanity. Such leniency was not enough for some individuals, who balked at the prospect of spending any time in jail and who threatened to withdraw from the peace process and expose their dealings with government officials. The boundary between the official state, which claimed legitimacy, and its violent, unofficial offshoots then began to erode.

A perilous moment for government officials then ensued. In 2006, a public scandal over revelations about the connections between paramilitaries and politicians, known as the parapolítica, began to unfold when a few paramilitary leaders revealed some of their dealings and alliances with government officials in public testimony. These revelations led to the jailing or investigation of more than one hundred members of Congress and governors, including several politicians from Santander province, such as Convergencia Ciudadana founder and Senator Luis Alberto Gil, Representative Luis Alfonso Riaño, Senator Oscar Josué Reyes, and Governor Hugo Aguilar, who received seven- to nine-year jail terms for their ties to the BCB. In addition, the former national DAS director, Jorge Noguera, was convicted of collaborating with the AUC to murder trade unionists and other political opponents. In 2008, in an effort to prevent the scandal from reaching into the presidential office, then president Álvaro Uríbe extradited fourteen top paramilitary commanders—including jailed BCB leaders Carlos Mario Jiménez and Ivan Roberto Duque—to the United States, where they were wanted on drug trafficking charges and where they were less likely to face questioning about their connections to high-ranking government officials in Colombia. Over the next two years, more details of the paramilitary-state relationship were revealed through a series of shocking scandals, but as Jasmine Hristov (2010) notes, what all the scandals had in common was the location of paramilitarism in the past, implying a rupture with the present in which paramilitarism officially no longer existed.

Neither the government nor the major media acknowledged the emergence of neoparamilitary groups, such as Águilas Negras and Los Rastrojos, which continued to use violence to suppress dissent, dispossess working people, and accumulate capital on behalf of a retooled right-wing alliance purged of its most noxious elements. Similarly, they ignored how parties tainted by the parapolítica scandal reorganized under new names to guarantee the continued influence and local political power of the scandal's heirs. A new designation—*bandas criminales* (BACRIM)—disappeared new paramilitary groups into the realm of common thieves and youth gangs; "emergent bands of criminals" became responsible for continuing violence, according to the government. Such linguistic sleight of hand severed the connection between those who used violence to accumulate capital, political leaders, and the security forces, and it reestablished the illusion of separation between the official state and the paramilitaries. By locating paramilitarism in the past, ridding themselves of former allies who had become a liability, and denying any connection to violent, illegal forms of capital accumulation and dispossession in the present, government officials reasserted their claim to rule by legitimizing the illegitimate (Hristov 2010).

The capacity to obscure historical connections, select and naturalize certain beliefs about the past, and obfuscate violent forms of inequality was part of a deepening rightward shift in processes of state formation in which the vision of a state that took care of its citizens' basic needs was diminished. In the Middle Magdalena, state formation turned on the control of the drug traffic, the consolidation of landownership, the command of space, and the unmaking of Barrancabermeja's working class, whose demands for better working conditions, land, public services, and democracy were silenced. The spaces that the institutional state had once filled or never occupied were taken over by new authoritarian, paramilitary networks, which frequently blurred with the institutional state and generated new worries about who acted in the state's name. Regulating a fragmented assemblage of authoritarian, clientelistic relations and normalizing BCB rule proved difficult, as reproducing a social order through fear and terror, with limited moral legitimacy, posed serious long-term problems.

The BCB was responsible for creating much of the disorder that it had to subsequently control. To the extent that paramilitary networks incorporated men and women into new relations of criminalized labor and indebtedness, they tended to further stigmatize and marginalize destitute people, who had no legal protections against threats or the arbitrary use of force meted out by individual commanders, and then eroded the relationships and understandings that had once constituted a vibrant working-class culture. These mercenary networks were not based on long-term, face-to-face interactions with neighborhood residents that inspired trust; they were undergirded by fear and intimidation. What emerged in Barrancabermeja between 2002 and 2006 was a highly unstable, violent configuration of private and public power that succumbed to the weight of its own murderous behavior. Yet after the most discredited paramilitary leaders were extradited to the United States, the mercenary blocs demobilized, and the numerous scandals involving government officials and paramilitaries had run their course, a newly sanitized institutional state reemerged in defense of a neoliberal social order that had been created by paramilitary violence and counterinsurgency and that was undemocratic to the core. How long this new order can continue to reproduce itself remains uncertain, as chronic insecurity, economic marginalization, and continuing fear define the daily lives of many working people in the city.

SIX

NARROWING

POLITICAL OPTIONS

AND HUMAN RIGHTS

. . .

On a steamy morning in February 2007, the Espacio de Trabajadores y Trabajadoras de Derechos Humanos (Workers' Space for Human Rights) convened an emergency meeting to respond to the attempted kidnapping of a street vendor. The Espacio had arisen in 2000 from the deepening violence of Barrancabermeja's dirty war to model itself after the defunct Coordinadora Popular. After years of state and paramilitary attacks against Barranca's popular organizations, it united a loosely knit coalition of surviving unions, neighborhood organizations, and human rights defenders. Although the Espacio lacked the depth, breadth, and organizational power of the Coordinadora, it convened every week to discuss problems, especially human rights concerns, and to propose solutions and bring popular pressure to bear on state officials. There was, however, nothing routine about this meeting.

Representatives from the teachers' union, a displaced persons organization, two international-based human rights groups, a regional human rights organization, the Juanist religious order, SINALTRAINAL, the USO, and the state's human rights office—the Defensoría del Pueblo—were among those crowded around a table in the second-floor headquarters of the OFP, which hosted Espacio meetings. Alfredo Arango hunched over the table.[1] A slightly built, middle-aged man with a thin mustache and gray-flecked hair that flowed away from his forehead, Arango cast nervous glances around the room. He was no stranger to Barrancabermeja. He had worked in the municipal slaughterhouse for nearly two decades before the BCB occupied the city and systematically murdered members of his union. Driven by fears of persecution and economic necessity, he spent the next several years on the move, never remaining in one place very long, and for the last sixteen months, he and his family had lived in the departmental capital, Bucaramanga, where Arango sold fast food on the street, and his wife took in laundry. His return to Barrancabermeja two days earlier had been terrifying and unexpected. He now hoped to get out of town again as soon as possible.

In a halting voice, Arango explained to the assembled audience how three soldiers dressed as civilians had kidnapped him off the street and accused him of controlling the FARC's financial resources for the conflicted region of southern Bolívar province, located upriver from Barrancabermeja on the Magdalena's western bank. "They thought that they caught a big fish," he said. Flashing a taut smile and stroking his chin, he wondered aloud how the armed forces could believe that he was the FARC's finance chief, given that he had so little formal education. "How could someone like me manage all the FARC's money," he asked rhetorically, and "why would I be so poor, if it were true?" These facts were apparently of little concern to his kidnappers, who stuffed him into the back of a car and threatened to kill him if he refused to cooperate. Because denying their charges seemed futile, Arango decided to string them along and buy time for himself by promising to lead the men to a large arms cache in Barrancabermeja, where he hoped that someone might help him.

Pausing frequently to hold back tears, Arango described how the soldiers drove down the mountainous road from Bucaramanga to the tropical plains of the Middle Magdalena and on to the barrio Boston, arriving at the place, on the edge of a field, where he indicated the weapons were buried. Because the hard-packed earth had clearly not been disturbed in a long time, his tormentors immediately became suspicious. They ordered him to dig up the alleged stockpile but lost patience when his efforts yielded only a large hole in the ground. The terrified street vendor insisted that he had made a mistake and convinced them to go to another neighborhood, where his relatives lived. After a short drive, they parked near his sister's house and started walking toward it. Arango recognized several local residents, but he did not greet them or even act like he recognized anyone. When Arango realized that his sister's front door was open, he made a bold, spur-of-the-moment decision to escape. Bolting into the house, he screamed at his shocked sister that men were trying to kill him and then disappeared out the back door and into a deep ravine. He made his way to his mother-in-law's home, where he hid until his sister contacted the OFP, which employed her. The organization was currently providing him with temporary sanctuary.

As the men and women seated around the table took in Arango's dramatic story, the OFP's director, Yolanda Becerra, entered the room and recounted the details of a two-hour meeting in the office of the public prosecutor (*fiscalía*), where she had filed a public denouncement (*denuncia*) against the army for violating Arango's human rights. The ensuing discussion focused on two concerns: how to protect Arango, and how to safeguard his family in Bucaramanga and Barrancabermeja. The group decided to ask the fiscalía to provide the Arango family with protective measures and to notify the Office of the Inspector General (Procuraduría), a public institution charged with investigating misconduct by state offices, of the kidnapping. To place additional pressure on municipal, departmental, and national state officials, each representative signed an urgent action alert that was e-mailed to other human rights organizations, religious groups, trade unions, and popular organizations, both in Colombia and abroad, asking recipients to immediately protest the army's treatment of Arango by telephoning, faxing, and e-mailing various government offices.

As an older vision of dealing with the state, based in collective claims to labor protections, social citizenship and national sovereignty, succumbed to the dirty war, human rights became a new form of claims making and political practice. Beginning in the late 1970s and accelerating in the 1990s, the global politics of "rights" sought to protect persecuted individuals from the overwhelming violence of the state and uphold new developments in international law. Rooted in liberalism, especially in the primacy accorded to the individual, and advocated by liberal elites, global human rights frameworks focused on empowering individuals and the socially excluded. "Rights talk," however, concerned itself less with class politics than with transcending politics and the restrictions of the territorially bounded nation-state. Human rights appealed to a moral vision of a global community that was not hemmed in by any political system. It represented a form of internationalism that replaced anticolonialism and communism, that emphasized collective self-determination and national sovereignty, rather than individual privilege, and that underscored the importance of the state, rather than the supremacy of international law (Chandler 2002; Moyn

2010). As Samuel Moyn observes, "It was not only the loss of faith in the nation-state but also the desertion of the stage by alternative promises to transcend the nation-state that accounts for the relevance of human rights in the last three decades" (2010: 212–13). Yet in Latin America, "alternative promises," such as socialism, anti-imperialist nationalism, social democracy, and liberation theology–inspired Christian humanism, were less deserters of the scene than crushed under the boot of authoritarian regimes that came to power in the middle decades of the twentieth century. Leftist activists in the Southern Cone, for example, adopted the language of human rights in the 1970s and 1980s, as repressive military dictatorships threatened their lives, dismantled left political projects, and forced them into exile in search of new allies. Neither political liberalism nor individualistic notions of human rights, they believed, addressed the social and economic problems that afflicted their societies, but they adopted the human rights frame to end state repression against people like themselves and to establish minimal rules for political participation. In this way, the left used global rights discourse to formulate its own opposition to cold war repression (Markarian 2005; Stites 2013).

Like these activists, many people in Barrancabermeja would not have framed their struggles in terms of human rights, if the ferocious repression had not shattered their world, torn individuals from relationships of solidarity, and forced them to build new alliances and support networks. And they did not adopt global human rights discourse whole cloth or see it as a replacement for the social and economic equality that they had long demanded from the state. Rather, I argue, the emergence of a new politics of human rights in Barrancabermeja was the by-product of decades of repression that narrowed political visions of a different world and blocked avenues of political practice. Making credible human rights claims took place within a constricted sense of political possibilities in which rights activists depended upon the appearance of objectivity and separation from left politics and could do little more than appeal to international law. Human rights then further hindered the development of progressive politics, because of its growing detachment from collective notions of liberation and social transformation.[2]

Activists in Barrancabermeja adopted the language and practice of human rights at a moment when the vibrant tradition of radical trade unionism and civic activism was in decline, and political violence was tearing apart older relationships of solidarity. They did so to challenge the assertion that the institutional state was the locus of rule and that its bureaucracies and shadowy allies could dispense violence with impunity.[3] The prioritization of human rights concerns gave rise to new institutions, networks, alliances, and international funding, as ascendant neoliberalism, with its narrow vision of legal equality and personal freedom, threatened to absorb a growing global human rights movement. In Barrancabermeja, human rights became an organizing concept and a political demand that brought together a diverse spectrum of people, who were often deeply divided, to act on the basis of what they did share: stopping the repression against them and regaining control over their lives and neighborhoods. To what extent, this chapter asks, was human rights activism able to suture together the fragments of Barrancabermeja's devastated social movements and transcend the individualism embedded in liberal notions of human rights and deepened by economic restructuring?

Human rights became part of the "language of contention" in Barrancabermeja and the Middle Magdalena, that is, "a common material and meaningful framework for talking about and acting upon social orders characterized by domination" (Roseberry 1994: 361), as working people were confronted again with the challenge of organization, institution building, and self-education that they had faced in the past but not in exactly the same way. Nongovernmental organizations dedicated to the defense of human rights arose from the shreds of Barrancabermeja's mutilated social fabric and arrived from elsewhere. The Barrancabermeja-based organization CREDHOS was founded, in 1987, by the Coordinadora Popular and supported by the Bogotá-based Centro de Investigación y Educación Popular (Center for Research and Popular Education, CINEP), a Jesuit-operated human rights organization. It was later joined by European-based and North American–based NGOs, such as Peace Brigades, Pax Christi, and Christian Peacemaker Teams, whose young "internationalists" provided protective accompaniment to threatened social leaders. Human Rights Watch, Amnesty International, Witness for Peace, and the Center for International Policy, among others, also monitored local events and reported on them from headquarters in Europe and the United States. The growth of human rights organizing opened new kinds of political possibilities and engagements when radical uncertainty was the central experience of working people in Barrancabermeja.

My analysis demonstrates how human rights also infused vener-able popular organizations with a different language and form of prac-tice. Unions, popular organizations, and development projects, such as the USO, the OFP, and the World Bank–funded Development and Peace Program for the Middle Magdalena, which began in 1995, integrated human rights concerns into the ways that they addressed labor con-flicts, advocated for poor women, and approached development issues, respectively. And in a variation of Bourdieu's metaphor of "the left hand and the right hand of the state,"[4] new bureaucratic government agencies—the Defensoría del Pueblo—championed the protection of human rights to legitimize government support of an idealized vision of the modern, law-abiding state, while the army incorporated human rights into its military strategy (Tate 2007: 256–89). As Greg Grandin observed, the strength of the idea of human rights was "that we as-sume that everyone means the same thing, when in fact the mean-ing is keenly contested. Not only is the context of the idea unsettled (do human rights entail social and economic rights or just individual rights?), but the application of the idea has been two edged, used either at the service of or in opposition to power" (2007: 194). Human rights were open to interpretation from different political perspectives, be-coming the ultimate "empty signifier" (Cmiel 1999: 1248). The con-cept allowed disparate groups with unequal access to power to infuse the notion with their own understandings and shape it in accord with changing political agendas (Markarian 2005; Tate 2007).

For social justice advocates and survivors of Barrancabermeja's unfolding dirty war, human rights activism straddled their fears and hopes about the institutional state. While the violence of state secu-rity forces and their long-standing collusion with paramilitaries had generated views of the state as predatory, murderous, unaccountable, and impenetrable, the practice of human rights held out the promise of holding the state accountable and making its institutions responsive to the law, which would, in turn, broaden the scope of liberal democ-racy. This chapter closely examines how a diverse group of social justice advocates drew on the idea and practice of human rights to challenge the legitimacy of the institutional state and to reconstruct a popular movement, as they maneuvered to stay alive amid the ferocious repres-sion targeted against them. Their various efforts were at times a class struggle and at times a struggle that moved on the edges of other cate-gories. What sorts of political possibilities did rights activism open and foreclose? Rather than juxtaposing a period of class-based struggles to an era of legalistic human rights activism, I paint a more complicated picture of continuities and discontinuities between the past and the present, as I explore the kind of social justice project that human rights activism represented in Barrancabermeja.

First, I examine how human rights activism emerged from earlier forms of class-based political organizing and claims making, and I take stock of the connections and the breaks with older forms of oppositional politics. The discussion then explores the contentious politics that surrounded efforts to incorporate the concerns of women and gays into the new alliances and forms of claims making created by human rights activism, as the tradition of class-based militancy was under siege. Finally, I consider how unarmed "accompaniment" by international human rights volunteers reshaped the understanding of international solidarity in Barrancabermeja in a period when the state could not provide basic security and the left could not protect its own people. Human rights activism, I argue, was a defensive move that arose in Barrancabermeja from the violent destruction of class-based forms of political protest and the discrediting of older utopian visions of socialism. Because of how political terror dismantled social movements into individual survival strategies and, together with neoliberalism, reconfigured the relationship between self and society, paramilitary repression and economic restructuring created the kind of vulnerable individuals about whom human rights claims could be made.[5] Although the idea and practice of human rights opened a new space for politics to emerge from the ashes of the dirty war, they simultaneously narrowed the parameters of what was both politically possible and imaginable and contributed to the deepening impoverishment of politics.

The Rise of Human Rights and the Defense of Life

Human rights activism developed in Barrancabermeja in the 1980s as a form of political organization and claims making to address state violence against the left, and it grew out of earlier forms of radical politics in Colombia (Tate 2007) and other Latin American countries that aimed to end the nightmare of military dictatorship (Markarian 2005). As the violence intensified in Barrancabermeja, a debate arose within the city's trade unions about the very notion of "rights," a conceptual category that had not figured prominently in workers' understanding of the world and how to change it. The United States had used the notion of human rights to attack the Soviet Union, and when the Carter administration adopted human rights rhetoric in its policy toward Central America, many trade unionists viewed the concept as a thin cover for escalating U.S. militarism in Nicaragua, Honduras, and El Salvador in the name of these rights. They also felt uncomfortable with the way that human rights discourse pushed political struggles into the legal realm and handed them over to lawyers, distracting attention from the strikes, meetings, popular assemblies, and other concrete actions associated with class struggle. As retired oil worker and longtime USO member Ramón Rangel observed, "The USO was a union characterized by concrete actions [*acciones de hecho*]. If anything happened, we organized a civic strike, a labor strike, or a meeting right away. We were formed that way as trade unionists, and that's how we were. We didn't value legal struggles, and we didn't think that anything would be solved through legalistic discussion with the state."[6] Similarly, SINALTRAINAL initially saw little value in human rights; the national directorate even opposed William Mendoza's participation in CREDHOS. According to Mendoza, the union directorate "debated whether or not to give me permission to attend CREDHOS events and to cover my expenses on these occasions. . . . There wasn't one [SINALTRAINAL] local that addressed the issue of human rights. I was the first person to start. Later, the union policy changed when [the directorate] came to understand that addressing human rights was part of what it meant to be an integral union leader, and they stopped screwing around with me."[7]

Although some Colombian unionists initially viewed human rights organizing as "bourgeois," the violent dismantling of the left moved them to embrace human rights as both an immediate problem and a strategy to build political support. Ramón Rangel explained how it became impossible for the USO to engage in collective bargaining with ECOPETROL, much less support the broader social struggles of peasant and urban popular organizations, because of the assassinations of the union's most prominent leaders and the sense of menace that hovered over their lives: "The death of Manuel Gustavo Chacón [a charismatic leader of the USO] is significant in the sense that it marked the beginning of the extermination of the union by the Colombian state, and from there we can say that since 1989, more than ninety-five compañeros have been killed inside the company. . . . We could not engage in collective bargaining because we had to defend our lives." He then emphasized that "life is not negotiated."[8] By the early 1990s, the USO and ECOPETROL had created a joint human rights commission to address the grave security risks faced by oil workers, and Rangel was one of its members. Members of SINALTRAINAL, too, began to participate in Permanent Peoples' Tribunals, convened in Bogotá and modeled after the Russell Tribunals on Vietnam, that addressed collective rights violations through an alternative judicial system—the people's tribunal—and heard evidence collected by unions, NGOs, legal scholars, and others about the crimes of the Colombian state and multinational corporations operating on Colombian territory. The tribunals' findings were presented in public ceremonies and then published in the hope of raising national and international awareness of political violence in Colombia.

In the late 1980s, human rights received national impetus with the creation of a Constitutional Assembly, which brought together a broad array of political forces, including indigenous groups, trade unionists, former guerrillas, religious organizations, and representatives of the traditional political parties. It presented an opportunity to relegitimize the state and served as a vehicle for demobilized guerrillas to participate in national political life, and the 1991 Constitution that emerged from its deliberations specified that the state would "adopt measures to protect groups who are discriminated against or marginalized," such as indigenous peoples and Afro-Colombians whose lands were being usurped by paramilitaries and threatened by development projects.[9] By displaying a new recognition of marginalized groups within Colombian society, the Constitution ceded certain rights to these groups and opened political space for talking about "diversity" and "inclusion," yet it remained silent about institutional racism, homophobia, and class inequality. It encouraged certain working people to demonstrate their membership in identity-based groups (indigenous, afro-descendant, gay/lesbian, etc.) at a time when the privatization of public entities, the retrenchment of state-supported social welfare services, free-trade policies, and new antilabor laws were driving more people into poverty. In this way, the state drew on notions of what Hale calls "neoliberal multiculturalism" to grant rights to disenfranchised groups and steer protest away from the deepening economic inequalities that were driving more and more people into poverty, but even these modest reforms failed because there was no political force strong enough to guarantee their enactment.[10]

The Constitution also created a new legal framework that established a state human rights agency—the Defensoría del Pueblo—assigned the task of helping victims of political violence. Yet it granted little investigative or enforcement power to the Defensoría, and, even more ominously, the Constitution had very little to say about the security forces (Tate 2007: 61). It should come as no surprise, therefore, that the rights and guarantees elaborated by the 1991 Constitution arrived stillborn. The FARC and the ELN had opted out of the Constituent Assembly, distrusting any agreement with the government after the annihilation of the Patriotic Union, and rededicated themselves to war through the embrace of kidnapping, drug trafficking, and extortion. The ensuing political and military centralization of regional paramilitary groups not only aimed to wipe out the ELN and the FARC, which had grown more powerful, but also took aim at the legal left, which had been legitimized by the Constituent Assembly and the new constitution (Valencia and Celis 2012: 77–78). Because of the escalating violence, defending the right to life superseded the popular struggles around labor, social citizenship, and national sovereignty that had defined an earlier era. Between 1990 and 2001, 87 percent of the strikes that occurred in the Middle Magdalena region addressed human rights violations, including the assassination or disappearance of labor leaders and community activists, illegal arrests, and generalized threats and political insecurity (Delgado 2006: 103).

From its office in Barrancabermeja, the working-class human rights activists of CREDHOS reached out to a membership in the small towns along the Magdalena River. They documented and denounced abuses by the security forces and the paramilitaries, and in conjunction with CINEP, they offered workshops and organizational support to local groups that were forming at the time and provided participants with the language of rights that was subsequently used to address state officials (Tate 2007). William Mendoza observed that, during his early involvement with CREDHOS, "our initial purpose was to conduct work around civil and political rights, but we never imagined that, after a short time, the struggle would be concentrated on the defense of life."[11] Activists' primary weapon was the denuncia—a public report that typically focused on paramilitary threats, assassinations, kidnapping, disappearances, and torture. It was directed at government officials in a high-risk effort to breach the alliance between them and paramilitaries. Human rights defenders demanded that the police and the military hold paramilitary perpetrators accountable for human rights violations and then denounced them for complicity when they failed to act. Not surprisingly, they increasingly found their own lives under threat.

If, as scholars have noted, the production of bureaucratic documents was one way that state agents and their interlocutors created the reality of the state and the proof of state power (e.g., Folch 2013; Hetherington 2011), Barrancabermeja's activists used the ritualistic prose of the denuncia to paint a dark picture of the Colombian state, and they amassed information that defied official representations of events and underscored denials and evasions. This "information game," Kregg Hetherington noted in the Paraguayan context, was "all about commanding the authority to represent the real" (2011: 159). Colombian human rights defenders not only aimed their denuncias at state officials but also sent them to other human rights organizations, unions, religious groups, and supporters, nationally and internationally, to garner support in pushing state officials to act morally and to uphold the law. In this way, they sought to "command the authority to represent the real," that is, to claim that their representations of human rights violations were truthful, by documenting abuses, shaming the security forces and government bureaucrats for their alleged complicity with the paramilitaries, and drawing on international connections and an evolving body of human rights law to bolster their claims.

By so doing, they expressed a vision of an accountable, law-abiding state, one that Winifred Tate (2015) calls an "aspirational state." Creating such a state depended on the reconstruction of a vibrant network of grassroots solidarity that could push demands for change, yet paradoxically, the practice of human rights required no social base. As human rights became increasingly professionalized and less about movement building, a major objective of human rights organizations became the compilation of objective information and the public dissemination of this information. Grassroots organizing and mass mobilizations were not necessary. And in order for the denuncias and claims of abuses to be "credible," activists had to separate themselves from any appearance of being "political," such as being tied to the political projects of victims and pressing an agenda for organizing society in a different way. Human rights activism, which emerged at a moment of narrowing political possibilities, thus ran the risk of further shrinking the space for politics by distancing itself from an agenda for transformative social change.

From the USO to the OFP: Continuities and Discontinuities

Between the 1980s and the early twenty-first century, human rights activists in Barrancabermeja belonged to a generation, a social class, and a political culture that viewed collective struggle as an important means to achieve social well-being and eradicate injustice. Yet while leadership and alliances in the 1970s and 1980s had depended on unions, peasants, students, neighborhood organizations, left political parties, and the Catholic Church, the old allegiances no longer held, and international financial aid flowed to organizations that promoted human rights. These organizations became important reference points for what remained of the urban popular movements. Although the Espacio—like the 1980s era Coordinadora Popular—united the surviving fragments of Barrancabermeja's trade unions and civic groups under one umbrella, decades of violence had weakened its popular base and political power. The outsized presence of the USO had substantially declined. Assassinations had claimed the USO's most dynamic leaders; factionalism had divided those leaders who remained; subcontracting and paramilitary infiltration had weakened the union's negotiating power; violence had disrupted its ties to rural social movements and poor urban neighborhoods; and the central office had moved to Bogotá. By the dawn of the twenty-first century, the women of the OFP had assumed leadership of the traumatized, diminished, but still-struggling popular movement. Human rights had replaced references to *el pueblo* and the language of class as the privileged political category, and the rights of women and sexual minorities had found a niche on activists' agendas.

The OFP had severed its ties to the Catholic Church in the late 1980s and was one of the only popular organizations in Barrancabermeja that managed to expand in the middle of the war, even though many of its leaders were harassed by the paramilitaries and its offices attacked. The OFP grew in part because it shifted from a church-based, neighborhood group to an independent, NGO that developed regional, national, and international connections. Financial support from European development agencies enabled the OFP to construct a solid institutional structure with several paid staff members and to offer courses on female reproductive health, domestic violence, nutrition, and human rights to poor women in Barrancabermeja and several small towns along the Magdalena River. The organization also operated soup kitchens and

FIG. 6.1 OFP women symbolically reweave the social fabric with brightly colored ribbons and burn military clothing.

provided a range of services to residents of the northeast through its "Casa de la Mujer." Yet as political violence engulfed every facet of daily life, the OFP became known less as a social service provider than as a human rights organization because of its leadership of the Espacio and its origins in the liberation theology–inspired Catholic Church of the 1970s.

The OFP became a refuge and a reference point for those experiencing political persecution, and it coordinated much of the public opposition to political violence after the paramilitary takeover of the city. The OFP articulated an antiwar political program around the slogan "Women do not give birth to sons and daughters and raise them for war" (*Las mujeres no parimos ni forjamos hijos y hijas para la guerra*) that condemned the violence perpetrated by "armed actors"—the guerrillas, the paramilitaries, and the state security forces—against "civil society." Yet even as the OFP attracted international financial support and won recognition for its defense of human rights, it restricted the range of interpretations through which the dirty war, past and present, was understood. It did so by creating a polarity between so-called armed actors and civil society, a distinction that was being widely adopted by human rights organizations, some academics, and government officials. At one extreme, the armed actors (e.g., the guerrillas, paramilitaries, and state security forces) were understood as the perpetrators of violence, but their political programs, constituencies, tactics, and relative power became conflated, even though the OFP held the paramilitaries responsible for the vast majority of rights violations and rarely denounced the guerrillas. At the other extreme, an amorphous civil society encompassed the individual victims of political violence who were usually portrayed as passive, despite their activism and participation in social movement organizations. This nomenclature obscured histories of class conflict and mobilization and reified violence in the present. It also did a disservice to the history of insurgent-pueblo relationships that were in fact supportive of the broad-based labor and civic demands of the progressive movement. The silencing of past forms of contentious politics complicated discussions about the social, political, and economic cleavages and diverse forms of political mobilization that continued to drive the conflict, while the liberal discourse of human rights addressed the abuses suffered by decontextualized victims.[12]

The OFP's articulation of a critical stance to all forms of violence in the 1990s came at a time when many unions and popular organizations were distancing themselves from the insurgencies and questioning the *combinación* strategy, which was increasingly perceived as a threat to them and their leaders. And it arose at a moment of extreme terror, when the scaffolding of Barrancabermeja's social movements was being disassembled and alternative analyses muzzled. The OFP's opposition to all forms of violence expressed the exhaustion of many urban residents worn down by the dirty war, and it enabled the organization to strengthen its institutional base with foreign financial support and to then garner political capital and legitimacy through its association with the "international community," that is, major Western organizations that funded development projects and supported human rights in the global South. "We could bring a thousand people out for a march because we had acquired a lot of credibility and international recognition," explained Yolanda Becerra. "We were the ones making the denuncias, and the international community responded with a lot of solidarity."[13] In contrast, human rights organizations and Western development agencies generally did not concern themselves with labor struggles. Neither the notion of class solidarity nor workaday conceptualizations of trade unionism occupied a central place in human rights discourse, which addressed working people only after they became victims of violence, and they were not encompassed by neoliberal concepts of "development," which sought to free up the creative energies of so-called microentrepreneurs.

The OFP was unlike many professionalized human rights organizations that limited themselves to filing denuncias and engaging in legal battles, and that had no use for a political base in the traditional sense. It organized street demonstrations to pressure municipal authorities to uphold the law and understood its network of programs and projects as part of its political base. Only a few days after the Espacio confronted the plight of Alfredo Arango, the OFP was again in crisis mode, following the early morning kidnapping of the twenty-year-old sister of one of the organization's leaders. Several unions and popular organizations, including the OFP, had recently received death threats that mentioned family members of activist leaders as possible targets. Such individuals were easier marks than their more politically prominent relatives, who often benefited from the protection of bodyguards and other security measures, and their death or disappearance could extract a high emotional price from family members and reverberate beyond particular institutions. While the kidnapping was an enormous shock to the women of the OFP, it came as no surprise; attacks on OFP leaders and their family members had happened before.

The Espacio hastily organized a caravan of protesters to focus public attention on the crime. The plan was to travel through key urban neighborhoods under paramilitary control and then stage a street demonstration that would block rush hour traffic on the highway leading out of town. Despite the short notice, by three o'clock a crowd of more than a hundred people had gathered in front of the OFP's headquarters, where they congregated in dispersed pools of shade under a row of trees that shielded the sidewalk from the blistering afternoon sun.

The caravan set off on a circuitous route through some of the most conflicted areas of Barranca with a red pickup truck in the lead. The OFP's director, a trade unionist from the USO, the state's human rights ombudsman, and the kidnapped woman's sister huddled inside the cab. A contingent of lumbering SUVs followed like a herd of docile bulls. In the backseats behind darkened windows sat trade union leaders, while their armed bodyguards piloted the vehicles. A swarm of motorbikes brought up the rear. Guided by students, rank-and-file trade unionists, NGO employees, nuns from the Juanist religious order, foreign human rights volunteers, and OFP project beneficiaries, they buzzed in and out of the throng of buses and taxis like bees on a mission.

As the caravan entered Barranca's poor neighborhoods, protest leaders spoke out over two loudspeakers strapped in the back of the pickup, addressing an invisible paramilitary audience as well as the merchants and residents who handed over a portion of their income to the mercenaries for "protection." They demanded that the kidnapped woman be returned alive and in good health; they condemned the extortion; and they lambasted the security forces for their indifference. The protest paused briefly in the desperately poor Arenales neighborhood on the river's sandy floodplain, where, people said, killers had dismembered their victims during the paramilitary takeover and thrown severed limbs into the river. As the procession moved along the waterfront, it passed a marketplace where fishermen were gutting and cleaning a fresh catch, and the smell of fish hung in the air. The men watched the protest in silence, betraying neither support nor opposition. Once again, the march leaders called for the immediate release of the kidnapped woman, condemned the security forces for inaction, and insisted to curious onlookers that Barrancabermeja was not at peace, despite the highly touted paramilitary demobilization. The exhortations and demands were repeated at every stop.

The march wound down in a candlelight vigil at the As de Copa, a site charged with the symbolism of past labor protests, where demonstrators stopped traffic into and out of the city for more than two hours. Groups of women from the OFP, dressed in black smocks, periodically chanted, "Women do not give birth to boys and girls and raise them for war," and the protest music of Victor Jara and Mercedes Sosa was interspersed with speeches that denounced paramilitarism, the kidnapping of innocent people, and the impunity that reigned in the city. The vigil and the march that preceded it demonstrated how human rights claims united, at least temporarily, a variety of individuals and organizations because it cut across diverse sectoral agendas. The protest also displayed the boldness and tenacity of the surviving social justice advocates in Barrancabermeja, where, unlike in the other small towns and hamlets of the Middle Magdalena, the embers of resistance had not been snuffed out. Yet the size of the protest was considerably diminished from the past, when the USO still had the organizational power to mobilize thousands of demonstrators to protest the deaths of labor leaders and the victims of paramilitary massacres. Despite Becerra's claims of bringing out a thousand people, demonstrators at human rights protests in the first decade of the twenty-first century typically numbered in the hundreds, or even less. Several people lamented the callousness and indifference toward human rights crimes that seemed to have settled over the city in comparison to the past, when every death and disappearance was marked with a much larger outpouring of rage. As one exasperated activist observed, "Nowadays there is a sort of culture of death in the sense that if there are not twenty deaths, nobody cares. There is no pain."[14] Such apparent apathy was tied both to the weakening of working-class institutions and relations and to the professionalization of human rights activism in which legitimacy in the eyes of foreign funders rested on separation from broader, alternative political agendas.

Although the goal of the OFP march was the immediate return of the kidnapped woman and, more generally, the rule of law, the end of impunity, and justice, there were continuities between the protests of the present and the past, and it would be an error to sharply differentiate the rights-based demonstrations of the present and the class-based mobilizations of the past. The USO and other trade unionists participated in the OFP protest, and one OFP member was married to a labor leader. As OFP director Yolanda Becerra explained the history of collaboration:

> The USO became an important referent [in the twentieth century], and anything that happened in the city passed through [it]. If somebody needed to bury a relative, the USO accompanied them; if you needed to fight for water in Barranca, the USO was there. The USO provided security in some ways—to be in a place with the USO, one felt secure. . . . But with the OFP, many compañeros from the USO created a very strong relationship of solidarity. The USO always pro-

vided space for the OFP . . . we were always available to each other. We walk hand in hand with the USO on many occasions.[15]

Even when they disagreed, trade unionists and OFP activists, who had often grown up in the same neighborhoods, suffered persecution because they advocated for a variety of deeply felt class concerns, such as fair wages, health care, community services, housing, and human dignity.

Most of the activists who participated in the OFP, CREDHOS, and the Espacio more generally started their political careers in organizations that represented both the radical and reformist left, such as the Communist Party, Catholic-influenced neighborhood organizations, and trade unions, and they were formed politically by the revolutionary politics and tumultuous civic strikes that defined the 1970s and 1980s. Yet the political passions nurtured and unleashed by these organizations and experiences exposed new fault lines that affected women and gay activists in contradictory ways. Mariana Menacho, a demobilized ELN guerrilla who had connected with the insurgency in the 1980s through the student movement in Bucaramanga, was harshly critical of the sexism in the USO. She condemned male oil workers for whom the practice of having multiple illegitimate children was a sign of virility and, even worse, meant that these children did not have access to the generous health care and education benefits available to the legitimate offspring of oil workers.

Similarly, the Stalinist homophobia of the Communist Party and the patriarchal morality of the Catholic Church reinforced traditional notions among leftists that women's role was to serve men and that homosexuality was counterrevolutionary and depraved. Yet the groundswell of political organizing that characterized Barrancabermeja's working-class neighborhoods in the 1970s and 1980s served as a training ground for a generation of women and gay activists who began to chafe at the deep-seated sexism and homophobia within the organized left. What developed from the new political possibilities opened by human rights activism was neither cohesion nor conformity but "politics," which, as Frederick Cooper (2000: 65) observes, is about getting people who disagree to act on the basis of what they have in common.[16]

Yolanda Becerra's midlife recognition of the debilitating effect of sexism on women built on her earlier political formation within a leftist, working-class political culture in which the rights of women were inextricably linked to the expansion of social and economic equality. Although organizing women was initially a way to strengthen urban popular movements, Becerra, the OFP director, explained that "the debates [in the 1970s and 1980s] were about politics and not gender. I didn't understand why women had to organize apart from men. I belonged to the civic movements and the youth movements, which were mixed. The OFP was a social organization, not a feminist one, and so there wasn't a lot of debate about gender. . . . but after I got married, I began to see the world differently and understand why women needed their own organizations."[17] Her new gender awareness also arose from greater domestic and international travel, which exposed her to feminist thinking in large Colombian cities, as well as Europe and the United States.

A new gender consciousness was also awakening among urban gays and lesbians. The rise of the Internet in the mid-1990s allowed for the development of transnational networks and connections that helped propel the emergence of an unevenly imagined, global understanding of "gay" that was differently shaped within particular social and political contexts. This vision took "gay" to mean men who had sex with other men, and it privileged a broad agenda of inclusiveness based on the right to marry, parental rights, and ending employment discrimination, issues that were key to gay rights debates in the United States and Europe. In Colombia, it was articulated most forcefully by upper-middle-class men in Bogotá, Medellín, and other large cities. Yet in the working-class neighborhoods of Barrancabermeja, not all men who had sex with other men were considered homosexuals, nor were they equally stigmatized for their behavior. Only the passive partner in a same-sex relationship was derided as effeminate and viewed as a source of amusement and contempt. The active partner was neither disgraced nor defined as a homosexual, and he could even enhance his macho credentials by sleeping with numerous passive men.[18] Indeed, based on his fieldwork in the working-class neighborhoods of Managua, Nicaragua, Roger Lancaster argues that "the nature of the homosexual transaction . . . is that the act makes one man a machista and the other a cochón [effeminate man]. The machista's honor and the cochón's shame are opposite sides of the same coin. The line that this transaction draws is not between those who practice homosexual intercourse and those who do not (for this is not a meaningful distinction at all in Nicaragua's popular classes) but between two standardized roles in that intercourse" (1992: 243).

As in Managua, Western understandings of gay and homosexual did not graft neatly onto the sexual practices and understandings of working-class Barrancabermeja. Yet some working-class activists seized on Western notions of gay and the methods associated with North American and European gay rights movements to advance their concerns in Barrancabermeja and establish their own organizations. They did so at a moment in the 1990s when metropolitan, upper-middle-class Colombians who identified as gay started to successfully advance a political agenda that played out in the legal sphere, where the Colombian Constitutional Court began handing down a series of rulings that validated the rights of Colombian sexual minorities. In 1995, for example, it recognized the rights of same-sex couples to engage in civil unions, a right it had granted to heterosexuals in 1990; in 1998, it ruled that public school teachers could not be fired for disclosing their sexual identity; and in 2007 and 2008, three decisions granted same-sex couples the pension, social security, and property rights accorded to heterosexuals.

For beleaguered working-class activists in Barrancabermeja, embracing a Western vision of gay rights seemed to offer a way to connect to international human rights organizations and the resources and protection they offered at a time when violence was crashing over their city. Indeed, two recently arrived human rights groups—Peace Brigades and Christian Peacemaker Teams, which began operations in 1995 and 2001, respectively—incorporated a Western understanding of gay identity into their conceptualization of human rights. They also provided legitimacy for gay rights struggles in a city that existed beyond the political radar of big city, upper-middle-class Colombian gays, who enjoyed better access to security and benefited from vibrant gay subcultures. They did so by attending events organized by gay activists, denouncing paramilitary threats and abuses of them, and occasionally providing emergency financial support.

Yet not only was the Anglo-American understanding of "gay" incommensurate with the range of sexual practices and understandings in working-class Barrancabermeja; the activism associated with it had little to say about the material needs of sexual minorities who suffered from the numerous problems—insecure employment, exorbitant rents, and lack of public services—experienced by working people in the city.

In addition, placing the specific concerns of Barrancabermeja's sexual nonconformists under the same human rights tent as women, peasants, and trade unionists was a complex affair. How the practice of human rights would integrate these groups remained a source of tension that is well illustrated by Enrique Jaraba's efforts, beginning in the twenty-first century, to use a fundamentally middle-class, Anglo-American notion of homosexuality to incorporate Barrancabermeja's sexual minorities into the fight for human rights.

Human Rights for Whom?

Enrique Jaraba, like Yolanda Becerra, formed a deeper understanding of exploitation and a more secure understanding of himself as an effective working-class activist through collective action associated with the left.[19] Jaraba, who spearheaded the struggle for lesbian, gay, bisexual, and transgender (LGBT) rights at the beginning of the twenty-first century, was too young to remember the 1970s, but he came from a family that he described as "very revolutionary." When he was a child, his parents immigrated to Barrancabermeja from the rural hinterland, after his father decided to cast his lot with other impoverished peasants who left the countryside in search of jobs in the oil industry. Under cover of darkness, the family acquired an urban lot through one of the organized land seizures that were taking place on Barrancabermeja's periphery. "People populated these spaces," he told me in 2010, "with a lot of struggle . . . and that is how I was formed politically around groups of neighbors, community leaders, and political groups that were active at that time."[20] As a young boy in the 1980s, he attended civic strikes with his aunts and imbibed the political discussions that constantly took place among relatives in his household. He credited an exiled uncle with teaching him "how to organize an operation."[21] Generally speaking, he noted, "The left strengthened Barrancabermeja, and logically one is influenced while growing up by the political forces that exist at any particular moment. Our thinking—a little to the left—was born that way. From the ideas of rights, from the idea of revolution, to protesting if something isn't correct, the spirit of defending things began there."[22]

Not surprisingly, however, many men and women who desired same-sex relationships eschewed left politics because the Catholic Church condemned homosexuality as perverse and immoral, and the

Communist Party defined it as a form of "bourgeois decadence." They carved out spaces in bars, discos, and other semipublic venues where they could develop romantic attachments and create supportive social networks away from the prying eyes of disapproving family members and the wider society. Within this semipublic world of same-sex eroticism, known as the *ambiente* (environment), a variety of suppressed sexualities flourished. Lesbians and transvestites, who symbolized homosexuality for many heterosexuals, occupied one extreme, and married men who maintained heterosexual relationships but also had sex with other men occupied another. Transvestites organized beauty pageants for which they sold tickets to anyone interested in watching them parade in elegant gowns and swimsuits, and lesbians gathered in the Barrio El Cerro to play *tejo*, a popular game that involves throwing a metal puck at small, explosive targets filled with gunpowder and embedded in moist clay. In addition, sexual behavior modeled along the traditional active/passive dichotomy existed alongside the decision of some men to embrace the word "gay" to define themselves and to indicate that both partners in a sexual relationship were homosexual.[23]

For Enrique Jaraba, embracing the human rights frame enabled him to adopt a usable category at a desperate moment when intensifying violence was closing down the ambiente and eviscerating the limited political spaces once available for the expression of stigmatized sexualities and the sharing of experiences. He did so as international human rights organizations with offices in Barrancabermeja tied the metropolitan notion of gay rights to human rights, and as individual activists who either worked for these institutions or visited the city on delegations sponsored by them expressed support for his struggles. Turning to human rights was thus a political move to advance particular claims and create new tactical alliances. Yet Jaraba's struggle would follow a long, torturous, and lonely path.

As a young man newly awakened to sexual desire, he had initially turned to an evangelical church in the hope of redirecting his sexual feelings toward women. "I heard that God could change you, that God liberated, that God gave, and that he could change the life of a person in many ways. So I started attending the church with the objective of changing my life," he explained. For a while, he almost succeeded. His pursuit of a pure relationship with God gave him a plausible excuse to spurn the attentions of women, and his personal charisma helped him establish a successful ministry in the northeast. Because of his skills as an orator and his ability to sing, his star began to rise among Barrancabermeja's evangelicals, and invitations to visit other congregations testified to his growing success. But it all came to an end after his sexual orientation was disclosed to a church elder, and a panel of deacons expelled him from the church and prohibited him from ever preaching again.

Sometime thereafter, in the late 1990s, Jaraba decided to dedicate himself to the cause of gay rights. The notion of human rights and the defense of the right to life had taken hold in Barranca's popular organizations, but the idea that sexual minorities had rights was only beginning to be expressed by activists in a few international organizations; it was not part of the conversation in most human rights organizations, trade unions, neighborhood groups, and social movement associations in the Middle Magdalena. "The only space available to me was with human rights," he explained, "but even there [in Colombian human rights and popular organizations] it was a joke. I was afraid of these organizations . . . but they talked a lot about the right to life, so I thought, OK, I could also be in those spaces." Breaking in was not easy. Jaraba's eyes welled with tears as he described to me how a Colombian human rights defender had beaten him up after a meeting in which he had raised the issue of paramilitary attacks against gay men. He insisted that, with few exceptions, Barranca's social movement organizations had difficulty recognizing that sexual minorities had rights, too. "Human rights for whom?" he asked rhetorically.[24]

Jaraba had good reason to be disgusted. During my visits to Barrancabermeja, trade unionists that I knew well often told me that "my friend" was in fact a child molester. Despite my efforts to defend Jaraba, one unionist, who had visited the United States, maintained that "homosexuals in the U.S. are not like the ones in Colombia," whom I could presumably never understand. Indeed, the stories that trade unionists told me about the paramilitary assault on Barrancabermeja were usually silent about the intentional targeting of effeminate men and transvestites, who suffered less for their political beliefs than for their sexual orientations. Homophobia also appeared to have intensified with the spread of HIV/AIDS, which placed men who had sex with other men in the spotlight and complicated understandings of solidarity with them. Most of the male trade unionists I encountered in Barrancabermeja expressed this homophobia through the casual use of the term *maricón* (effeminate man) as an offhand insult or form of one-upmanship between heterosexual men, as well as a more direct denigration of the passive partner in same-sex relationships. Such unmediated discrimination made developing alliances between gay activists like Jaraba and the labor movement very difficult.

Because of this rejection, Jaraba created, in 2000, an organization called People in Action to advocate for the rights of LGBT people and to shield the organization behind the public promotion of "human diversity." This proved an exceptionally hard task, as the notion of human diversity proved to be an inadequate bulwark against the growing repression. On the eve of the BCB takeover, Jaraba organized a gathering of teenagers to discuss the notion of rights, and as the meeting got under way, two unknown men on a motorcycle came looking for him. Jaraba denied that he was the person they were seeking, but in the days, months, and years that followed, he became the target of continual death threats, harassing phone calls, and, on one occasion, a botched kidnapping. After the BCB takeover, when many locales in the ambiente closed, paramilitaries targeted effeminate men and transvestites in so-called social cleansing campaigns. Yet the repression cracked open the door for new alliances, as BCB mercenaries declared homosexuals, trade unionists, and a broad swath of the legal left "military targets."

The persecution and the climate of fear that existed in Barrancabermeja forced People in Action to become less a social movement than a one-man campaign that projected a broader institutional existence through a web page that Jaraba established in 2011. But the repression was not the only hindrance to the development of a social movement. Building an activist group of LGBT *barranqueños* proved difficult for a number of reasons. Gays, lesbians, and bisexual and transgender peoples held various political views and understandings about themselves, their sexuality, and the sexual desires of others. Metropolitan classifications obscured sexual identifications in Barrancabermeja and had little to say about the growing economic precariousness that affected all working people in the city. Some sexual minorities had colluded with the paramilitaries. Others occasionally supported Jaraba's work but chose neither to disclose their sexuality nor to associate too closely with a threatened activist. Jaraba frequently expressed his exasperation with gays who "spent all their time gossiping and criticizing others" as opposed to transvestites who were "more unified." Not surprisingly, he had difficulty inspiring sexual nonconformists to become involved with activities that risked their public exposure, placed them in physical danger, and did little to address their economic vulnerability.

Yet Jaraba persisted. He organized seminars for young people who were just discovering their sexuality; he provided aid and comfort to AIDS patients, who had difficulty acquiring medications and endured social stigmatization and the rejection of family members; he counseled transvestites who wanted to change their names; and he brought gay-themed theater productions to Barrancabermeja. Moreover, he regularly denounced the murder, harassment, and torture of homosexuals through his regular participation in the Espacio. The ability to withstand repression and abuse was part of the heroic imaginary of the left, in which militants identified with suffering and self-sacrifice (Markarian 2005; Tate 2007), and he won grudging admiration from some straight human rights defenders because of his tenacity. The OFP helped him temporarily relocate to Bogotá, after a death threat forced him to leave town, and one trade unionist conceded, in 2012, that "he's gay but he is more macho than anybody. He's a guy with firm convictions, and I respect him because he knows his work. . . . He is the one who positioned gay rights in Barrancabermeja."[25]

Sexual minorities and straight human rights defenders needed each other, but even though Jaraba made some inroads with human rights organizations, he faced considerable problems articulating an LGBT agenda to heterosexual audiences. For example, several of the city's social organizations convened a public forum to commemorate the Colombian bicentennial in the Club Infantas, the venerable ECOPETROL social and recreation center.[26] While the heroes of the nineteenth-century war of independence against Spain were commemorated on national television and in speeches by government officials, Barrancabermeja's popular organizations used the opportunity to discuss what was wrong with the present and gathered representatives from peasant, union, neighborhood, and human rights organizations throughout the Middle Magdalena region to denounce the rights violations plaguing their communities and neighborhoods.

A panel entitled "Human Rights and Victims" convened on the last day of the event and drew an audience of well over one hundred people, many of whom were peasants who had suffered displacement and threats to their livelihoods over the years. It was chaired by a former human rights ombudsman, and the panelists included representatives from displaced peoples' organizations, the Catholic Church, and CREDHOS. Although not officially on the program, Jaraba had given the CREDHOS representative a copy of a flyer that described his organization, and the individual, whom Jaraba knew well, offered him the opportunity to speak at the end of the event.

Jaraba and I sat next to each other as one speaker after another denounced ongoing human rights violations in the Middle Magdalena, especially the intimidation faced by displaced peasants who sought to reclaim their stolen lands. As his time to speak approached, Jaraba told me that he was going to lay out the crimes against LGBTs in Barrancabermeja in detail—the extrajudicial executions, the torture, and the constant harassment—and drive home the persistent discrimination that defined their daily lives. Yet after ascending the stage and taking the microphone, he equivocated. During his ten-minute presentation, Jaraba never mentioned the words "gay," "lesbian," or "transgender," nor did he say anything about the persecution and discrimination suffered by them, choosing instead to reference the "sexual diversity" that characterized Colombia's heterogeneous population and to call on the audience to respect it. Afterward, I asked him to explain. Jaraba said that, as he looked out over the audience, the large number of peasants in attendance had intimidated him and made him worry about his own safety. "They come from a very patriarchal culture," he told me, and "they have a very provincial way of thinking [*muy de pueblo*]."[27] He felt that the rural people would not have understood words like "gay," which was not used in the countryside; more important, he feared that, if they fully grasped the kinds of sexual identities and relationships that he was asking them to respect and accept as normal, the tone of the meeting might have changed. Even though his presence on the stage testified to the partial success of his efforts to elevate the concerns of Barrancabermeja's LGBTs, Jaraba still felt the need to use coded language among would-be allies for fear of reprisals, and his fear about discussing the paramilitary persecution, murder, and disappearance of gays foreclosed an opportunity to link one aspect of the experiences of LGBT barranqueños to those of peasants, who were primarily concerned with the theft of their lands and physical displacement.

Enrique Jaraba's efforts to connect the rights of LGBT barranqueños to the struggle for human rights proceeded in fits and starts. Sometimes, the looming threat of murder, kidnapping, or torture was enough to unite working people across their differences; but at other times, deep-seated prejudices and different agendas kept sexual non-conformists and heterosexuals apart. Moreover, some attempts to advance the cause of LGBT barranqueños steered a careful path away from human rights, which, because of its leftist roots and the persecution suffered by activists, was viewed as too controversial and dangerous (see chapter 7). The Polo de Rosa (Pink Pole), for example, arose in 2005 within the Polo Democrático Alternativo (Democratic Alternative Pole) political party to encourage greater LGBT electoral participation and to support LGBT candidates, but its Barrancabermeja representative did not participate in Espacio meetings or publicly denounce the human rights violations committed against LGBT residents, preferring to keep a lower public profile.

Jaraba's activism illustrates the strengths and weaknesses of the turn to a politics of human rights. Human rights opened a limited political space for the articulation of "gay" concerns that was marginally more amenable to Jaraba's agenda than the unions, and it offered the possibility of building alliances with other persecuted groups. Yet being gay was the basis of Jaraba's political organizing. It represented a claim to rights and recognition that spoke less to the understandings and concerns of Barrancabermeja's working-class sexual minorities than to the political sensibilities and identifications of well-heeled, big-city gay urbanites and the international human rights activists who legitimized his struggles locally. Such a vision might have inspired more people had the paramilitaries not had a stranglehold on the city, but it nevertheless raised questions about the nature of political action. There was a difference between, on the one hand, grafting a new identity onto the already established leftist ideas and practices of human rights associated with the city's social movements and, on the other hand, harnessing this identity to the remnants of an older, class-based politics in order to articulate a new vision of progressive politics that sought to change the world and lay claim to the future. Human rights activism lacked a political vision that could address working-class experience in the neighborhoods and workplaces of the city, as the USO and the Coordinadora Popular had done in the past, and that could link this experience to the lives of sexual minorities and peasants struggling to hold onto or to recover their lands and their livelihoods. Amid the violence and social decomposition of the late twentieth and early twenty-first centuries, creatively fusing gay rights and class politics into a new form of claims making and an alternative vision of society was a tall order, not least because of the homophobia of the Old Left itself and the limited political resources that middle-class notions of gayness offered to activists like Enrique Jaraba in Barrancabermeja.

The Politics of Human Rights Accompaniment

While social contact with international human rights volunteers facilitated the development of Western models of sexuality, the influx of internationals, mostly from North America and Europe, also provided an assist to Barrancabermeja's beleaguered human rights defenders and social movement leaders by offering them unarmed "accompaniment." Colombian activists believed that having an "international" escort raised the cost of violent attacks for the perpetrators, and although daily life was more complicated and uncertain than this understanding suggests, many leaders of popular organizations embraced international accompaniment in response to a pressing need and in the hope that, because it connected them to a broader network of concerned citizens, international NGOs, and interstate organizations, any aggressive act against them would be met by an international outcry. Indeed, my long association with Enrique Jaraba arose, in part, because of his wish "to be seen in the presence of foreigners." Whenever I was in town, we would display our relationship by walking around the northeast and the port area on weekends, when the ebb and flow of urban life subsided and he felt most vulnerable. Yet even as accompaniment validated social struggles that were condemned by broad sectors of society, connected activists to a broader national and international network, and offered threatened leaders a sense of safety, it underscored the dependency of social movement militants on foreigners at a time when the social relations that had once sustained leaders and popular movements were being demolished, impunity was rampant, and the Colombian state was not providing security.

As political violence ripped through the Middle Magdalena, some European-based and North American–based human rights organizations, which were small and underfunded, began to provide unarmed volunteers to go along with persecuted social movement leaders during their daily activities and to stake out a visible presence during the public events of imperiled groups. Peace Brigades pioneered the strategy in Barrancabermeja. It was followed by other groups, such as Christian Peacemaker Teams, Pax Christi, and Witness for Peace, which

offered occasional accompaniment when staff members or a delega-
tion of North Americans visited the city. Volunteers clad in T-shirts,
vests, and hats that identified them as human rights defenders made
it known that they were prepared to report on abuses to their international support base and to intervene in a nonviolent fashion, if forced
to do so. Through their physical presence, the internationals sought to
reassure members of popular organizations that they were not alone,
even though their nationality, race, and class usually made them safer
than the Colombians.

The rationale behind accompaniment was that because of the political relationships that the Colombian state maintained with other
powerful states, especially the United States and Western European
democracies, and because of the economic aid that it received from
them, government officials wanted to minimize the political fallout from gross human rights violations and avoid the sanctions that
might result if a foreigner witnessed a human rights crime. Similarly,
the reasoning was that paramilitary leaders allied with the Colombian
security forces did not want to draw international attention by com-
mitting atrocities in the presence of international observers. Consequently, those activists accompanied by foreigners—especially North
Americans and Europeans—were arguably less vulnerable to assault
than others.[28]

One longtime Colombian activist recalled how unviable the notion
of unarmed accompaniment seemed in the 1990s. "The internationalists," she explained, "came from a different culture" and did not understand the nature of the dirty war that was gaining momentum. "What
were they going to defend me with?" she asked rhetorically. "People at
the time thought that the guerrillas would protect them. Even without asking them, the guerrillas were not going to let us get killed. So
[the idea of unarmed international accompaniment] was a big conceptual change."[29] Her understanding reflected a benevolent view of the
guerrillas, who were seen as allies of working people, and it expressed
dismay that young, unarmed strangers could offer any protection, a
notion that stuck many other people as preposterous, too. These views
changed, however, as the paramilitary stranglehold on Barrancabermeja's working-class neighborhoods intensified, and insurgents could
not defend unarmed civilians and became complicit in their abuse, by
switching sides and fingering their supporters. As the dirty war degen-
erated and working people found themselves at the mercy of the BCB,

international human rights organizations and their young volunteers became new, highly visible participants in the struggle for social justice in Barrancabermeja. Accompaniment became a different way of doing politics, one that was rooted in a fervent claim to neutrality and that based itself in the principles of international law. It rested on the race and class privileges of foreigners and the universalism of human rights law. It also required no political base and threatened to become a kind of philanthropy on behalf of threatened Colombian activists that could not substitute for older forms of solidarity in which working people struggled together to advance political agendas that envisioned a reordering of society.

I appreciated the strengths and limits of international accompaniment when, in 2007, Jackeline Rojas, a member of the OFP, asked me to accompany her on a day trip to Cantagallo, a small river port north of Barrancabermeja where the organization operated a soup kitchen. Rojas always felt apprehensive in Cantagallo because several years earlier, paramilitaries had encircled her on a street and threatened to kill her, and the mayor had told her that he could not guarantee her safety. Although she had since returned a number of times and the BCB had demobilized, a sense of foreboding overcame her every time she made the journey because of widespread evidence that much remained unchanged as neoparamilitary groups arose in the same territory once claimed by the disbanded BCB. She invited me to accompany her in the hope that my presence would provide her with a modicum of security and peace of mind while she conducted a series of workshops. Although I neither worked for a human rights organization nor had any training in the practice of accompaniment, everyone who knew me assumed that I "worked in human rights." My nationality, fair complexion, and foreign-accented Spanish also sent a clear signal that I was an international, just like other human rights defenders who, in some cases, were my friends. This unofficially qualified me as a sort of second-string protection plan, which indicated the level of anxiety felt by activists at the time. I received frequent requests to hang around with people as they went about their daily lives and had to constantly explain that I had nothing to offer in the event of an emergency. Rojas understood my limitations but insisted that I come along anyway.

As we waited on the dock for the boat to take us downriver, the neoparamilitaries were hard to ignore. Rojas pointed out several men, dressed in civilian clothing, who appeared to be monitoring the river traffic not far from where we were seated. "They are paramilitaries," she told me, "but don't look at them." I focused my gaze on the crew loading packages and a refrigerator onto our vessel, which we finally boarded, along with some fifteen other passengers, and sat swaddled in life vests on hard, wooden benches. The captain eased the boat away from the shore and into the swift current. Globs of brownish foam excreted from the oil refinery bobbed along the surface of the water, and a moist breeze blew through the cabin.

Before reaching our destination, we stopped briefly in Puerto Wilches, a center of African palm cultivation across the river from Cantagallo. Several travelers disembarked, and new ones took their place. Dockworkers pulled cargo off the roof and hoisted up new bundles, causing the boat to rock back and forth and nauseating some continuing travelers who sought firmer footing on the dock. Rojas called my attention to a young man surveying the hustle and bustle. He, too, was a paramilitary, she whispered, and he was known by the alias Iguano. Iguano appeared to be a young man in his late twenties. He was rail thin with closely cropped hair and a large pendant dangling around his neck. A pair of tight blue jeans clung to his legs, and a T-shirt emblazoned with the image of an action hero fell loosely below his waist. From behind a pair of dark sunglasses, Iguano chatted casually with people on the dock until the boat was ready to leave.

Several hours later in Cantagallo, Iguano reappeared. Rojas and I were having lunch in the OFP's soup kitchen, after a long morning of workshops with local women. As we chatted about the organization's work, I watched the cooks serve up bowls of soup and plates of rice, fried bananas, cassava, and stewed chicken and place these offerings in the kitchen window, where diners picked up their orders. Suddenly Rojas stopped talking. Her expression changed, and she focused an intense stare on a space behind me. Something was obviously wrong, but I did not appreciate what was happening until Iguano and three companions approached from behind and sat down next to us. As the group talked loudly among themselves and appeared to ignore us, Rojas got up, walked to the kitchen window, and instructed the staff not to serve them. Fastening a withering glare on Iguano, she then returned to her seat. Soon thereafter, one of the men attempted to place an order, but the cook told him that the food had run out. He reported this information to his companions, who then departed as quickly as they had arrived. I was stunned; poor women had just refused to feed aggressive men.

According to Rojas, the symbolism of my presence that day, as well as the numerous other international ties developed by the OFP, helped to empower the women and create more political space in a small town where paramilitarism had established a firm foothold and remained dug in despite the demobilization. But even though the OFP women had prevailed that particular day, the confrontation with Iguano vanished into a void of public silence. When workshop participants had returned from their homes and Rojas reconvened the afternoon session, no discussion of what had happened took place. And at the end of the day, Rojas and I departed, leaving local women to deal with any consequences from the encounter with Iguano alone. Had the presence of an international restrained the paramilitaries from harming the women, or had it helped to create a situation that jeopardized their security after Rojas and I were gone? The answer was not clear.

My visit to Cantagallo provides a disturbing commentary on the extent of the left's defeat in the Middle Magdalena and a statement about what international solidarity has become. Faced with neoparamilitary groups and an institutional state that do not hesitate to unleash violence against any critic of the status quo and unable to protect their own, the activist survivors of Colombia's dirty war must dedicate an inordinate amount of time and energy to ensuring their basic security. Although some of them, like Rojas, can turn to a few small, underfinanced international organizations for accompaniment, these groups cannot come even close to addressing the full extent of the need. So an untrained international like me can become a prospect for accompaniment, because I, too, have a foreign body and am therefore not that different from my better-trained compatriots in human rights organizations. Human rights accompaniment is a symptom of both the crisis of security in the Middle Magdalena and the debilitation of the relationships, networks, and institutions that once sheltered people and defined their self-understanding.

Although human rights activism forged new connections among activists and between them and national and international constituencies, the class concerns that had animated an earlier era of popular struggle were pushed to the margins or silenced. Disparate human rights agendas never coalesced into a political force that was powerful enough to reunite the fragmented pieces of Barrancabermeja's traumatized working class in a way that could articulate a vision of rights that encompassed justice, economic equality, and the guarantees of citizenship. Persistent violence ensured that the idea and practice of human rights remained focused on the right to life and survival, while pervasive fear made overcoming difference difficult and undermined the articulation of a vision of the future that went beyond what was wrong with the present.

Despite the limitations of contemporary human rights activism and practice, the struggle over rights and universal principles has certainly not ended. Building new understandings of rights and forms of solidarity to replace the heterogeneous working-class formation of the mid-twentieth century remains a work in progress. Whether and how people accomplish this task in the "aftermath of counterinsurgency" is far from clear.

SEVEN

THE AFTERMATH OF
COUNTERINSURGENCY

. . .

"I am afraid that we are becoming more isolated," commented William Mendoza, as we finished our Cuban sandwiches in the overpriced food court of the San Silvestre shopping mall. Upscale clothing stores surrounded us. Sleek escalators escorted shoppers to the mall's multiple floors, and ATMs spit cash into the hands of eager consumers. Air-conditioning offered welcome relief from the sweltering streets outside. The mall epitomized the new geography of exclusion in Barrancabermeja. Although the steamy neighborhoods of the northeast, where Mendoza spent much of his life until the paramilitaries arrived, were only a ten-minute drive away, the distance felt much greater. We could have been in Miami.

It was July 2013, and the irony of meeting in this glass-encased citadel of consumption, disconnected from the popular matrix of urban life, was hard to escape. The vision of democracy that forty-eight-year-old Mendoza had spent much of his life fighting for—a vision that embraced equality through living wages, public services, and agrarian reform—was buried under the condominiums and office buildings that were sprouting up in the vicinity of the mall. Decades of political terror had converted Barrancabermeja and its surrounding hinterland into a mecca for capitalist investment that was secured by the continual use of violence against people like Mendoza and anyone who questioned the status quo. Drug money and the anticipated expansion of the oil refinery for biofuel production had energized a construction boom, but Barranca's overcrowded, working-class neighborhoods were decaying. Chronically high unemployment rates refused to budge because large national and international oil industry contractors shunned skilled, local workers with a reputation for militancy and instead imported cheaper, foreign laborers to conduct routine maintenance and repair operations. Local contractors complained that they could no longer compete. Rents were expensive and the quality of basic services poor. Mendoza could not afford the clothes and the techno-gadgetry on display around us, but he felt safe within the closely monitored, authoritarian space of the mall, where private security guards prowled the passageways and guarded the entrances, and throngs of buyers and gawking window-shoppers calmed his feelings of vulnerability.

The new political order remains hostile to democratic practices and opposed to any challenge from below. Although Barrancabermeja's radical tradition survives as a more influential minority political current than in other Colombian cities, this long-established way of thinking and relating to others totters on ever-weaker legs. There is no common memory about the past, just competing and opposed stories about the city's violent history. Nowadays, human rights activism has diminished, and working people chart crooked pathways through a disordered, unstable present in which the violence of the past is not over, and fears and anxieties obscure the future. Holding perpetrators to account has been a slow, uneven process, and impunity remains rampant. In the aftermath of the terror of the paramilitary takeover and subsequent demobilization, the city is characterized less by peace than by a low-intensity disorder, a term I use to denote social conditions that block the emergence of shared understandings about the past and about intensifying vulnerability in the present, and that kicks open the door for those in power to define the problems and pose solutions.

Because of the persistent threat and reality of violence and because of the ways that dispossession, physical displacement, disorganization, and social fragmentation have disrupted the lives of working people over and over again, crafting lives that are truly "theirs" is a major challenge for people who have been forced to live in extremis. How to claim an everyday life—and not just a daily existence of one thing after another—raises issue of control over the material, social, and emotional realities that make a dignified life and a sense of the future possible. As Gerald Sider observes: "People ordinarily try to make and to claim some kind of ordinary—some stability to today, some continuity between yesterday and tomorrow, in some parts of their lives at least. In this sense . . . what we call everyday life does not name a feature or an aspect of social existence . . . but a high-stakes struggle" (2008: 124–25). It is a struggle that many *barranqueños* are losing.

How can working people in Barrancabermeja create a peaceful co-existence and imagine a better future when they hold different memories about what happened and continues to happen? This chapter explores how fragmented memories, disempowerment, and radical uncertainty, engendered by years of political violence and neoliberal restructuring, affect people's capacity to establish a modicum of control over their lives, workplaces, and neighborhoods. The dirty war has torn apart social solidarities, forcing men and women to find their way through the violent netherworld of capitalist modernization alone. War-related immigrants are cut off from rural life, while many long-time residents have fled to other cities. Scores of popular leaders who once challenged the power of the state, the oil company managers, and the agrarian bourgeoisie have lost their lives, and the infrastructure of human rights organizations is ill equipped to address the predations of neoliberalism, from the erosion of social services for the urban poor to the precarious conditions of employment. Reconfigured neoparamilitary groups contend with each other for control of drug trafficking corridors, land, and illegal enterprises and monopolize the popular economy of Barrancabermeja, while threatening anyone who questions the established order.

Far from ending, the war has entered a new phase. By focusing on radical uncertainty and the centrality of disempowerment in the lives of different people, we can better appreciate the chaos-producing consequences of past political violence. We can also better understand how the corrosive power of continuing violence shapes the limits of political possibility. The first part of the chapter analyzes the decline of the human rights movement and the fractured memories about Barrancabermeja's conflicted past that inform understandings of its still unstable present. The discussion then focuses on how radical uncertainty persists because of the social fragmentation and disempowerment that have reconfigured social life in working-class districts of the city. For many working people, the central concern is how to endure chronic uncertainty, rather than how to change it.

Contradictory Memories of Violence

There is little agreement among urban residents about what happened in the past and about how to understand the present. For a great many barranqueños, the paramilitary takeover ended a period of violent turmoil for which the guerrillas were responsible, even though some of these same people eventually came to see the paramilitaries as "worse than the guerrillas." For many others, it fragmented their lives and brought continuing persecution and economic hardship that made stitching the pieces back together nearly impossible. And for still others, it was only the most recent of a string of displacements and upheavals that had plagued their lives for years.

Barrancabermeja's human rights defenders, trade union leaders, former peasants, and civic activists remember the early twenty-first-century paramilitary takeover of the city as either the continuation or the beginning of a long period of persecution, rupture, and sometimes forced displacement that has still not ended. Their memories form what Steve Stern (2004: 105–6) calls "emblematic memory," a schema that organizes meaning, selects what is truthful about the past, and poses arguments about countermemories, while connecting personal experiences, or the stories told by friends, relatives, and acquaintances to individuals, into a larger, collective account. According to Stern, memories become emblematic when they manage to "capture an essential truth about the collective experience of society" (113). Yet the deaths of dynamic leaders, persistent threats and harassment from neoparamilitary groups, and the diminished vitality of working-class institutions have undermined explanations that connect past terror to the political nature of contemporary violence.

In 2013, many of the trade unionists and activists that I had met or interviewed in Barrancabermeja, since 2004, no longer lived in the city because of physical attacks and persistent threats to their lives, and deep feelings of foreboding had pushed others to question their commitment to social justice struggles. Assaults, death threats, and the invasion of their homes had forced the OFP's two most charismatic leaders, Yolanda Becerra and Jackeline Rojas, into internal exile; Rojas's husband, Juan Carlos Galvis of SINALTRAINAL, had left, too; David Ravelo, the former head of CREDHOS, was serving a long prison sentence for conspiring with the FARC to murder a politician linked to the paramilitaries at a time when Barrancabermeja was under siege; and

Enrique Jaraba spent long periods away from the city, as death threats made life in Barrancabermeja ever more untenable for him. Jaraba was also considering leaving the Espacio because, in his dismal assessment, it no longer had an impact on anything except provoking more death threats against its participants.

For many residents of the city, human rights had also become a toxic concept, one that they associated with the Espacio, CREDHOS, the OFP, and the USO, which had been stigmatized by the government for years as havens for guerrillas. Associating with these organizations, they believed, would do less to enhance their security than to threaten it. For example, when high school student Efraín Garcia led a student protest against the misuse of municipal education funds allocated for the construction of a new school, he began to receive death threats. Rather than report the threats to a human rights organization, however, his terrified parents pulled him out of school and started asking around about how to change their names. Garcia's mother fretted about her family becoming associated with the USO, which had supported the student demonstration. "What's wrong with the USO?" I asked, as we talked on a street corner. "Oh, nothing," she replied, looking away from me and changing the subject. "We just sell tamales. We have never been involved with anything." She quickly mounted her motorcycle and started the engine. I did not pursue the matter and waved as she sped off. Our brief interchange spoke loudly about the deep divisions that had fragmented a once-powerful, organized working class. The USO no longer represented a source of community support or a champion of the rights of working people for her frightened family. It had become part of the problem, and even the appearance of affiliation with it could be dangerous. She and her family turned instead to their evangelical faith for emotional sustenance.

In addition, the Espacio's capacity to coordinate and advance human rights claims had clearly diminished. At a meeting convened in the USO's library in July 2013 to discuss recent threats against several social justice advocates, the scant attendance was a departure from the packed gatherings of the past. Housed in a 1920s-era brick building that once contained the administrative offices of the Tropical Oil Company, the library's faded collection recalled a time when education for the legions of illiterate migrant workers who crowded into Barrancabermeja counted among the priorities of the budding labor movement. But not one of the eight people seated around a small conference table represented the USO. I recognized familiar faces from years past but slowly realized that some of the people were essentially there on their own behalf. The organizations that they had once led either barely functioned or existed in name only.

Over the previous month, several Espacio members and others had received manila envelopes with warnings of imminent annihilation from groups calling themselves Los Rastrojos, Los Urabeños, and the Ejército Anti-Restitución del Magdalena Medio, and two people had reported telephone calls in which a muffled voice warned them that they would be killed if they did not leave town. There was a lot of discussion about who was making these threats, how serious they were, and what should be done about them. Several people also complained about the failure of the police to investigate. The Espacio coordinator laid out a series of questions that no one seemed prepared to answer: "How do we continue defending human rights? What is happening with the social movement in the city? What can we do to regenerate it?" Luz Molina, a representative of the families of the paramilitary massacre of May 16, 1998, reported that jailed paramilitary boss Wolman Sepúlveda would be released from jail soon. He would likely move back to the city, she said.

Seven years after media-saturated ceremonies of mercenaries handing over their guns concluded the paramilitary demobilization process, targeted activists could be excused for thinking that the more things changed, the more they seemed to stay the same. Yet the situation was not identical to the past. The aftermath of the dirty war had given rise to new ways of fighting an old conflict. Neoparamilitary organizational structures were less cohesive than those of the former BCB: commanders no longer dictated orders from the occupied homes of urban residents, nor did they call entire neighborhoods to meetings in public plazas; the activities of the so-called gasoline cartel had visibly faded; and mercenaries wearing paramilitary insignia had ceased to conduct military drills in poor neighborhoods. Nevertheless, demobilized rank-and-file paramilitaries had filtered back into the city and taken up residence in the same neighborhoods that they had terrorized, while reconfigured paramilitary groups fought among themselves for the control of territory and each other's foot soldiers. Reports of mysterious armed men recruiting youth or patrolling the streets of some neighborhoods after dark circulated in the city's working-class districts, where neoliberal austerity policies had provided the armed right with legions of disillusioned, unemployed youth. Selective assassinations periodically punctuated the apparent calm.

Safety remains a constant worry for Espacio members, trade union leaders, and other social justice advocates, and many people still adhere to a range of security precautions that, years ago, they thought would be temporary. Furthermore, they are periodically stigmatized as "subversives" or "guerrilla auxiliaries," a practice that isolates them from others, tarnishes their reputations, and justifies the use of violence against them. Unlike the residents of the Southern Cone, Peru, and Central America who struggled with the legacy of dirty wars after the fall of military rulers or the official signing of peace accords, Colombians have wrestled with the trauma of collective violence as the government negotiated the incorporation of the armed right into society, while continuing to wage war against the depleted insurgencies in isolated frontier strongholds. All this informs how Espacio members and threatened activists understand the present as defined less by peace than by lasting rupture and enduring assaults on their lives and livelihoods. Although some acknowledge past "mistakes" made by the guerrillas, and others refer to contemporary insurgents as "terrorists," the behavior of the guerrillas, past and present, is of less concern to these individuals than the terror of the paramilitaries and their successors.

In contrast, some working people in Barrancabermeja dismiss the threats against human rights activists as self-manufactured propaganda designed to exaggerate the danger they face and to guarantee the continuation of government-authorized protective measures. These residents believe that the BCB brought peace to the city. Casimira Santos, for example, is a young hairstylist who works in a northeast beauty salon, just over the bridge that separates the immigrant neighborhoods from the city center. She insists that, when the BCB arrived in full force a decade ago, it ended years of guerrilla extortion and violence, and she maintains that barranqueños are much better off today because of its intervention. Although Santos did not work in the northeast when it was under guerrilla control, she claims to know a lot about the period of insurgent rule because of what another stylist, her friend Raisa, has told her. She tells me that the guerrillas extorted all the store owners. It was impossible, she says, for anyone to operate a business because of the constant pressure. And to make matters worse, the police turned potential customers back at the bridge because crossing into guerrilla territory was too dangerous. "Nice cars could not circulate in the northeast because of the guerrillas," she notes, "but thankfully, all that has changed" because the paramilitaries broke the invisible barrier, symbolized by the bridge, that delineated guerrilla-controlled, northeast Barrancabermeja from the urban center. In her estimation, they effectively unified the city and made daily life livable.

Like Santos, Rosalba Castillo, a small-scale merchant, believes that the paramilitaries pacified Barrancabermeja. Castillo lives in a neighborhood that was formerly a stronghold of the ELN and emphasizes that "now we are living in heaven" (*ahora estamos viviendo la gloria*), compared with the mayhem of the past. The turmoil that she describes took place during the BCB takeover of the northeast, when it was routing guerrilla militias from the city with the tacit support of state security forces. She describes how a stray bullet hit her husband in the leg while he was sitting on the patio of their home. And firefights broke out everywhere, she says, making it impossible for children to walk to and from school. Her daughter agrees. Once, she says, guerrillas, fleeing the paramilitaries, took refuge in her school. Mother and daughter blame this period of chaos on the insurgencies and insist that life got much better after they were gone, when the violence abated.

The accounts of Casimira and Rosalba form another memory framework for understanding the past, one that is shared by many other barranqueños. Memories of "the paramilitary takeover as peace" began to crystallize after 2002, when the BCB began to consolidate its control of the northeast. Media accounts of guerrilla atrocities burnished their truth value, as did the guerrillas' violent betrayal of each other. Yet in subsequent years, the "paramilitary takeover as peace" framework lost some of its explanatory power, as day-to-day experiences with the new overlords moved more people to conclude that the paramilitaries did not bring improvements to their lives. Nevertheless, it has remained an important way of understanding the past and imparting meaning to current events.

An official report on the dirty war, mandated by the 2005 Justice and Peace Law, has not adequately addressed conflicting memories of the past, ignoring the passions, shifting alliances, and interests that drove the conflict to a bloody climax in the early twenty-first century. Although it demonstrates that the paramilitaries committed the vast majority of massacres and extrajudicial executions, the account is primarily descriptive. It does not sufficiently explain why the dirty war happened and leaves important questions unaddressed, for example, what was at stake for different groups, what kinds of ideologies and opposing visions shaped the confrontation, why was the fighting more intense at some times and not at others, and how did violence arise from the clash of opposed forces? It also surrenders analytic clarity through the adoption of categories such as "armed actors" and "civil society."[1] These categories muddy the fault lines of the conflict and obscure the historical unfolding of the dirty war in which social life was repeatedly transformed through political action that arose from extreme social polarization (Grupo de Memoria Histórica 2013).

Making memories count is intertwined with whose voices matter. Contemporary memory battles are deeply embedded in struggles over power and legitimacy, and they may bubble to the surface on key dates and anniversaries, when organized groups or networks of individuals focus attention on the past in ways that push forgetfulness and contentious claims to the forefront of public debate. Stern (2004: 120–24) calls such moments of heightened consciousness, when the everyday flow of dominant ideas and beliefs is challenged and interrupted, "memory knots." One such moment of charged memory skirmishes arose in July 2010, when Colombia celebrated the bicentennial of its birth as a nation. The symbolically powerful date offered an opportunity to organize publicly and project historical interpretations into the public sphere. Hundreds of people from peasant organizations, student associations, labor unions, and human rights groups gathered in Barrancabermeja. Unlike government leaders who dominated official celebrations in Bogotá with paeans to the heroes of nineteenth-century independence wars, they engaged and updated a historical memory rooted in the labor and popular struggles of the Middle Magdalena and asserted that Colombians were still not independent.

During two days of human rights forums, cultural presentations, and commemorative events billed as the Bicentenary of the Peoples of the Northeast, they celebrated the region's radical democratic history. In one evening event called "Historical Referents," the lives of labor organizers Raúl Eduardo Mahécha and Maria Cano, assassinated oil workers Manual Chacón, Leonardo Pozada, and Orlando Higuita, and the revolutionary priest Camilo Torres, among others, were honored. These powerful referents allowed a series of speakers to ground a dissident emblematic memory in the struggles of the past. The speakers not only extolled their lives but also denounced the state for murdering them. They did so in a small plaza, located along the busy Avenida

Ferrocarril, a place that evoked their connection to the past and whose name had been the source of controversy for years.

In 1996, the USO and other popular organizations had planned to name the plaza after Camilo Torres, a popular Catholic cleric who had joined the ELN and been killed by the army during his first foray into combat. They intended to do so in a commemorative ceremony on the thirtieth anniversary of Torres's death. One day prior to the event, organizers placed a veiled bust of Torres in the plaza, but it was destroyed by a squad of paramilitaries who blew it apart with a high-powered rifle, in full view of the patrons at a nearby bar. For years thereafter, the plaza was known as the Parque del Descabezado (Park of the Headless One), but in 2010, those gathered in the plaza hoped that would change. Activists held a ceremony that had been delayed for fourteen years. After the speeches ended, they placed a wreath at the base of a statue, which held a new bust of Camilo Torres, and renamed the plaza Parque Camilo Torres (Camilo Torres Park). Yet death threats directed against them, before and after the commemoration, suggested that the park's identity was far from settled, and that activists' capacity to circulate and project dissident memories in the public sphere would remain limited.

How the past is remembered shapes understandings of the turbulence and disorder that continue to plague working-class neighborhoods. Ever since the paramilitary demobilization, considerable debate has surrounded a rising number of homicides that became a widespread concern in 2009, when some fifty killings took place in the first few months of the year. Were the murders the politically motivated work of reconfigured neoparamilitary groups, or were they purely criminal and opportunistic, as the mayor's office claimed? Colombian human rights organizations and the United Nations high commissioner for human rights had already sounded the alarm about the emergence of a new generation of "neoparamilitaries" and "successor groups." The government, however, insisted that the criminal violence of common thieves and youth gangs accounted for urban insecurity and that so-called criminal bands, or BACRIM, were an expected and transitory aspect of postconflict Colombia. As we saw in chapter 6, this sleight of hand was an effort to reestablish the illusion of a separation between government officials and those who used illegal violence to accumulate wealth and power, but it also built on a half-truth: like other Latin American cities in which crime waves followed the conclusion of civil wars and the enactment of neoliberal economic restructuring programs, common crime was a concern in Barrancabermeja's working-class precincts. It was both entangled with and separate from the reconfiguration of paramilitary entities.

Official assertions that paramilitarism no longer existed did little to calm activists' fears about the political motives behind the homicides of early 2009. The debate about the political or criminal nature of the deaths formed the backdrop of a conversation that I had with Viki, a Juanist nun who resided in northeast Barrancabermeja, about what had changed and what had remained the same in the northeast since the demobilization. Dressed in a flowing habit that covered her body from head to foot, the diminutive young woman greeted me at the door of a residence she shared with several other religious from the same Catholic order. She escorted me to a wicker rocking chair under a ceiling fan and brought out a pitcher of lemonade. As we sipped our drinks, she described how two young men had robbed her as she was walking home from the market a few days earlier. The individuals had approached from behind, snatched her purse, and fled. Neighborhood security was a serious problem, Viki said, because it was harder for people to make a living than in the past and because youth, in particular, had few opportunities after high school. She then moved quickly from describing her experience as a victim of petty crime to detailing the continuing paramilitary menace. For years, Viki and other Juanist religious had received death threats from the AUC for their support of African palm worker unions in the port towns north of the city, and the intimidation had not stopped with the demobilization. She underscored the political nature of the threats, past and present, that arose from her alleged support of the guerrillas, from being a "communist," and from purportedly bringing shame to the church, and she scoffed at the government's insistence that "criminal bands" were responsible for them. She also insisted that the spate of urban homicides, which were on everyone's lips, arose both from the competition and score settling among neoparamilitary groups in some cases and from the continued targeting of social justice advocates by these same entities in others. Political violence and criminal violence had become intertwined, making it easier to dismiss the deaths of social justice advocates as "nonpolitical" and thus ignore them.

Several days after this conversation, I sat down with Jairo, a young man who advised the mayor on human rights, in the hope of understanding how municipal authorities explained Barrancabermeja's enduring turbulence. The mayor's office was controlled by the centrist political movement — the Movimiento Alianza Social Indígena — whose homegrown candidate, Carlos Contreras, had won the mayoralty in elections the previous years with 31 percent of the vote. After taking my business card, Jairo peppered me with questions about the purpose of my visit and then launched into a long, vague monologue about the city's violent history that circled around and around but went nowhere. Finally, after much circumlocution, Jairo cut to the chase. "It is my personal opinion that trade unionists and human rights defenders are no longer at risk," he said. He insisted that criminals and mafiosi were the fundamental public security concerns and explained that most of the recent homicide victims were either hapless passersby in the wrong place at the wrong time or delinquents who bore responsibility for what happened to them.

Such views indicated that war continued in Barrancabermeja, but with new weapons. As government officials disappeared political violence into the realm of criminality, they blocked discussions of urban insecurity that were at odds with the peaceful image of Barrancabermeja they wanted to project. Three years after my meeting with Jairo, a new administration took the reins of the municipal government, and in a city council meeting the new mayor discouraged worried trade unionists from publicly complaining about the continuing violence. "The mayor told us that we shouldn't denounce all the assassinations, robberies, threats, and disappearances," an exasperated union leader told me, "because it will scare away foreign investment."[2]

Attracting foreign investment was a high priority for municipal officials. The Middle Magdalena had become a center for multinational investment in mining, African palm plantations, and hydroelectric projects, and the economic effervescence was evident in the new hotels that had sprouted in central Barrancabermeja; in the Avianca Airlines decision to include more flights on its Bogotá-to-Barrancabermeja route; and in an airport expansion project that had remade the old structure into a glittering symbol of the cosmopolitan city imagined by urban boosters. Although the power of the most notorious paramilitary bosses, such as Ernesto Báez, Julián Bolívar, and Macaco, had declined, their legacy lived on, as the booming economy expanded on the graves of thousands of people. Private political violence had created the conditions for a reinvigorated capitalism to flourish in the city center, while working-class neighborhoods remained integrated into neoparamilitary networks that controlled labor, commerce, transportation, drug trafficking, and protection and periodically surfaced to suppress challenges to the new order. As the municipal government—like its neoliberal counterparts in other Colombian cities and elsewhere—limited the definition of security to crime and excluded both politically motivated violence and the decline of well-being brought on by neoliberalism, working people felt more vulnerable and exposed to invisible forces beyond their control.

Daily Life and Radical Insecurity

"The big question," according to neighborhood council president Pablo Lucerna, "is who can you trust."[3] Lucerna posed this rhetorical question at a time when he faced an impossible dilemma. His terrified sister had arrived on his doorstep to inform him that men she presumed to be paramilitaries had threatened to kill her and an aunt if Lucerna did not hand over community development funds earmarked for a new soccer field. Too frightened to take the matter to the police, whom he distrusted, Lucerna consulted other council presidents, who reported that they, too, had experienced extortion demands and that, out of fear for their lives, they had surrendered the money. Lucerna then decided to approach the "politico" who was threatening him in the hope of resolving the problem. At the meeting, he sat next to a teenage hit man who described himself as "the business's best killer" and who bragged about the recent murder of the leader of a fisherman's association. Lucerna explained to the young man's boss that the funds were for community development projects, that he did not have access to them, and that the budget at his disposal was smaller than the politico believed. None of this convinced his tormentors, who gave him a few days to come up with the cash. Terrified about the consequences of refusal, Lucerna delivered the money but then faced a series of new problems. Paying off the extortionists was no guarantee that they would not return and threaten him again. Furthermore, Lucerna's long tenure as council president raised the possibility that he had already made concessions and accommodations with the shadow powers to keep his position and guarantee his relative safety. His more immediate concern, however, was that he could neither complete the construction of the soccer field nor account for the funds to local residents and the mayor's office. His only recourse was to explain to the mayor what had happened, but to his consternation, the mayor did not believe him. He accused Lucerna of embezzling the money and demanded that he repay it.

All of this raises disturbing questions about the ways that fear, uncertainty, and the absence of trust have become embedded into social life. Why, we might ask, did the mayor refuse to believe Lucerna's story, given a long history of paramilitary and guerrilla extortion in the city? Could the mayor's silence reflect pressure that he, too, was under? Was he also colluding with restructured paramilitary groups? In light of the city's past, such collaboration, either voluntary or coerced, was entirely within the realm of possibility. But had Lucerna actually stolen the money? The mayor's charges had the ring of plausibility, especially because Lucerna was unemployed. Municipal positions that provide access to public funds beckoned urban residents like ATMs, given the high level of unemployment and underemployment in the city. They not only allowed occupants to pilfer public coffers but also enabled the distribution of jobs and favors to friends. As one local resident complained, "Nobody talks about corruption because everyone is either stealing or hoping to steal when it is their turn to control the public till."

Answering these questions is nearly impossible. Lucerna's case, however, highlights how uncertainty and threats of violence infuse opaque, authoritarian relationships of inequality that remain too dangerous to openly challenge. These relationships are not only crucial for the survival of poor people; they pose economic and personal risks to those who try to separate from them. Lucerna's concerns about trust underscore the difficulty faced by ordinary people in creating a sense of social, economic, and emotional well-being over time and projecting it into the future. The violent unraveling of social relationships and popular organizations, and the loss of the trust, social connections, and relative stability that these relationships and organizations provided have vastly diminished the ability of people to create effective and enduring livelihood strategies. The explosion of competition in the absence of labor rights and regulations has made it very difficult for working people to reconfigure self-help networks and forms of mutual assistance. Everything is for sale—from a spot on the street to sell avocados to the "right" to work—and bribes and extortion undergird new hierarchies and forms of exploitation. People have to make do with fewer social, material, and emotional resources than in the past, and they have to find ways to remake their lives in the midst of circumstances that are mostly beyond their control. As they increasingly confront the world as autonomous individuals, it should come as no surprise that they focus less on challenging the power of those who are responsible for the precarious conditions that hem in their lives than on checking and channeling the activities of other people like themselves, in efforts to make their own lives more tolerable.

Human rights advocate Osvaldo Jiménez, for example, took money from his bodyguards on a monthly basis until the guards finally had enough and denounced him.[4] According to Jiménez, the two men—one of whom was a childhood friend—willingly gave him the government funds, allocated for their per diem expenses and to feed the government-owned, gas-guzzling SUV that transported him around town, when some of the money remained unspent at the end of the month. Jiménez asked for the money because of the intermittent and irregular nature of his work, which lurched from one short-term contract to another. These "contracts," which in most cases involved little more than unenforceable verbal agreements, ranged from providing the sound system for public events or private gatherings to leading human rights workshops for municipal and private sector employees. Even when Jiménez managed to arrange a deal, he was not always paid on time and sometimes was not paid at all. His precarious situation was a constant irritant in his relationship with his mother, who struggled, usually with minimal success, to sell natural health care products in order to cover the approximately $375 of monthly expenses for the house that she shared with her son. The unused funds from the bodyguards' expense account provided him with a very modest economic cushion that offset some of the uncertainty about paying his monthly bills, and they assuaged his tense relationship with his mother.

Yet for the bodyguards, there was nothing voluntary about the surrender of this money, which they would have preferred to keep for themselves and their own households. They understood Jiménez's request as payment for the right to continue working for him; it was, they believed, extortion in every respect. The conflict points to the fragile, impoverished economy of Barrancabermeja's working-class neighborhoods, where intense competition pits people against each other, creating new understandings of "income" and fragmenting the diminishing resources still available to residents. The pressures to pay one's bills, find work, put food on the table, and live a dignified life beyond mere survival are not new for residents of Barranca's working-class neighborhoods, but they have intensified. Working people have little choice but to fall back on each other—people like themselves who are equally hard-pressed.

Engaging in petty extortion and other illegal activities feeds dominant views of a criminal underclass on the urban periphery, even though these economic pursuits are often the requirement for survival in the absence of viable alternatives. Carola Gómez, for example, is a sporadically contracted ECOPETROL worker.[5] Single and in her thirties, Gómez makes good money—about a thousand dollars a month—when ECOPETROL hires her to perform quality control work in the refinery, and the accoutrements of her episodic prosperity, which include a large refrigerator, three overstuffed armchairs arranged around a glass-topped coffee table, and a five-piece dining room furniture set, ornament her small home. Gómez's relatively high wages allow her to weather periods between contracts—but not always. Sometimes, months pass with no word from ECOPETROL. During these tight economic times, she turns to illegal work as a motorcycle taxi driver (*mototaxista*) and sometimes sells hot dogs to prostitutes and their clients in the city's red-light district, where she must hand over a portion of her earnings to a local enforcer. The police have fined her on several occasions for both activities, but she views the fines as the cost of putting food on her table. Economic necessity creates "criminals," like Gómez, who are also misconstrued as "entrepreneurs." They have neither rights nor protections and are thus more vulnerable to manipulation, coercion, and police harassment.

The unease and social decomposition that have arisen from years of violence and economic restructuring are not completely controlled by the municipal authorities, the neoparamilitaries, or the private sector, which are unwilling and unable to incorporate poor urban residents into the neoliberal order in ways that guarantee their social reproduction. Indicative of the social restiveness were the tensions that shaped relations between unlicensed motorcycle taxi drivers and the licensed drivers of taxicabs. The ranks of both groups swelled with the downsizing, labor outsourcing, and trade union decline that accompanied the enactment of neoliberal policies in the city and the massive displacement of peasants from the countryside. In 2000, some 1,123,764 motorcycles circulated in Colombia, but by 2004 this figure had increased by more than 500,000, and sales of motorcycles increased 65 percent between 2003 and 2004 (Hurtado 2007). Discontentment among Barrancabermeja's urban transporters then deepened in the wake of the paramilitary demobilization, after hundreds of rank-and-file mercenaries took to the city's streets on motorcycles to offer their services as unofficial drivers, along with other young men who found themselves marginalized from legal forms of employment. Unlike the city buses, which were desperately slow and made numerous stops, the mototaxistas took passengers directly to their destinations for approximately the same fare as a city bus, one that undercut by 50 percent the fare that licensed cabbies charged.

The licensed cabbies, many of whom had been downsized from once-stable jobs and who worked extremely long hours to put food on their families' tables and to pay expensive licensing fees, felt threatened. "They [the mototaxistas] are criminals who steal money from people and abuse women," explained one exasperated driver. The mototaxistas not only operated illegally, which bolstered understandings of their presumed criminality, but some were also controlled by neoparamilitary groups, which obliged them to hand over a percentage of their income for the right to operate and used them to collect intelligence on the ebb and flow of life in the city. All of this made it relatively easy to stigmatize all mototaxistas, even as notions of legality and illegality divided working people from each other.

Worried about the erosion of their income by the mototaxistas, the licensed cabbies demanded that the municipal government do more to control the proliferation of the unlicensed drivers, and they staged a series of protests to this end. The mayor's office subsequently emitted a decree that excluded the mototaxistas from the crowded center of town, where prospective passengers were abundant, but did nothing to address the economic issues at the root of the problem. This, in turn, sparked counterprotests by the mototaxistas, who argued that public space could not be restricted in this way. Municipal officials then resorted to force to control the so-called dangerous classes who were disrupting the new urban order these officials hoped to preserve.

These conflicts illustrate how downsizing and dispossession on the one hand and the production of difference (illegality/legality) on the other hand are closely related processes. Together, they demonstrate how working people have to constantly struggle from within, and against, these divisions in order to develop a shared sense of purpose and identity. They highlight the unevenness and unpredictability of class formation in which popular struggles may generate new forms of exclusion and difference, rather than new relations of solidarity. All of this is very fluid, and none of it is predictable. And at a moment when strong leaders are needed to reconnect working people around a common purpose, these individuals face overpowering challenges of their own.

War as Peace Process

One of the notable features of the "postconflict" era is the readiness of state prosecutors to investigate accusations of misconduct against human rights defenders, trade unionists, and social movement leaders. This eagerness contrasts to their hesitance or failure to inquire about attacks, threats, and harassment directed at the same people. The investigations, which often result in spurious criminal charges, are often based on false information contained in intelligence reports and on allegations by demobilized paramilitaries and ex-guerrillas who have received financial support from the state as a means to entice them to demobilize and reintegrate into society (Human Rights First 2009). The 2005 Justice and Peace Law offered health benefits, protection and security, economic support, and reduced prison sentences (as little as eight years) to ex-combatants—mostly demobilized paramilitaries. In exchange for these benefits, individuals were required to confess their crimes in voluntary depositions (*versiones libres*) given in judicial hearings convened to establish the facts of particular cases, and to return stolen property to victims.

Yet the paramilitary "confessions" have done less to close the door on the violent past and lay the basis for reconciliation than to open up a new phase of conflict, recrimination, and revenge, demonstrated by the sensational parapolítica scandal that erupted in the aftermath of the demobilization in which mercenaries identified dozens of legislators who collaborated with them (see also Payne 2009). The "truths" related by the paramilitaries are selective and at best partial, in both senses of the word. The mercenaries have implicated some politicians, former guerrillas, and ordinary citizens in their murderous activities but have remained silent about other key supporters and alliances, especially the networks that connected them to entrepreneurs and businesses in the private sector. Sometimes they have offered details about their activities; at other times, they are intentionally obscure.

Viewing them and their testimonies with critical suspicion is imperative, but as Human Rights First reports, this "testimony is frequently neither properly evaluated nor corroborated, and many regional prosecutors assume that it is reliable and credible" (2009: 13), especially in cases involving human rights defenders. Indeed, for OFP director Yolanda Becerra, what is known as the peace process has served only to revictimize the victims. "In their depositions," she says,

> the paramilitaries have fingered us [as guerrilla collaborators]; they have stigmatized us, and they have said that we even worked with them, which is a very serious claim. . . . They have made our work more difficult, because of this ideological assault. . . . The last deposition nearly killed me. They have accused me of belonging to the FARC, the ELN, and the EPL, which I am prepared for, but when one of them said that I talked with the paramilitaries, that I met with them, it was something that I never expected. It was really hard for me. Of all the things that I have lived through, [this accusation] was the worst. It's a way of killing you morally and politically, and we feel that it is part of their strategy.[6]

When ex-BCB leader Rodrigo Pérez Alzáte, alias Julián Bolívar, was scheduled to testify in a Medellín courtroom, his appearance was anxiously anticipated by the BCB's victims and survivors in Barrancabermeja, some of whom watched his deposition on closed-circuit television. Sporting a buzz cut, the bespectacled, fair-haired mercenary confessed to at least twenty massacres in various municipalities of Santander province between 2000 and 2004 in which seventy-seven people died. He described one of the earliest slaughters in Barrancabermeja, in November 2000, when his men commandeered a city bus to facilitate their work. Accompanied by two deserters from the ELN, the paramilitaries drove through Barranca's working-class neighborhoods, stopping at the homes of ELN *milicianos* identified by the ex-guerrillas and then executing them. "The bodies were embarked in taxis and sent to the funeral homes," related Pérez Alzáte, "to impact and to demonstrate that the domination of Barrancabermeja remained in our hands" (Verdad Abierta 2009).[7]

Pérez Alzáte also used the public forum to target Yolanda Becerra and other activists whom the BCB had not killed. Juan Carlos Galvis and William Mendoza of SINALTRAINAL were two of those singled out by Pérez Alzáte. After asserting that he had never threatened the trade unionists, as they had claimed in a *denuncia*, the jailed paramilitary leader blamed Mendoza's ex-wife for the threats. More ominously, he then asserted that Galvis and Mendoza had provided information to a guerrilla group that enabled it to enter the Coca-Cola factory in the late 1990s and plant a bomb, which wreaked major destruction on the installation and paralyzed production for several months (Verdad Abierta 2008). His allegations could not be directly challenged by the victims, who could neither cross-examine nor interrogate Alzáte, and they ignited a prolonged period of intense anxiety for the labor leaders and others fingered by the paramilitary leader. Galvis, Mendoza, and Becerra worried that the state prosecutor would initiate an open-ended criminal investigation of them and feared the prospect of prolonged, arbitrary detention as the investigation took its course.[8] The public charges raised the real possibility of imprisonment, separation from their homes and families, and severe financial hardship. And they forced the two men to spend time and money defending themselves.

Although Galvis and Mendoza received support from SINALTRAINAL, they could no longer count on the backing of a strong popular movement in the same way as in the past, a movement that would protest their possible imprisonment, raise funds to support them and their families if necessary, and keep pressure on government officials. Torn from networks of popular solidarity, which had then disintegrated around them, the men organized their defense alone with their lawyers. Whatever the veracity of the charges and countercharges, there was no room for justifying violence as a legitimate form of social justice, even though many Coca-Cola workers believed in the late 1990s that management was actively colluding with the paramilitaries to murder and terrorize them. Times had changed. Human rights and liberal democracy had displaced the revolutionary use of violence as a means to obtain justice and as a tool of social transformation, even as the government, with support from the United States, waged a war by any means necessary against the remaining redoubts of insurgent power, which the middle and upper classes widely viewed as acceptable violence.[9] But even worse, the Coca-Cola plant bombing had apparently little to do with revolutionary values; it was, according to the trade unionists, a guerrilla reprisal for the corporation's failure to accede to an extortion demand and reflected the transformation of the insurgencies into criminal enterprises. In a time of popular defeat, disillusionment, and fragmented memories, when coherent alternatives to neoliberalism remained beyond the horizon of hope and expectation, defending themselves as the innocent victims of Pérez Alzáte, a deceitful sociopath, was the only option for Galvis and Mendoza.

Radical insecurity—political, social, economic—is the outcome of the defeat of a decades-old, working-class political culture and the fragmentation of an infrastructure of grassroots solidarity that sustained an understanding of how to act on the world, a broad sense of political purpose, and the hope that animated resistance. And it is the product of the impunity-based violence that made the defeat possible. Although Barrancabermeja is an extreme example of the violent "unmaking" of class and the enactment of a particularly severe form of neoliberalism, it is not the only place where working people have experienced periods of setback. The dismantling of once-powerful working classes has happened before, in other places and at other times, and spawned new labor relations and forms of struggle (Mason 2007). The fragmentation, vulnerability, and latent fear that characterize Barrancabermeja's neighborhoods are neither unique nor an end in themselves. The current situation of urban residents demonstrates how unresolved and contentious the process of class formation is when viewed up close in the present. Indeed, the present moment is best conceptualized as an interlude between the unmaking of one set of class relationships and the class relations of the future, which remain beyond contemporary political horizons.

CONCLUSION

. . .

Pedro Lozada is a survivor who believes that he has lived to celebrate his eighty-third birthday because of the grace of God. Frail and slowed by the infirmities of old age, Lozada resides with his son, daughter-in-law, and two granddaughters on a narrow street in a neighborhood that he and a wave of other peasant refugees created in the 1980s, when the army and allied paramilitaries drove them from the countryside. For much of his long life, Pedro Lozada pursued a vision of popular democracy that challenged the foundations of elite rule and the official state's pronouncements about national progress. Because of his insistence on far-reaching agrarian reform, the rights of workers to control the fruits of their labor, and the role of the state in promoting and protecting the common good, he and others like him unsettled local landlords and political bosses, who understood that a more open, democratic society posed a threat to their power. Lozada lived in the Middle Magdalena countryside for more than fifty years, struggling along with other peasant settlers to carve a productive farm from the jungle and withstand the pressures of acquisitive landlords and oil companies. He was an effective grassroots organizer for many years. With the backing of the Communist Party, Lozada established a rural school for peasant children in his community, and his various leadership positions — of a fisherman's association, of peasant committees, and of neighborhood councils — as well as his militancy in the Communist Party, his election to the Puerto Berrío city council, and his participation in the Patriotic Union, all attest to the ways that he developed a sense of confidence in himself, envisioned a world that was free of the stifling constraints of

Colombian society, and dared to hope that he and others could make their vision a reality.

Lozada's arrival in Barrancabermeja as a disoriented refugee was not the first time that he suffered violent, physical displacement. During the decades after World War II, Lozada endured multiple dislocations, death threats, economic marginalization, and the loss of friends and family members, as privatized terror fueled interrelated processes of dispossession, land concentration, and capital accumulation. His memories of the violence and persecution of the mid-twentieth-century Violencia and of the late twentieth-century counterinsurgent terror were continuous and uninterrupted, and his descriptions of the horrific ruptures that split his life apart in the 1980s were only the most dramatic of a series of upheavals that he had experienced and would continue to experience well into the twenty-first century. Paramilitaries, he said, transformed a region of "green gold" into a "land of cannibals" (*tierra de antropófagos*). They did not just force people to leave. According to Lozada, they gutted them, fried and consumed their internal organs, and threw the corpses into the river. The image of bloodthirsty cannibals symbolized how he and others like him experienced the dirty war as a devastating, horrific trauma. The savage inhumanity terrified him, tore him from the political and social networks that maintained him as a local leader, and demolished a form of collective politics that was meaningful and felt connected to social movements elsewhere.

Not surprisingly, Lozada most enjoys discussing his childhood memories, prior to the political turmoil of the last seventy years, and these memories are filled with nostalgia. "Life was very beautiful in those times," he says. "People were happy, and there was a lot of solidarity among them. . . . There was no hunger in the Middle Magdalena [because] food was abundant."[1] He fondly recalls the times that he and his brother fished under a full moon, when schools of catfish swarmed along the riverbank and rattled the reeds that grew in the shallow water, beckoning fishermen to pluck them into their nets. The steamboats that carried passengers up and down the river and the musical bands that accompanied them also held a special fascination for him. "In an airplane, you don't dance," he observed. "In a bus, nobody dances, and no one dances on a train, either, but on those boats, people danced while they traveled. [The boats] passed by with people dancing, and [we] would wave from the riverbank. It was beautiful." Lozada

<small>FIG. C.1</small> Pedro Lozada, his granddaughter, and neighborhood children.

remembers how the crews purchased yuca and plantains from peasants who lived along the river and offered plates of food to those who paddled their canoes near the steamboats. He believes that it is important to record this history, and he has taken great pains to preserve it in a personal memoir, which, despite failing eyesight and bouts of headaches, he continues to work on. During our periodic conversations over the course of several years, he enjoyed reading long excerpts that were filled with vivid descriptions of the flora and fauna and the idyllic nature of daily life in the Middle Magdalena countryside.

Lozada's romantic portrait of his past life along the river contrasts with the poverty and social fragmentation that characterize his current existence. Nowadays, the imperative to earn a living focuses the energies of residents in a city saturated with uprooted rural immigrants and downsized urban workers, and returning to a countryside transformed by the violent displacement of peasant communities, the spread of cattle ranching, and the emergence of African palm cultivation is impossible. Getting by in the present is difficult, too, because years of persecution, defeated political projects, violent displacement, and the murder of friends have created an emotional wasteland for him, where sustaining his spirit is a challenge. His son Alirio's conversion to evangelical Protestantism adds to his feelings of alienation.

Evangelicalism offers Alirio a refuge from his father's politics and the family's traumatic history. The elder Lozada tries to understand. He has attended services in different evangelical churches—the Jehovah's Witnesses, Light of Day, and Four Square—at the invitation of friends, yet he insists that he "has never heard an evangelical pastor talk about misery or inequality." He has also sought spiritual fulfillment in the Catholic Church but has been disappointed. Although he lives in the Catholic parish of Nuestra Señora de los Milagros, where liberation theology flourished from the 1960s into the 1980s, the current priests demonstrate little interest in community organizing. Lozada is especially critical of one cleric who cut funds for outreach to neighborhood groups and refused Lozada permission to hold a meeting of displaced peasants on church premises. The individual, according to Lozada, also painted over a mural depicting social movement and union struggles, and he evicted a school from church property to install a shrine that would attract donations from more well-heeled believers in other parishes.

Lozada's gauzy memories of dancing travelers, abundant food, and social solidarity remain both peripheral and integral to his life in contemporary Barrancabermeja. They provide a sense of attachment to a social world that he remembers as tranquil, satisfying, and intimately connected to others, and they remain important to an elderly man who has endured the fear, grief, and loneliness of decades of violent repression, death, and ruptured relationships. Yet they are disconnected from the politics and social movements that, for decades, gave meaning to his life. Raymond Williams (1973) urges us to place the city and the countryside, and the ideas and values associated with them, within the same analytic framework because they are, he suggests, changing historical realities that cannot be reduced to static archetypes. By examining them in relation to each other, we can begin to understand how capitalist processes—the drive to accumulate wealth, the changing division and valuation of labor, displacement and dispossession, power relations—generate starkly contrasting images of the rural past and the urban present and produce alienation, separation, and longing.

This book has focused on how dispossession and displacement re-configured the geography of political power in the Middle Magdalena, making and unmaking a working class, whose alliances spanned the city and the country, and remaking working people as individuals who have had to turn inward and find their way through the netherworld of capitalist development with little support, as old solidarities unraveled. It has argued that class is less an entity (e.g., wage laborers) that can be grasped and described at any particular moment than an emergent, dialectical relationship that arises around the tensions generated from capitalist development. These tensions have spawned assemblages of people that compose and recompose around the production and distri-bution of wealth and the organization and regeneration of social life. They have induced social and political struggles at multiple geographic scales and produced shifting configurations of power in which, at dif-ferent times, a foreign oil company, left-wing guerrillas, and right-wing paramilitaries tried to regulate the affairs of people within their do-main and to naturalize the particular social relations and ideological assertions associated with their rule. Yet the clash and bang of com-peting forces around the control of land, labor, mineral wealth, politi-cal office, and the illegal cocaine traffic has generated intense violence and an ongoing crisis of hegemony in the Middle Magdalena, where nowadays the institutional state turns away from the needs of work-ing people and guarantees a favorable investment climate for foreign corporations, while neoparamilitaries control the popular economy of working-class neighborhoods, repress challenges to the status quo, and oversee the violent accumulation of capital.

The violence that undergirds the contemporary social order is neither incidental nor peripheral to the process of class and state for-mation; it is an intrinsic part of it. Although Barrancabermeja is an extreme example of the violent making and unmaking of class and un-stable fields of power, it is indicative of a much broader pattern that we must understand in order to grasp how dispossession, displacement, and disorganization periodically unravel the institutions, relation-ships, understandings, and ways of life that undergird working-class power and force people to constantly struggle anew to reshape their lives and livelihoods. Indeed, if, as David Harvey (2005) argues, neolib-eralism involves the restoration of capitalist class power, the destruc-tion of nodes of concentrated working-class strength, from northern England and the American Midwest to highland Bolivia and Chile, illustrates how the upward redistribution of wealth emerges from a wellspring of imposed disorder.

The current moment of social fragmentation and radical insecurity in Barrancabermeja makes it hard to grasp why the concept of class remains an important analytic concept for comprehending the profound transformations that are reconfiguring social life in Colombia and the world. It might seem that concepts like "the poor" or "microentrepreneur" are more salient categories of analysis for understanding everyday life in urban "informal sectors." That is why I have adopted a long view of class formation and taken a step back from the simmering violence and disorganization of the present. When understood historically and processually, class helps us to grasp the emergent, open-ended, and always contingent ways that different kinds of working people come together as they try to make sense of their experiences and create livable lives. And, as Gavin Smith (2014: 150–76) notes, it also helps us to understand how, at times, the potential for collective action, always inherent in this "coming together," shifts from a latent possibility to an active rejection of the terms on which social life is organized.

For much of the twentieth century, class action in Barrancabermeja arose from the refusal of oil workers, displaced peasants, impoverished urbanites, petty merchants, and others to accept the working conditions, lack of public services, harassment, and repressive control of, first, the Tropical Oil Company, and then the Colombian state. It emerged as they made and remade their connections to each other amid the disruptions set in motion by the discovery and production of oil, the capitalist modernization of the countryside, migration and forced displacement, the explosion of urban shantytowns, dirty war, and economic restructuring, all of which re-created old inequalities and gave rise to new forms of difference. Working people found ways to downplay their divisions, construct organizational forms, pressure the TROCO and then ECOPETROL, and advance their own vision of the future that charged the institutional state with responsibility for the social and economic welfare of its citizens. They exercised a powerful democratizing force that went beyond the specific workplace concerns of organized labor to address facets of working-class experience in urban neighborhoods and rural communities.

By the late twentieth century, the democratizing momentum had crested. Popular struggles that sought to expand the parameters of political, economic, and social democracy increasingly became defined within the overheated, polarized rhetoric of the cold war, and Colombia and militarized states across Latin America targeted working people with violence in the name of fighting communism. Political violence wrenched individuals from networks of solidarity, tore them from their homes, dismantled popular organizations, eliminated the most dynamic leaders, and narrowed the horizons of what was politically possible. As Greg Grandin (2004) has so powerfully demonstrated, it laid the basis for neoliberalism to flourish, by reconfiguring the relationship between self and society and replacing broader, social understandings of democracy with a more limited notion in which personal liberties trumped efforts to overcome social inequality. Barrancabermeja was an extreme example, but it was not an exception.

As many scholars have observed, the cold war was less a contest between the United States and the Soviet Union, or a battle between proxies of the two superpowers, than "an attempt by the United States (and its local clients) to contain insurgencies that challenged post- (or neo-) colonial social formations predicated on dependent economies and class, ethnic, and gender inequalities" (Joseph 2010: 402; see also Grandin and Joseph 2010; Joseph and Spenser 2008; Saull 2006). Moreover, it did not end with the fall of the Berlin Wall and the collapse of the Soviet Union. The cold war wound down in Central America with the signing of peace accords in the 1990s but continued in Colombia under another name, the "war on drugs," which provided a gloss for ongoing counterinsurgency against so-called narco-guerrillas and justified continuing U.S. military aid for the Colombian security forces well into the twenty-first century.[2] In Barrancabermeja, it reached a violent denouement with the paramilitary takeover, the routing of the insurgencies, and the subsequent paramilitary demobilization, which were followed, in 2012, with the initiation of peace talks between the Colombian government and a vastly weakened FARC. The strength of mid-twentieth-century social movements in the Middle Magdalena was a measure of the savagery directed against people who were unwilling to accept a violently unjust social order as their cross to bear.

Barrancabermeja became less an example of a militant outpost of working-class power in a conservative country than a typical instance of the devastation wreaked by the new, neoliberal order that counterinsurgency, backed by the U.S. and Colombian governments, had brought into existence. Together with frontier regions such as Putumayo, the Guajíra, Meta, and Caquetá, working people in Barrancabermeja were incorporated into the neoliberal nation on terms that were not their own. They became part of violent, authoritarian hierarchies, under the control of paramilitaries and their successors, in which they enjoyed neither rights nor protections. At the same time, the spatial coordinates of class power recohered around regional poles of development based in extractive industries, such as coal, gold, oil, cattle ranching, African palm cultivation, and cocaine trafficking. These nodes of capitalist power represented the demise of an older vision of citizenship and social security in which the nation-state was responsible for social well-being. They represented a recalibration of national space for global commodity flows that were produced through organized violence and intensified capital accumulation, and they constituted a new form of labor discipline in which efforts to regulate the harshest aspects of the market were replaced by a no-holds-barred approach to the exploitation of labor.[9] Such assemblages of public and private power demonstrated how the making and remaking of spaces of capital accumulation were never entirely contained. They were tied to government policies and social struggles unfolding in different spatial fields, from the defeat of working people in Barrancabermeja and the rise of narco-paramilitarism to U.S. security doctrine and the advent of neoliberalism.

In the neighborhoods of northeast Barrancabermeja, the privatization of state agencies, the rise of paramilitaries and neoparamilitaries, the strength of violent networks, and deepening poverty continue to raise questions about who speaks in the name of the state and where "it" is located. This study has demonstrated that the state is not a container for social, political, and economic processes that operates exclusively through the apparatus of government institutions. It has shown how, for more than a century, class struggles, the imperial power of the United States and its corporations, counterinsurgent war, and the violent narco-economy have shaped the command of space and conflicting claims to legitimate rule. "The state" has always worked through alliances with "nonstate" actors, such as corporations and clandestine paramilitary groups, who shape how "it" is conceived. Nowadays, working people must grapple with constant insecurity as they contend with reconfigured, neoparamilitary networks whose contours are only partly visible, whose links to past terror are obscured by government claims that they represent little more than a contemporary manifestation of common criminality, and who do not hesitate to repress any challenge to the established order, as the boundaries between political and criminal violence grow more opaque. Because violent networks control many of the economic opportunities available to poor men and women, separating from them not only poses risks to working-class livelihoods but also endangers people's lives, as neoparamilitary and criminal entities who have their own agendas prey on newly vulnerable people. Such a dismal scenario is similar to that faced by working people in many other parts of the world, where criminals, landlords, employers, and politicians, often with connections to the security forces, use coercion and violence to regulate social life in the absence of labor rights and other protections (e.g., Breman 2003). All of this has consequences for how neoliberal democracy is practiced at a time when wealth and power are being redistributed upward, and points to the importance of new economic opportunities and relationships for urban residents.

I appreciated what was lost in Barrancabermeja, as well as how still unresolved its future is, one sweltering afternoon in 2013, when I looked over a collection of striking photographs with the archivist of the USO. One dramatic image showed a large crowd of protesters outside the oil refinery in 1986, carrying a sign that read "The people speak, the people rule." Another photograph captured a group of young men defending a street barricade during a 1977 civic strike. And still another caught oil workers in broad-brimmed straw hats marching on the mayor's office, during one of the first labor strikes in the 1920s. They all illustrated how, at different moments, people had organized, pushed back against the established order, and become protagonists in the making of history. They radiated hope and a sense of possibility that had moved people to understand existing conditions in their workplaces and their neighborhoods as transitory. I asked the archivist what made Barranca special. "People in this city always fight back," he said.

Indeed, during certain moments in the history of the city and the Middle Magdalena, movements against domination have always arisen, from the Barranca Commune, the peasant Bolsheviks, and the labor strikes of the early twentieth century to the civic strikes of the 1960s and 1970s and more recent protests against human rights violations. And working people have always found ways to organize and construct institutions—unions, neighborhood associations, peasant associations, coordinating committees, and so forth—to advance their claims on the powerful. How they might do so in the future is impossible to predict. Yet the sheer persistence of Pedro Lozada, William Mendoza, Enrique Jaraba, Yolanda Becerra, Juan Carlos Galvis, Jackeline Rojas, and other people encountered in this book, despite everything that has happened to them, speaks to the resilience of the human spirit and to their persistent struggles not just to survive from one day to the next but to strengthen the tattered threads of the social fabric and demand justice. We can see this persistence in Pedro Lozada's treks from his home in the northeast, over the bridge, and into the city center to meet with other displaced peasants to discuss how they are going to reclaim stolen lands. We can appreciate it in William Mendoza's leadership of SINALTRAINAL — the scrappy union that never succumbed to paramilitary terror and corporate efforts to dismantle it — and in the inspiration he has found in the popular struggles taking place in neighboring Venezuela, where working people have challenged neoliberalism and established new institutions and practices. And we can hear it in Yolanda Becerra's worries from internal exile that NGOs are assuming too much importance in the Middle Magdalena, supplanting the strikes, assemblies, and marches of once-powerful social movements with circumscribed development projects. "The country has become NGOized," she frets. "The work of an NGO is valuable but it is not the same as a social movement. . . . I think that we have a lot of work to do to reconstruct a social movement. If there are not strong social movements, it is impossible to advance a peace process."[4] These people force us to appreciate that, even in periods of intense repression and hopelessness, possibilities for crafting a different social order are always present. They experienced, and in some cases helped to bring about, the rise of powerful social movements in the Middle Magdalena and then lived through their subsequent demise, but the eclipse of Barrancabermeja's radical political culture is not complete. The embers of critical consciousness still glow in the daily lives of people who refuse to "forget" in a country awash in amnesia.

When I first arrived in Barrancabermeja, in 2004, and was cast in the role of human rights observer, the activists I met were a source of inspiration and hope, and they still are. They were full of insightful political analyses that were not taking place in my home country and were relentless in their condemnation of the Uríbe administration and the paramilitarism that they associated with it. Yet their struggles for human rights reflected less the birth of a new political force with the power to challenge an emergent narco-bourgeoisie and the policies of the Colombian and U.S. governments than defensive, rearguard actions that represented a desperate call for help from a social movement that was largely defeated. This book has argued that, although human rights activism created some room for a new politics to take shape in the repressive environment of late twentieth-century Barrancabermeja, it shrunk understandings about what was politically possible and narrowed visions of a different world. It did so by placing human rights testimonies outside of politics, removing working people from their conflicted history of political struggle, and treating them as long-suffering victims. All of this happened as extreme violence was destroying the class identities and organizations that had shaped how working people understood the world. Indeed, the practice of human rights required no social base, and human rights activists were obliged to separate themselves from the politics of the victims in order to establish their legitimacy in the eyes of international organizations, an imperative that further aggravated the narrowing of political possibilities.

What is at stake in Barrancabermeja is how ordinary people speak to each other about their lives and histories in ways that bring them together and keep them talking, despite the different ways that the past is silenced and neoparamilitaries threaten their safety. Repairing the social fabric means coming to terms with the deep divisions that violence and neoliberalism have created among them, constructing a historical narrative that links the past to the present, and forging new alliances and institutional forms to channel popular demands and lay claim to the future, all of which are fundamentally projects for working people. Despite the current limitations of human rights discourse and practice, the struggle over universal principles and conceptions of rights has not ended. Even though human rights activism has remained a defensive movement in Barrancabermeja that has not rearticulated a common class project, it does not necessarily follow that decent jobs, minimum wages, adequate health care, potable water, and quality education cannot be expressed in the language of rights, together with respect and equality for gays, indigenous peoples, Afro-Colombians, and women. Anthropologist Karen Ann Faulk (2013), for example, describes how working people in post-dictatorial Argentina have demanded that the neoliberal state uphold notions of collective well-being by expanding the notion of human rights to include freedom from corruption and impunity. Which rights are demanded in the future and how they are conceptualized will depend on whether and how diverse working people in Barrancabermeja rebuild social, institutional, and personal ties to each other. It will also depend on their ability to develop wider coalitions and alliances to provide them with both broader societal credibility and the capacity to oppose repression and the impunity that accompanies it.

The issue for scholars who want to create an alternative is how to support working people, if asked to do so, during a period of demobilization and defeat, when they are regrouping and figuring out the way forward once again. Practicing a critical anthropology is about negotiating the shoals of daily life with our research subjects, as they confront the challenges of daily life. It means doing our best to appreciate the goals and understandings during the brief time that we are with them, documenting their setbacks and detours, and negotiating when and how to prod the process of social change along. The outcome of the struggles of ordinary barranqueños remains an open question.

Introduction

1   The rationale behind international accompaniment was that because of the political, economic, and military connections between the United States and, to a lesser extent, the European Union, the Colombian government and allied paramilitaries seek to minimize the political fallout of gross human rights violations that might arise if a foreigner witnessed a human rights crime. According to this thinking, Colombian activists accompanied by foreign — especially EU and North American observers — were less vulnerable to attack (Mahoney and Eguren 1997).

2   Although I coordinated the visits of two delegations of U.S. activists to Colombia with the U.S.-based human rights organization Witness for Peace in July 2006 and again in 2010, I never worked for a human rights organization. I always introduced myself as a U.S.-based university professor writing a book about political violence in Colombia.

3   To this end, I am deeply indebted to the work of August Carbonella and Sharryn Kasmir and have benefited from many fruitful discussions with them.

4   For notable anthropological exceptions, see, for example, Sider (1986) and Striffler (2002).

5   E. P. Thompson, for example, did not focus just on the workplace but also explored how the British working class was "made" in neighborhoods and churches. Although Thompson's work has shaped the development of labor history over the last half century, a brief interdisciplinary engagement of anthropology with working-class and labor history prompted by Thompson's writings was marginalized and never fully developed (e.g., Cooper 2000; Kalb 2000).

6   See, for example, Nugent (1997) for an important discussion of state formation in Chachapoyas, Peru.

7   See Appel (2012) for an interesting discussion of how oil corporations seek to control labor on an offshore oil rig and remove it from entanglements with onshore social life. Appel calls this process "modularity."

8   See Striffler (2002) and Striffler and Moberg (2003) for a discussion of the transformation of foreign-controlled banana enclaves.

9   For more on the CIA program, see Priest (2013).

10   Colombian government estimates of the number of displaced persons continue to rise. See the web page of the Red Nacional de Información at www.rni.iunidaddevictimas.gov.co. The NGO Consultoría para los Derechos Humanos y Desplazamiento (Human Rights and Displacement Consultancy, CODHES) has documented the process of forced displacement in Colombia for many years. For more information, go to www.codhes.org.

11   The political neutrality of Human Rights Watch has also been called into question, as a number of its board members have close ties with the U.S. government, including the CIA (Bhatt 2013). See also Tate (2007) for an interesting discussion of the professionalization of human rights practice in Colombia and its separation from the programs and practices of the left.

Chapter One. Black Gold, Militant Labor

1   Beliefs about national development emerged from a vision of economic liberalism in which free trade, individual sovereignty, propertied citizenship, and "whitening" through *mestizaje* would produce national prosperity. Although Colombia's Liberal Party and Conservative Party were divided during the nineteenth and early twentieth centuries, male elites in both parties embraced the liberal vision to a considerable degree. See Safford and Palacios (2002). See also Tinker Salas (2009) on Venezuela, where oil and national development were closely intertwined.

2   In total, the TROCO paid 10 percent royalties to the Colombian state on the oil produced from the wells around Barrancabermeja. This "tax" was considered high by foreign investors (van Isschot 2015: 219).

3   See LeGrand (1998) for a discussion of the Caribbean banana zone that challenges traditional notions of tightly bounded enclave economies.

4   See Santiago (2006) and Tinker Salas (2009) for insightful accounts of the development of the Mexican and Venezuelan oil industries, which was happening at the same time as oil production was expanding in Colombia.

5   The practice of hiring West Indian workers extended beyond Barrancabermeja to Standard Oil operations in Venezuela. Miguel Tinker Salas

cites a Standard Oil official in Venezuela who described the West Indians as "British Negros" who could "more easily learn our ways" and who were less likely to mix with Venezuelan workers and unionize (Tinker Salas 2009: 111).

6 The lands claimed by the Texas Petroleum Company were located in what was then known as the "territorio Vásquez."

7 Interview with Pedro Lozada, Barrancabermeja, July 2011.

8 The tendency to mythologize the relationships between oil workers and prostitutes is still alive in Barranca today. Several oil workers whom I interviewed characterized these relationships as warm, long-term, and committed based on what they had read or heard from others.

9 Women did not win the right to vote until 1954.

10 For an insightful discussion of the land conflicts that shaped late nineteenth-century and early twentieth-century Colombia, see LeGrand (1986).

11 Some of the children of the so-called Bolsheviks would participate in the Liberal guerrilla movement of Rafael Rangel, after the 1948 assassination of Liberal presidential candidate Jorge Eliécer Gaitán. They were also among the founding members of the ELN in the 1960s. For example, the father of ELN leader Nicolás Rodríguez (aka "Gabino") was one of the leaders of the uprising in San Vicente de Chucurí (A. Vargas 1992: 57–58).

12 Santiago (2006) makes a similar point for the Mexican Huasteca.

13 Interview with Pedro Lozada, Barrancabermeja, July 2011.

14 Interview with Ramón Rangel, Barrancabermeja, July 5, 2009.

Chapter Two. Cold War Crucible

1 Van Isschot (2015) uses the expression "state-run company town" to describe Barrancabermeja during the two decades that followed the departure of the TROCO.

2 See Giraldo and Camargo (1985) for a broader discussion of Colombian civic strikes.

3 Interview with Pedro Lozada, Barrancabermeja, July 2007.

4 Interview with Pedro Lozada, Barrancabermeja, July 2007.

5 Interview with Pedro Lozada, Barrancabermeja, July 2007.

6 See Grandin (2004) for a similar description of how participation in the Communist Party provided an avenue for mid-twentieth-century Guatemalan indigenous to forge a workaday understanding of democracy and develop a collective sense of entitlement. Grandin also makes the important point that Marxism did not impose a rigid ideological uniformity on the indigenous who engaged with it but, rather, facilitated the development of a sharpened sense of individual agency.

7   Interview with Pedro Lozada, Barrancabermeja, July 2007.

8   E-mail communication, December 27, 2012.

9   See Fischer (2014) for a discussion of how fears of communism shaped perceptions of shantytown life in mid-twentieth-century Latin America.

10 See Striffler (2004) for a useful discussion of the uneven relationship between class formation, industrialization, and urbanization.

11 German Pinzón, "De Barranca sale la unidad sindical," *La Calle*, December 5, 1958, cited in Vega, Núñez, and Pereira (2009: 222–23).

12 The suspension illustrates the intensity of cold war tensions in this period and the oil company's antipathy toward the Communist Party, which likely organized the trip.

13 See Rabe (2012) for a good summary of the United States' involvement in cold war Latin America.

14 Plan Lazo was one such early initiative. Adopted in 1962, it was the creation of General Alberto Ruíz Novoa, who commanded a battalion of Colombian soldiers who fought with the United States in the Korean War. The idea behind Plan Lazo was to isolate the peasant support base of the guerrillas by providing development assistance in conflicted parts of the country. At the heart of the plan was the militarization of peasant communities through the creation of a network of collaborators and paramilitary units trained to find and kill alleged subversives.

15 According to Alejo Vargas (1992), many peasants around Barrancabermeja saw the arrival of the ELN as a continuation of the struggle waged by the Liberal guerrillas of Rafael Rangel.

16 Interview with former ELN guerrilla, Bogotá, March 7, 2009.

17 Forrest Hylton (2014) argues that a key explanation for the cold war defeat of the Colombian left was the failure to build popular power in the exploding urban shantytowns.

18 Interview with William Mendoza, Barrancabermeja, July 9, 2006.

19 Interview with Yolanda Becerra, Bucaramanga, July 18, 2009.

20 Interview with Yolanda Becerra, Bucaramanga, July 18, 2009.

21 Interview with teacher, Barrancabermeja, July 20, 2010.

22 Interview with Eduardo Díaz, July 15, 2013.

23 Interview with Yolanda Becerra, Bucaramanga, July 18, 2009.

24 Interview with Ramón Rangel, Barrancabermeja, July 5, 2009.

25 Interview with urban resident, Barrancabermeja, July 10, 2006.

26 The Colombian government would use the military court system, in which defendants had none of the protections of the civilian system, to try oil workers throughout the 1970s.

27 Interview with Jubencel Duque, Barrancabermeja, July 30, 2009.

28 *El Bogotano*, October 31, 1977, qtd. in Vega, Núñez, and Pereira (2009: 346).

29 Interview with Pedro Lozada, Barrancabermeja, July 2007.

30 Paramilitaries assassinated thousands of UP militants around Colombia and literally exterminated the party. For more on the Patriotic Union, its relationship to the FARC, and its decimation at the hands of the paramilitaries, see Dudley (2004).

31 See Ballvé (2012) for a useful discussion of this process in the Urabá region.

32 Most of the urban militias belonged to the ELN and were divided into two groups: the Frente Urbano de Resistencia Yarigués (FURY) and Capitán Parmenio. They were followed by the FARC's Milicias Bolivarianas and the EPL's Milicias Obreras.

33 Interview with urban resident, Barrancabermeja, July 1, 2009.

34 Interview with social movement leader, Barrancabermeja, July 2009.

35 Interview with former member of the Coordinadora Popular de Barrancabermeja, Barrancabermeja, July 2009.

36 The PCC elaborated the thesis of the combination of all forms of struggle during its ninth party congress in 1961, but it was a strategy that was adopted, with less doctrinaire fanfare, by other insurgencies as well. It would later be used to most devastating effect by the AUC.

37 Interview with a leader of a popular organization, Barrancabermeja, July 2007.

Chapter Three. Terror and Impunity

1 My account of Yesid Peña's abduction draws on interviews with his father, Jaime Peña, in Barrancabermeja in 2007.

2 More than one thousand people were murdered and three hundred others forcibly displaced between 2000 and 2003 (CINEP/CREDHOS 2005). In 2000, Barrancabermeja, a city of 250,000, had a homicide rate of 227 per 100,000 inhabitants. Los Angeles, a city of almost 10 million, had a homicide rate of 6 per 100,000, and Washington, DC, the U.S. capital of 550,000, had a homicide rate of 44 per 100,000 (Human Rights Watch 2001: 53). Between January and February of the following year, one resident of the city died every twelve hours (Madero 2001).

3 See Klein (2007) for a discussion of the ways that crisis fuels capitalist transformation.

4 Interview with human rights worker, Barrancabermeja, February 2007.

5 Interview with William Mendoza, Barrancabermeja, July 2010.

6 These betrayals intensified conflict between the EPL and the FARC, which had long competed with the EPL in Barrancabermeja and elsewhere. See Chomsky (2008: 195–207) for a discussion of the right-wing shift of the EPL in the Urabá banana zone.

7 Interview with Barrancabermeja resident, Barrancabermeja, February 2007.

8 Many residents reported that guerrillas who initially collaborated with the paramilitaries were subsequently killed, once they were no longer useful.

9 Interview with urban resident, Barrancabermeja, July 2009.

10 Interview with urban resident, Barrancabermeja, July 2010.

11 Excessive extortion demands also turned onetime peasant supporters away from the FARC in the Puerto Boyacá–Puerto Berrío region of the southern Middle Magdalena region. The FARC initially won the support of peasants and even some cattle ranchers after it brought theft and cattle rustling under control. However, when the insurgents leaned too heavily on their support base for "contributions," they quickly fell out of favor. It was middle peasants, such as future paramilitary chieftain Ramón Isaza, who formed so-called self-defense groups and collaborated with the armed and local elites to fight the guerrillas.

12 Interview with urban resident, Barrancabermeja, July 2007.

13 A similar process of militia decline and guerrilla defeat was simultaneously taking place in Medellín, Colombia's cocaine capital. The military coordinated Operations Orión, Mariscal, and Estrella VI with the paramilitaries, and by 2003, "Don Berna" had vanquished the guerrilla militias, as well as a rival paramilitary group, the Bloque Metro. With the consolidation of paramilitary power, violent crime then dropped dramatically. An abundant literature documents the shifting boundaries between youth gangs, guerrilla militias, and paramilitaries in Medellín (Aricapa 2007; Ceballos-Melguizo 2001; G. Medina 2006).

14 Amelia González is a pseudonym. The interview took place in Bogotá in July 2007.

15 Gerald Sider (2008) makes a distinction between an everyday life in which people enjoy a relative stability and can more or less effectively organize a livelihood, and a daily life characterized by chronic insecurity and unpredictability.

16 See Narotzky and Besnier (2014) for an insightful discussion of crisis, hope, and livelihood strategies.

17 Interview with Pedro Lozada, Barrancabermeja, July 2013.

18 Interview with urban resident, Barrancabermeja, February 2007.

19 Tania Li (2009) notes the importance of connecting political and economic processes that generate and shape fear to the actual experience of it. See also the collection of articles that address the question of fear in the same issue.

20 Interview with urban resident, Barrancabermeja, March 2007.

21 Linda Green (1999) writes about fear as a way of life among Mayan widows in rural Guatemala in the aftermath of the civil war.

22 In 2011, two men broke into the Galvis home at a time when Jackeline

and her daughter, who suffers from cerebral palsy, were home alone. One of the intruders put a gun to the young girl's head and threatened to kill her if Jackeline did not reveal the whereabouts of her husband and son. They then defaced the walls with red paint and sprayed paint onto Jackeline, before leaving with several of the couple's valued possessions. Because of this incident, the family moved to another city.

23 Juan Carlos Galvis, for example, was one of the plaintiffs in a case brought in U.S. court against the Coca-Cola corporation in which the company was accused of collaborating with paramilitaries to terrorize and murder trade unionists. Jackeline repeatedly spoke out against the paramilitaries in public forums and denounced their threats and harassment of others to the public prosecutor in Barrancabermeja.

24 Interview with urban resident, Barrancabermeja, March 2007.

25 Interview with former TELECOM worker, Barrancabermeja, March 2007. The name is a pseudonym.

26 Although the guerrillas repressed homosexuality within their ranks, they did not target gay-friendly establishments to the same degree as the paramilitaries, according to several local people.

27 Interview with urban resident, Barrancabermeja, July 2010. The name is a pseudonym.

28 Interview with urban resident, Barrancabermeja, July 2010.

Chapter Four. Unraveling

1 Interview with Osvaldo Torres, Bogotá, May 2004.

2 The combinación tactic was first articulated by the FARC, and it was embraced more by this insurgency than any other.

3 Telephone interview with Adolfo Cardona, August 2004.

4 Interview with SINALTRAINAL president, Javier Correa, May 2004.

5 See Romero and Torres (2011) for a comparative discussion of Chiquita and Drummond, which operated on the north coast of Colombia.

6 In 1999, there were eleven anchor bottlers around the world, including Coca-Cola Enterprises in the United States, South Africa's SABCO, and Mexico's FEMSA.

7 Spatial fixes, according to David Harvey (1996), periodically arise from the contradictions that shape the uneven history of capitalist development. "The tensions between place-bound fixity and spatial mobility of capital," he notes, "erupt into generalized crisis . . . when the landscape shaped in relation to a certain phase of capitalist development . . . becomes a barrier to further accumulation. The geographical configuration of places must then be reshaped" (296).

8 Interview with Barrancabermeja worker, Barrancabermeja, August 2006.

9 The Federación Sindical Mundial is an international federation of labor unions that was founded in Paris in 1945. It has backed struggles against apartheid, racism, colonialism, capitalism, and the policies of the United States and NATO.

10 This is a pseudonym. Interview conducted in Barrancabermeja, June 2007.

11 This is a pseudonym. Interview conducted in Barrancabermeja, July 2006.

12 Interview with Efraín Zurmay, Barrancabermeja, June 2009.

13 This is a pseudonym. Interview conducted in Barrancabermeja, July 2007.

14 Interview with Efraín Zurmay, Barrancabermeja, June 2009.

15 Interview with Efraín Zurmay, Barrancabermeja, June 2009.

16 This is a pseudonym. Interview conducted in Barrancabermeja, June 2007.

17 Interview conducted in Barrancabermeja, June 2007.

18 Interview conducted in Barrancabermeja, June 2007.

19 This is a pseudonym. Interview conducted in Barrancabermeja, July 2007.

20 Interview conducted in Barrancabermeja, July 2007.

21 Interview with Efraín Zurmay, Barrancabermeja, July 2009.

22 Interview with Efraín Zurmay, Barrancabermeja, July 2009.

23 Edilberto Araújo is a pseudonym.

24 Quotations in this section are taken from interviews with William Mendoza conducted in Barrancabermeja in 2009 and 2010.

25 Saul Ramírez is a pseudonym.

26 Interview with Juan Carlos Galvis, Barrancabermeja, June 2004.

27 E-mail communication from William Mendoza, October 2012.

Chapter Five. Fragmented Sovereignty

1 See Hylton (2010) for a similar analysis of the city of Medellín, where a different regional power bloc established the social and political conditions for the emergence of a finance, insurance, real estate, and service-sector economy underwritten by cocaine profits.

2 In a move to reorient discussion away from the law and formal ideologies of rule, Thomas Blom Hansen and Finn Stepputat understand de facto sovereignty as "the ability to kill, punish and discipline with impunity" (2006: 296).

3 Christopher Krupa and David Nugent (2015) raise these questions in a discussion of state formation and daily life in the Andes.

4 See, for example, Joseph and Nugent (1994); Krupa (2010); Krupa and Nugent (2015); Nugent (1997).

5 Castaño had turned against Medellín cartel leader Pablo Escobar and joined with his brother, Fidel, to form a vigilante group that fought the cartel until Escobar's death in 1993. The group, called Personas Perseguidas por Pablo Escobar (People Persecuted by Pablo Escobar, "Los Pepes"),

was allegedly financed by the Calí cartel and linked to the Colombian national police. It represents an early instance of ties between the future leader of the AUC and state security forces. For more on "Los Pepes," see Bowden (2001).

6 Because of the success of the counterinsurgency war, the guerrillas have been substantially weakened over the last decade, and in some parts of the country, they have devolved into criminal enterprises with little explicit political program. The ELN has been virtually defeated, except in Arauca department, where it survives on revenues extorted from the oil industry. And the FARC, since 2012, has been negotiating peace with the government, after suffering serial defeats at the hands of the Colombian armed forces and losing several key leaders. Ramírez (2011) claims that nowadays in Putumayo department, the FARC is less interested in replacing the state than in coexisting with it. Moreover, as a result of the increasing involvement of the guerrillas in the narcotics traffic, the insurgents have reportedly collaborated with paramilitary groups in some parts of the country.

7 Jonathan Fox (1994: 153) defines authoritarian clientelism as an unequal bargaining relationship in which clients are subordinated through the threat of violence.

8 See Romero, Olaya, and Pedraza (2011) for a fuller accounting of the privatization of the health care system and the theft of public resources in northern Colombia.

9 A widely circulated 2001 video shows Iván Roberto Duque Gaviria, alias Ernesto Báez, proselytizing for another candidate of Convergencia Ciudadana, the cattle rancher Carlos Clavíjo, before an audience in Barrancabermeja. He states, "Gentlemen, leaders of Barrancabermeja . . . with the leadership of the Autodefensas Unidas de Colombia, we are launching a single list for the Senate of the republic for the entire Middle Magdalena. A list headed by Carlos Clavíjo and Carlos Higuera" (www.youtube.com /watch?v=Iox9ydYCL4). Clavíjo was subsequently elected and served in the Colombian Senate from 2002 to 2006. It was widely believed that, following the BCB takeover of Barranca, Duque controlled the municipal budget, and any decisions about expenditures passed through him.

10 Interview with former union leader, Barrancabermeja, July 2006.

11 Interview with former union leader, Barrancabermeja, July 2006.

12 Interview with former union leader, Barrancabermeja, July 2006.

13 Interview with former union leader, Barrancabermeja, July 2006.

14 Juan Sebastián Sánchez is a pseudonym.

15 Interview with Barrancabermeja resident, Bogotá, July 2006.

16 See Narotzky and Smith (2006) for an interesting discussion of how fear and uncertainty regulated social life in post–Civil War Spain.

17 See CINEP/CREDHOS (2005) for a full list of the rules.

18 At the time, two thousand pesos were worth slightly less than US$1.

19 Interview with urban resident, Barrancabermeja, 2007.

20 Interview with urban resident, Barrancabermeja, 2010.

21 In the case of Urabá, Ballvé (2012) documents the extensive involvement of paramilitaries, through the JACs, in a range of development projects, such as street lighting, water and sewage systems, and trash collection, financed through public monies channeled through paramilitary front companies.

22 See Auyero (2009) for a discussion of clientelism that focuses on the daily "problem-solving" capacity of clientelistic networks rather than simply their capacity to deliver votes in exchange for favors at election time.

23 Leonardo Páez is a pseudonym.

24 Interview with urban resident, Barrancabermeja, July 2010.

25 The front was named for the late brother of AUC leader Carlos Castaño.

26 E-mail communication with Barrancabermeja human rights defender, September 2013.

27 Interview with Pedro Lozada, Barrancabermeja, July 2013.

28 Winifred Tate (2007: 215–55) argues convincingly that even though state human rights agencies presented opportunities for action against rights violations, especially at the local level, they had no enforcement capacity and ended up producing impunity through the endless circulation of reports and information.

29 In addition to providing security, the DAS issued visas, controlled immigration, and collected intelligence on both domestic and international threats. Because of repeated scandals, it was dissolved in 2011 and replaced by the National Directorate of Intelligence.

30 Interview with Barrancabermeja union leader, Barrancabermeja, February 2007.

31 Interview with Gloria Gaviria, Ministry of Social Protection, Bogotá, April 2007.

32 Interview with Rafael Bustamante, Ministry of Interior, Bogotá, April 2007.

33 Interview with William Mendoza, Barrancabermeja, March 2007.

34 See Mitchell (1991) for a discussion of the state as "the effect" of spatial and temporal arrangements, surveillance, and social and political process that create the distinction between state and society.

Chapter Six. Narrowing Political Options and Human Rights

1 Alfredo Arango is a pseudonym.

2 Compare Luis van Isschot (2015), who argues that human rights activism in Barrancabermeja was mainly about the continuation of preexisting

projects of social change. See Striffler (2015) for an important discussion of how the rise of human rights was transforming the practice and understanding of U.S.–Latin American solidarity at the same time.

3 Several important studies demonstrate how the understandings and practice of human rights become vernacularized, as groups use international legal frameworks and concepts of rights to make claims on the state, while simultaneously shaping new notions of human rights that emerge from specific social, cultural, and political histories (e.g., Faulk 2013; Merry 2006; Tate 2007).

4 Pierre Bourdieu interviewed by Droit and Ferenczi (2008).

5 I am following Greg Grandin (2004), who makes this argument more generally about cold war Latin America.

6 Interview with Ramón Rangel, Barrancabermeja, July 2009.

7 Interview with William Mendoza, Barrancabermeja, July 2009.

8 Interview with Ramón Rangel, Barrancabermeja, July 2009. Manuel Chacón was murdered by a navy death squad in 1988. He not only had been a charismatic leader of the USO but also was one of the leaders of the Coordinadora Popular and was associated with the ELN-affiliated legal, political movement A Luchar.

9 Quotation from Article 13 of the Colombian Constitution, http://confinder .richmond.edu/admin/docs/colombia_const2.pdf.

10 Charles R. Hale (2002) argues that "neoliberal multiculturalism" divided indigenous peoples in Central America into those who were "acceptable" to the state and those who were not. See also Speed (2008), Gustafson (2009), and Postero (2006) for additional discussion on the politics of multiculturalism under neoliberalism.

11 Interview with William Mendoza, Barrancabermeja, July 2009.

12 Barrancabermeja was similar to postwar Guatemala as described by Oglesby (2007). See also Jelin (2003).

13 Interview with Yolanda Becerra, July 2009.

14 Interview with human rights activist, Barrancabermeja, February 2007.

15 Interview with Yolanda Becerra, July 2009.

16 Frederick Cooper challenges scholars to understand the past and the present "with a vision wide enough to appreciate multiple forms of social connections and imagination and to recognize power and exploitation where they are constituted, with all their limits, contingencies, and vulnerabilities to new forms of imagination and connection" (2000: 67).

17 Interview with Yolanda Becerra, July 2009.

18 See Lancaster (1992: 235–79) for a more detailed discussion of the meaning and practice of homosexuality in Managua's working-class neighborhoods.

19 Enrique Jaraba is a pseudonym.

20 Interview with Enrique Jaraba, Barrancabermeja, July 2010.

21 Jaraba is referring obliquely to the kinds of political and military actions once organized by the guerrillas when they occupied the Northeast.

22 Interview with Enrique Jaraba, Barrancabermeja, July 2010.

23 See J. Green (1999) for an interesting discussion of the development of male homosexual identities and their politicization in twentieth-century Brazil.

24 The quotations in the two previous paragraphs come from an interview with Jaraba on July 15, 2010, in Barrancabermeja.

25 Interview with trade unionist, Barrancabermeja, June 2012.

26 ECOPETROL constructed the Club Infantas in 1954 to address the "recreational, sporting, and cultural needs" of its workforce.

27 Interview with Enrique Jaraba, Barrancabermeja, July 2012.

28 See Mahoney and Eguren (1997) for more on the philosophy and practice of international accompaniment.

29 Interview with social movement activist, Bogotá, July 2009.

Chapter Seven. The Aftermath of Counterinsurgency

1 Forrest Hylton noted this conceptual problem in a presentation at the conference of the Latin American Studies Association in Chicago in 2014.

2 Interview with William Mendoza, Barrancabermeja, July 2013.

3 Pablo Lucerna is a pseudonym.

4 Osvaldo Jiménez is a pseudonym.

5 Carola Goméz is a pseudonym.

6 Interview with Yolanda Becerra, July 2009.

7 On August 30, 2013, Pérez Alzáte was convicted of a long series of offenses, which included aggravated homicide, kidnapping, forced disappearance, torture, terrorism, acts of barbarism, and hydrocarbon theft. He was sentenced to eight years in prison.

8 At the time, the leaders of a peasant organization headquartered in Barrancabermeja were detained in a prison as state prosecutors investigated their alleged links to the FARC. After a long imprisonment, they were freed, and the charges were dropped.

9 From the first decade of the twenty-first century, the CIA and the National Security Agency operated a covert action program in Colombia funded by a multimillion-dollar black budget that was separate from the millions of dollars channeled to the Colombian military through Plan Colombia. This program helped the Colombian security forces kill at least two dozen rebel leaders, including FARC commander Raúl Reyes (Priest 2013).

Conclusion

1 Interview with Pedro Lozada, Barrancabermeja, July 2011.
2 Even as the "war on drugs" provided a gloss for counterinsurgency in Colombia, it targeted poor minority communities in the United States and criminalized them. Initiated by Richard Nixon and escalated under the Reagan and Clinton administrations, the domestic drug war allowed whites to channel their antipathy toward African Americans in race-neutral language that focused on crime and to oppose the reforms won by the civil rights movement.
3 Deborah Cowan and Neil Smith (2009) describe this process as a shift from geopolitical to geoeconomic logics.
4 Interview with Yolanda Becerra, July 8, 2009.

REFERENCES

Abrams, Philip. 1988. "Notes on the Difficulty of Studying the State." *Journal of Historical Sociology* 1 (1): 58–89.

Almario, Gustavo. 1984. *Historia de los trabajadores petroleros*. Bogotá: Ediciones Cedetrabajo.

Álvarez, Jaime. 1983. *Las putas tambien van al cielo*. México City: Costa Amic Editores.

Amnesty International. 1999. "Barrancabermeja: A City under Siege." Accessed August 2013. www.amnesty.org/en/library/info/AMR23/036.

Appel, Hannah. 2012. "Offshore Work: Oil, Marginality, and the How of Capitalism in Equatorial Guinea." *American Anthropologist* 39 (4): 692–709.

Applebaum, Nancy P. 2003. *Muddied Waters: Race, Region, and Local History in Colombia, 1846–1948*. Durham, NC: Duke University Press.

Aranguren, Mauricio. 2001. *Mi confesión: Carlos Castaño revela sus secretos*. Bogotá: Editorial Oveja Negra.

Archila, Mauricio. 1978. *Aquí nadie es forastero*. Bogotá: CINEP.

———. 1991. *Cultura e identidad obrera: Colombia, 1910–1945*. Bogotá: CINEP.

Aricapa, Ricardo. 2007. *Comuna 13: Crónica de una guerra urbana*. 2nd ed. Antioquia: Editorial Universidad de Antioquia.

Arredondo, Leon. 2005. "Liberalism, Working-Class Formation, and Historical Memory: Dockworkers in a Colombian Frontier." PhD diss., City University of New York.

Auyero, Javier. 2009. *Routine Politics and Violence in Argentina: The Grey Zone of State Power*. New York: Cambridge University Press.

———. 2012. *Patients of the State: The Politics of Waiting in Argentina*. Durham, NC: Duke University Press.

Auyero, Javier, and Débora Swistun. 2009. *Flammable: Environmental Suffering in an Argentine Shantytown*. New York: Oxford University Press.

Ávila, Ariel Fernando. 2010. "Injerencia política de los grupos armados." In . . . *y refundaron la patria: De cómo mafiosos y políticos reconfiguraron el Estado Colombiano*, ed. Claudia López, 79–213. Bogotá: Debate.

Ávila, Ariel Fernando, and Tatiana Acevedo. 2010. "Monografía político electoral: Departamento de Santander, 1997–2007." In . . . *y refundaron la patria: De cómo mafiosos y políticos reconfiguraron el Estado Colombiano*, ed. Claudia López. Annex [CD]. Bogotá: Debate.

Ballvé, Teo. 2012. "Everyday State Formation: Territory, Decentralization, and the Narco Landgrabs in Colombia." *Environmental Planning D: Society and Space* 30: 603–22.

Bejarano, Ana Maria, and Eduardo Pizarro. 2004. "Colombia: The Partial Collapse of the State and the Emergence of Aspiring State-Makers." In *States-within-States: Incipient Entities in the Post–Cold War Era*, ed. Paul Kingston and Ian S. Spears, 99–118. New York: Palgrave Macmillan.

Bergquist, Charles. 1986. *Labor in Latin America: Comparative Essays on Chile, Argentina, Venezuela, and Colombia*. Stanford, CA: Stanford University Press.

————. 1996. *Labor and the Course of Latin American Democracy: U.S. History in Latin American Perspective*. London: Verso.

Bhatt, Keane. 2013. "The Hypocrisy of Human Rights Watch." NACLA *Report on the Americas*, winter: 55–58.

Bjork-James, Carwil. 2015. "Hunting Indians: Globally Circulating Ideas and Frontier Practices in the Colombian Llanos." *Comparative Studies in Society and History* 57 (1): 98–129.

Bonilla, Laura. 2007. "Magdalena Medio: De las luchas por la tierra a la consolidación de autoritarismos subnacionales." In *Parapolítica: La ruta de la expansión paramilitar y los acuerdos políticos*, ed. Mauricio Romero, 341–90. Bogotá: Corporación Nuevo Arco Iris.

Bowden, Mark. 2001. *Killing Pablo: The Hunt for the World's Greatest Outlaw*. New York: Penguin.

Breman, Jan. 1994. *Wage Hunters and Gatherers: Search for Work in the Urban and Rural Economy of South Gujarat*. New York: Oxford University Press.

————. 2003. *The Labouring Poor in India: Patterns of Exploitation, Subordination, and Exclusion*. New York: Oxford University Press.

Broderick, Walter J. 2000. *El guerrillero invisible*. Bogotá: Intermedio.

Bucheli, Marcelo. 2006. "Multinational Oil Companies in Colombia and Mexico: Corporate Strategy, Nationalism, and Local Politics, 1900–1951." Paper presented at the International Economic History Conference, Helsinki, Finland.

Bushnell, David. 1993. *The Making of Modern Colombia: A Nation in Spite of Itself.* Berkeley: University of California Press.

Carbonella, August. 2014. "Labor in Place / Capitalism in Space: The Making and Unmaking of a Local Working Class in Maine's 'Paper Plantation.'" In *Blood and Fire: Toward a Global Anthropology of Labor*, ed. August Carbonella and Sharryn Kasmir, 77–122. New York: Berghahn.

Carbonella, August, and Sharryn Kasmir. 2014. "Introduction: The Anthropology of Labor." In *Blood and Fire: Toward a Global Anthropology of Labor*, ed. August Carbonella and Sharryn Kasmir, 1–29. New York: Berghahn.

Castro, Jaime. 1998. *Descentralizar para pacificar*. Bogotá: Editorial Ariel.

Ceballos-Melguizo, Ramiro. 2001. "The Evolution of the Armed Conflict in Medellín." *Latin American Perspectives* 116 (28): 110–31.

Chandler, David. 2002. *From Kosovo to Kabul: Human Rights and International Intervention*. London: Pluto.

Chernick, Marc, and Michael Jiménez. 1993. "Popular Liberalism, Radical Democracy, and Marxism: Leftist Politics in Contemporary Colombia, 1974–1991." In *The Latin American Left: From the Fall of Allende to Perestroika*, ed. Barry Carr and Steve Ellner, 127–49. Boulder, CO: Westview.

Chomsky, Aviva. 2008. *Linked Labor Histories: New England, Colombia, and the Making of a Global Working Class*. Durham, NC: Duke University Press.

CINEP/CREDHOS. 2005. *Barrancabermeja: La otra versión: Paramilitarismo, control social y desaparición forzada, 2000–2003*. Bogotá: CINEP/CREDHOS.

Cívico, Aldo. 2012. "'We Are Illegal, but Not Illegitimate': Modes of Policing in Medellín, Colombia." *Political and Legal Anthropology Review* (POLAR) 35 (1): 77–93.

Cmiel, Kenneth. 1999. "The Emergence of Human Rights Politics in the United States." *Journal of American History* 86 (3): 1231–50.

Contreras, Victor. 1970. *Barrancabermeja: Estudio socioeconómico y administrativo del município*. Bogotá: Centro de Estudios sobre Desarrollo Económico de la Universidad de Los Andes.

Cooper, Frederick. 2000. "Farewell to the Category-Producing Class." *International Labor and Working-Class History* 57: 60–68.

Cowan, Deborah, and Neil Smith. 2009. "After Geopolitics? From the Geopolitical Social to Geoeconomics." *Antipode* 41 (1): 22–48.

Davis, Mike. 2006. *Planet of Slums*. London: Verso.

Delgado, Álvaro. 2006. "El conflicto laboral en el magdalena medio." In *Conflictos, poderes, e identidades en el magdalena medio, 1990–2001*, ed. Mauricio Archila, Ingrid Johanna Bolívar, Álvaro Delgado, Martha Cecilia García, Fernán E. González, Patricia Madariaga, Esmeralda Prada, and Teófilo Vásquez, 85–164. Bogotá: CINEP/COLCIENCIAS.

Denning, Michael. 2010. "Wageless Life." *New Left Review* 66: 79–98.

de Soto, Hernando. 1989. *The Other Path: The Invisible Revolution in the Third World*. New York: Harper and Row.

Díaz, Apolinar. 1988. *Diez días de poder popular: El 9 de abril en Barrancabermeja*. Bogotá: FESCOL/El Labrador.

Droit, R. P., and T. Ferenczi. 2008. "The Left Hand and the Right Hand of the State: Interview with Pierre Bourdieu." *Variant*, no. 32 (summer). www .variant.org.uk.

Dudley, Steven. 2004. *Walking Ghosts: Murder and Guerrilla Politics in Colombia*. New York: Routledge.

Duncan, Gustavo. 2006. *Los señores de la guerra: De paramilitares, mafiosos y autodefensas en Colombia*. Bogotá: Planeta.

El Tiempo. 1992. No más apoya a insurgentes. November 29. www.eltiempo.com.

———. 1994. Piratería se toma las vias. August 29. www.eltiempo.com.

ENS (Escuela Nacional de Estadística). 2002. *Structural Adjustment Process in Colombia*. Bogotá: ENS.

Farmer, Paul. 1997. "On Suffering and Structural Violence: A View from Below." In *Social Suffering*, ed. Arthur Kleinman, Veena Das, and Margaret Lock, 261–83. Berkeley: University of California Press.

Farnsworth-Alvear, Ann. 2000. *Dulcinea in the Factory: Myth, Morals, Men, and Women in Colombia's Industrial Experiment, 1905–1960*. Durham, NC: Duke University Press.

Faulk, Karen Ann. 2013. *In the Wake of Neoliberalism: Citizenship and Human Rights in Argentina*. Stanford, CA: Stanford University Press.

Ferguson, James. 2005. "Seeing Like an Oil Company: Space, Security and Global Capital in Neoliberal Africa." *American Anthropologist* 107 (3): 377–82.

Fischer, Brodwyn. 2014. "A Century of the Present Tense: Crisis, Politics, and the Intellectual History of Brazil's Informal Cities." In *Cities from Scratch: Poverty and Informality in Urban Latin America*, ed. Brodwyn Fischer, Bryan McCann, and Javier Auyero, 9–67. Durham, NC: Duke University Press.

Folch, Christine. 2013. "Surveillance and State Violence in Stroessner's Paraguay: Itaipú Hydroelectric Dam, Archive of Terror." *American Anthropologist* 115 (1): 44–57.

Fox, Jonathan. 1994. "The Difficult Transition from Clientelism to Citizenship: Lesson from Mexico." *World Politics* 46 (2): 151–84.

García, Marta Cecilia. 2006. "Barrancabemeja: Ciudad en permenente disputa." In *Conflictos, poderes e identidades en el Magdalena medio, 1990–2001*, ed. Mauricio Archila, Ingrid Johanna Bolívar, Álvaro Delgado, Martha Cecilia García, Fernán E. González, Patricia Madariaga, Esmeralda Prada, and Teófilo Vásquez, 243–312. Bogotá: CINEP/COLCIENCIAS.

Gibb, George Sweet, and Evelyn H. Knowlton. 1956. *History of Standard Oil Company (New Jersey): The Resurgent Years, 1911–1927*. New York: Harper and Row.

Gill, Lesley. 2004. *The School of the Americas: Military Training and Political Violence in the Americas*. Durham, NC: Duke University Press.

———. 2009. "The Parastate in Colombia: Political Violence and the Restructuring of Barrancabermeja." *Anthropologica* 51 (2): 313–26.

————. 2010. "The Limits of Solidarity: Labor and Transnational Organizing against Coca-Cola." *American Ethnologist* 36 (4): 667–80.

Giraldo, Javier, and Santiago Camargo. 1985. "Paros y movimientos cívicos en Colombia." *Controversia* 128: 11–42.

Gledhill, John. 1999. "Official Masks and Shadow Powers: Towards an Anthropology of the Dark Side of the State." *Urban Anthropology* 23 (3–4): 199–251.

González, Estefaní, and Orián Jiménez. 2008. *Las guerras del Magdalena Medio.* Bogotá: Intermedio.

Government of Colombia. 1927. *Exposición del poder ejecutivo al congreso de 1927 sobre turbación del orden público en los municípios de Ambalema, Barrancabermeja, Beltrán, Girardot y La Dorada.* Bogotá: Imprenta Nacional.

Grandin, Greg. 2004. *The Last Colonial Massacre: Latin America in the Cold War.* Chicago: University of Chicago Press.

————. 2007. "Human Rights and the Empire's Embrace: A Latin American Counterpoint." In *Human Rights and Revolutions*, ed. Jeffrey N. Wasserstrom, Lynn Hunt, and Marilyn B. Young, 191–212. Lanham, MD: Rowman and Littlefield.

————. 2010. "Living in Revolutionary Times: Coming to Terms with the Violence of Latin America's Long Cold War." In *A Century of Revolution: Insurgent and Counterinsurgent Violence during Latin America's Long Cold War*, ed. Greg Grandin and Gilbert M. Joseph, 1–44. Durham, NC: Duke University Press.

Grandin, Greg, and Gilbert M. Joseph, ed. 2010. *A Century of Revolution: Insurgent and Counterinsurgent Violence during Latin America's Long Cold War.* Durham, NC: Duke University Press.

Green, James. 1999. *Beyond Carnival: Male Homosexuality in Twentieth-Century Brazil.* Chicago: University of Chicago Press.

Green, Linda. 1999. *Fear as a Way of Life: Mayan Widows in Rural Guatemala.* New York: Columbia University Press.

Green, W. John. 2000. "Sibling Rivalry on the Left and Labor Struggles in Colombia during the 1940s." *Latin American Research Review* 35 (1): 85–117.

Gruber, Helmut. 1991. *Red Vienna.* New York: Oxford University Press.

Grupo de Memoria Histórica. 2013. *Basta ya! Colombia: Memorias de guerra y dignidad.* Bogotá: Centro Nacional de Memoria Histórica.

Gustafson, Bret. 2009. *New Languages of State: Indigenous Resurgence and the Politics of Knowledge in Bolivia.* Durham, NC: Duke University Press.

Hale, Charles R. 2002. "Does Multiculturalism Menace? Governance, Cultural Rights and the Politics of Identity in Guatemala." *Journal of Latin American Studies* 34 (3): 484–525.

Hansen, Thomas Blom, and Finn Steppputat. 2006. "Sovereignty Revisited." *Annual Review of Anthropology* 35: 295–315.

Harvey, David. 1996. *Justice, Nature and the Geography of Difference.* Oxford: Blackwell.

———. 2003. *The New Imperialism.* New York: Oxford University Press.

———. 2005. *A Brief History of Neoliberalism.* New York: Oxford University Press.

———. 2010. *Rebel Cities: From the Right to the City to the Urban Revolution.* London: Verso.

Havens, A. Eugene, and Michel Romieux. 1966. *Barrancabermeja: Conflictos sociales en torno a un centro petróleo.* Bogotá: Universidad Nacional.

Hetherington, Kregg. 2011. *Guerrilla Auditors: The Politics of Transparency in Neoliberal Paraguay.* Durham, NC: Duke University Press.

Hristov, Jasmine. 2010. "Self-Defense Forces, Warlords or Criminal Gangs? Towards a New Conceptualization of Paramilitarism in Colombia." *Labour, Capital and Society* 43 (2): 14–56.

Human Rights First. 2009. *Baseless Prosecutions of Human Rights Defenders in Colombia: In the Dock and under the Gun.* New York: Human Rights First.

Human Rights Watch. 1996. *Colombia's Killer Networks: The Military-Paramilitary Partnership and the United States.* Washington, DC: Human Rights Watch.

———. 2001. *The "Sixth Division": Military-Paramilitary Ties and U.S. Policy in Colombia.* Washington, DC: Human Rights Watch.

———. 2010. *Paramilitaries' Heirs: The New Face of Violence in Colombia.* Washington, DC: Human Rights Watch.

Hurtado, Julia C. 2007. "'Llevaremos la situación hasta las últimas consequencias': Motopiratas." *Vanguardia Liberal*, July 9. www.vanguardialiberal.com.

Hylton, Forrest. 2006. *Evil Hour in Colombia.* London: Verso.

———. 2010. "The Cold War That Didn't End: Paramilitary Modernization in Medellín, Colombia." In *A Century of Revolution: Insurgent and Counterinsurgent Violence during Latin America's Long Cold War*, ed. Greg Grandin and Gilbert M. Joseph, 338–70. Durham, NC: Duke University Press.

———. 2014. "The Experience of Defeat: The Colombian Left in the Cold War That Never Ended." *Historical Materialism* 22 (1): 67–104.

Hylton, Forrest, and Sinclair Thompson. 2007. *Revolutionary Horizons: Past and Present in Bolivian Politics.* London: Verso.

Isacson, Adam. 2001. *The New Masters of Barrancabermeja: A Report on CIP's Trip to Colombia, March 6–8, 2001.* Washington, DC: Center for International Policy.

Jaramillo, Rafael. 1934. *Barrancabermeja: Novela de proxenetas, rufianes, obreros y petroleros.* Bogotá: Editorial E.S.B.

Jelin, Elizabeth. 2003. *State Repression and the Struggles for Memory.* London: Latin American Bureau.

Joseph, Gilbert M. 2010. "Latin America's Long Cold War: A Century of Revolutionary Process and U.S. Power." In *A Century of Revolution: Insurgent and Counterinsurgent Violence during Latin America's Long Cold War*, ed. Greg Grandin and Gilbert M. Joseph, 397–414. Durham, NC: Duke University Press.

Joseph, Gilbert M., and Daniel Nugent, eds. 1994. *Everyday Forms of State Formation: Revolution and the Negotiation of Rule in Modern Mexico*. Durham, NC: Duke University Press.

Joseph, Gilbert M., and Daniela Spenser, eds. 2008. *In from the Cold: Latin America's New Encounter with the Cold War*. Durham, NC: Duke University Press.

Kalb, Don. 2000. "Class (in Place) without Capitalism (in Space)?" *International Labor and Working-Class History* 57: 31–39.

Kalb, Don, and Herman Tak. 2005. "Introduction: Critical Junctures: Recapturing Anthropology and History." In *Critical Junctions: Anthropology and History beyond the Cultural Turn*, ed. Don Kalb and Herman Tak, 1–27. New York: Berghahn.

Kasmir, Sharryn. 2014. "The Saturn Automobile Plant and the Disorganization of Labor." In *Blood and Fire: Toward a Global Anthropology of Labor*, ed. August Carbonella and Sharryn Kasmir, 203–49. New York: Berghahn.

Klein, Naomi. 2007. *The Shock Doctrine: The Rise of Disaster Capitalism*. New York: Metropolitan Books.

Kramer, Paul. 2011. "Power and Connection: Imperial Histories of the United States in the World." *American Historical Review* 116 (5): 1348–91.

Krupa, Christopher. 2010. "State by Proxy: Privatized Government in the Andes." *Comparative Studies in Society and History* 52 (2): 319–50.

Krupa, Christopher, and David Nugent. 2015. "Introduction: Off-Centered States: Rethinking State Theory through an Andean Lens." In *State Theory and Andean Politics: New Approaches to the Study of Rule*, ed. Christopher Krupa and David Nugent, 1–34. Philadelphia: University of Pennsylvania Press.

Lancaster, Roger. 1992. *Life Is Hard: Machismo, Danger, and the Intimacy of Power in Nicaragua*. Berkeley: University of California Press.

Larson, Brooke. 2004. *Trials of Nation Making: Liberalism, Race, and Ethnicity in the Andes, 1810–1910*. New York: Cambridge University Press.

Lazar, Sian. 2008. *El Alto: Rebel City*. Durham, NC: Duke University Press.

Leal, Francisco, and Andrés Dávila. 1990. *Clientelismo: El sistema política y su expresión regional*. Bogotá: IEPRI/TM.

LeGrand, Catherine C. 1986. *Frontier Expansion and Peasant Protest in Colombia, 1830–1936*. Albuquerque: University of New Mexico Press.

———. 1998. "Living in Macondo: Economy and Culture in a United Fruit Company Banana Enclave in Colombia." In *Close Encounters of Empire: Writing the Cultural History of U.S.–Latin American Relations*, ed. Gilbert M. Joseph, Catherine C. Legrand, and Ricardo D. Salvatore, 333–68. Durham, NC: Duke University Press.

Levenson, Deborah. 2013. *Adios Niño: The Gangs of Guatemala City and the Politics of Death*. Durham, NC: Duke University Press.

Levenson-Estrada, Deborah. 1994. *Trade Unionists against Terror: Guatemala City, 1954–1985*. Chapel Hill: University of North Carolina Press.

Li, Tania. 2009. "Reflections on the Ethnography of Fear." *Anthropologica* 51 (2): 363–66.

Loingsigh, Geróid. 2002. "La estrategia integral del paramilitarismo en el Magdalena Medio de Colombia." Manuscript.

López, Claudia, ed. 2010. *. . . y refundaron la patria: De cómo mafiosos y políticos reconfiguraron el Estado Colombiano*. Bogotá: Debate.

Madero, Regulo. 2001. "Human Rights Violations: Manifestations of a Perverse Model of Governance." Accessed May 2007. http://www.colhrnet.igc.org/newsletter/y2001/spring01art/regulo101htm.

Mahoney, Liam, and Luis Enrique Eguren, eds. 1997. *Unarmed Bodyguards: International Accompaniment for the Protection of Human Rights*. West Hartford, CT: Kumarian.

Mallon, Florencia. 2005. *Courage Tastes of Blood: The Mapuche Community of Nicolás Ailío and the Chilean State, 1906–2001*. Durham, NC: Duke University Press.

Marín, Evangelina. 2006. "Eramos unos soñadores." In *Colombia: Terrorismo de estado: Testimonio de la guerra sucia contra los movimientos populares*, ed. Vladimir Carrillo and Tom Kucharz, 349–65. Barcelona: Icaria.

Markarian, Vania. 2005. *Left in Transition: Uruguayan Exiles and Latin American Human Rights Networks, 1967–1984*. New York: Routledge.

Mason, Paul. 2007. *Live Working or Die Fighting: How the Working Class Went Global*. Chicago: Haymarket Books.

Medina, Carlos. 1990. *Autodefensas, paramilitares, y narcotráfico en Colombia: Origen, desarrollo y consolidación*. Bogotá: Editorial Documentos Periódicos.

———. 2001. *Elementos para una história política del Ejército Nacional de Liberación*. Bogotá: Rodríguez Quito Editores.

Medina, Gilberto. 2006. *Una historia de las milicias en Medellín*. Medellín: Instituto Popular de Capacitación.

Merry, Sally Engle. 2006. *Human Rights and Gender Violence: Translating International Law into Local Justice*. Chicago: University of Chicago Press.

Mitchell, Timothy. 1991. "The Limits of the State: Beyond Statist Approaches and Their Critics." *American Political Science Review* 85 (1): 77–96.

Molano Brazo, Alfredo. 2009. *El medio del magdalena medio*. Bogotá: CINEP.

Moyn, Samuel. 2010. *The Last Utopia: Human Rights in History*. Cambridge, MA: Harvard University Press.

Murillo, Amparo. 1994. *Un mundo que se mueve como el río: Historia regional del Magdalena Medio*. Bogotá: Instituto Colombiano de Antropología.

Narotzky, Susana, and Niko Besnier. 2014. "Crisis, Value, Hope: Rethinking the Economy." *Current Anthropology* 35 (supplement 9): S4–S16.

Narotzky, Susana, and Gavin Smith. 2006. *Immediate Struggles: People, Power, and Place in Rural Spain*. Berkeley: University of California Press.

Nordstrom, Carolyn. 2000. "Shadows and Sovereigns." *Theory, Culture and Society* 17 (4): 35–54.

Nugent, David. 1997. *Modernity at the Edge of Empire: State, Individual, and Nation in the Northern Peruvian Andes, 1885–1935.* Stanford, CA: Stanford University Press.

Oglesby, Elizabeth. 2007. "Educating Citizens in Postwar Guatemala: Historical Memory, Genocide, and the Culture of Peace." *Radical History Review* 97 (winter): 77–98.

Palacios, Marco. 2006. *Between Legitimacy and Violence: A History of Colombia, 1875–2002.* Durham, NC: Duke University Press.

Payne, Leigh. 2009. "Performances of Power: Paramilitary Confessions in Colombia." Paper presented at the IILJ International Legal Theory Colloquium "Virtues, Vices, Human Behavior, and Democracy in International Law." New York University Law School, February 12.

Pizarro, Eduardo. 1989. "Los orígenes del movimiento armado comunista en Colombia (1949–1966)." *Análisis Político* 7 (May–August): 7–31.

———. 1991. *Las FARC: De la autodefensa a la combinación de todas las formas de lucha.* Bogotá: Tercer Mundo Editores.

Postero, Nancy. 2006. *Now We Are Citizens: Indigenous Politics in Postmulticultural Bolivia.* Stanford, CA: Stanford University Press.

Priest, Dana. 2013. "Covert Action in Colombia: U.S. Intelligence Bomb Kits Help Latin American Nation Cripple Rebel Forces." *Washington Post*, December 21. www.washingtonpost.com.

Rabe, Steven G. 2012. *The Killing Zone: The United States Wages Cold War in Latin America.* New York: Oxford University Press.

Ramírez, Maria Clemencia. 2011. *Between the Guerrillas and the State: The Cocalero Movement, Citizenship, and Identity in the Colombian Amazon.* Durham, NC: Duke University Press.

Restrepo, Laura. 1999. *La novia oscura.* Bogotá: Aleaguera.

Richani, Nazih. 2002. *Systems of Violence: The Political Economy of War and Peace in Colombia.* Albany: SUNY Press.

———. 2005. "Multinational Corporations, Rentier Capitalism, and the War System in Colombia." *Latin American Politics and Society* 47 (3): 113–44.

———. 2007. "Caudillos and the Crisis of the Colombian State: Fragmented Sovereignty, the War System and the Privatisation of Counterinsurgency in Colombia." *Third World Quarterly* 28 (2): 403–17.

Roldán, Mary. 2002. *Blood and Fire: La Violencia in Antioquia Colombia, 1946–1963.* Durham, NC: Duke University Press.

Romero, Mauricio. 2003. *Paramilitares y autodefensas, 1982–2003.* Bogotá: IEPRI.

Romero, Mauricio, Ángela Olaya, and Hernán Pedraza. 2011. "Privatización, paramilitares y política: El robo de los recursos de salud en la Costa Caribe." In *La economia de los paramilitares: Redes de corrupción, negocios y política*, ed. Mauricio Romero, 15–74. Bogotá: Debate.

Romero, Mauricio, and Diana Fernanda Torres. 2011. "Drummond, Chiquita y paramilitares: Adaptación y negociación de ventajas en medio del conflicto." In *La economia de los paramilitares: Redes de corrupción, negocios y política*, ed. Mauricio Romero, 149–90. Bogota: Debate.

Roseberry, William. 1994. "Hegemony and the Language of Contention." In *Everyday Forms of State Formation: Revolution and the Negotiation of Rule in Modern Mexico*, ed. Gilbert M. Joseph and Daniel Nugent, 355–66. Durham, NC: Duke University Press.

Safford, Frank, and Marco Palacios, eds. 2002. *Colombia: Fragmented Land, Divided Society*. New York: Oxford University Press.

Sánchez, Gonzalo. 1976. *1929 Los "bolcheviques" del Líbano*. Bogotá: Ediciones El Mohan.

———. 1983. *Los días de la revolución: Gaitanismo y 9 de abril en provincia*. Bogotá: Centro Cultural Jorge Eliécer Gaitán.

Santiago, Myrna I. 2006. *The Ecology of Oil: Environment, Labor, and the Mexican Revolution*. New York: Cambridge University Press.

Saull, Richard. 2006. "Reactionary Blowback." In *The War on Terrorism and the American "Empire" after the Cold War*, ed. Alejandro Colás and Richard Saull, 65–90. New York: Routledge.

Scheper-Hughes, Nancy, and Philippe Bourgois. 2004. "Introduction: Making Sense of Violence." In *Violence in War and Peace: An Anthology*, ed. Nancy Scheper-Hughes and Philippe Bourgois, 1–32. Malden, MA: Blackwell.

Schneider, Cathy. 1995. *Shantytown Protest in Pinochet's Chile*. Philadelphia: Temple University Press.

Schneider, Jane, and Peter Schneider. 2003. *Reversible Destiny: Mafia, Antimafia, and the Struggle for Palermo*. Berkeley: University of California Press.

Schulman, Sam. 1967. "Family Life in a Colombian 'Turgurio.'" *Sociological Analysis* 28 (4): 184–95.

Semana. 2006. "Como se hizo el fraude." April 8. http://www.semana.com.

Sider, Gerald. 1986. *Culture and Class in Anthropology and History: A Newfoundland Illustration*. New York: Cambridge University Press.

———. 2008. "Anthropology, History and the Problem of Everyday Life: Issues from the Field and for Discussion." In *Alltag, Erfahrung, Eiginnsin: Historisch-anthropologische Erkundungen*, ed. Belinda Davis, Thomas Lindenberger, and Michael Wildt, 120–32. Frankfurt: Campus.

SINALTRAINAL (Sindicato Nacional de Trabajadores de la Industria de Alimentos). n.d. "Breve histórico de SINALTRAINAL-Colombia." Files of SINALTRAINAL. Bogotá, Colombia.

Smith, Gavin. 2014. *Intellectuals and (Counter-) Politics: Essays in Historical Realism*. New York: Berghahn.

Solidarity Center. 2006. *Justice for All: The Struggle for Workers' Rights in Colombia*. Washington, DC: Solidarity Center.

Speed, Shannon. 2008. *Rights in Rebellion: Indigenous Struggle and Human Rights in Chiapas*. Stanford, CA: Stanford University Press.

Standing, Guy. 2011. *The Precariat: The New Dangerous Class*. London: Bloomsbury.

Stern, Steve. 2004. *Remembering Pinochet's Chile: On the Eve of London 1998*. Durham, NC: Duke University Press.

Stites, Jessica, ed. 2013. *Human Rights and Transnational Solidarity in Cold War Latin America*. Madison: University of Wisconsin Press.

Striffler, Steve. 2002. *In the Shadows of State and Capital: The United Fruit Company, Popular Struggle, and Agrarian Restructuring in Ecuador, 1900–1995*. Durham, NC: Duke University Press.

———. 2004. "Class Formation in Latin America: One Family's Enduring Journey between Country and City." *International Labor and Working-Class History* 65: 11–25.

———. 2015. "Latin American Solidarity: Human Rights and the Politics of the U.S. Left." In *Palgrave Encyclopedia of Imperialism and Anti-imperialism*, ed. Immanuel Ness and Zak Cope. New York: Palgrave Macmillan.

Striffler, Steve, and Mark Moberg, eds. 2003. *Banana Wars: Power, Production, and History in the Americas*. Durham, NC: Duke University Press.

Tate, Winifred. 2007. *Counting the Dead: The Culture and Politics of Human Rights Activism in Colombia*. Berkeley: University of California Press.

———. 2011. "Paramilitary Forces in Colombia." *Latin American Research Review* 46 (3): 191–200.

———. 2015. "The Aspirational State: State Effects in Putumayo." In *State Theory and Andean Politics: New Approaches to the Study of Rule*, ed. Christopher Krupa and David Nugent, 234–56. Philadelphia: University of Pennsylvania Press.

Taussig, Michael. 2003. *Law in a Lawless Land*. New York: New Press.

Tax, Sol. 1963. *Penny Capitalism: A Guatemalan Indian Economy*. Chicago: University of Chicago Press.

Thompson, Edward P. 1963. *The Making of the English Working Class*. New York: Vintage.

———. 1978. "Eighteenth-Century English Society: Class Struggle without Class?" *Social History* 3 (2): 133–65.

Tinker Salas, Miguel. 2009. *Oil, Culture, and Society in Venezuela*. Durham, NC: Duke University Press.

Valbuena, Martiniamo. 1947. *Memorias de Barrancabermeja*. Bucaramanga: Editorial El Frente.

Valencia, León, and Juan Carlos Celis. 2012. *Sindicalismo asesinado: Reveladora investigación contra los sindicalistas colombianos*. Bogotá: Random House Mondadori.

van Isschot, Luis. 2015. *The Social Origins of Human Rights: Protesting Political*

Violence in Colombia's Oil Capital, 1919–2010. Madison: University of Wisconsin Press.

Vargas, Alejo. 1992. *Colonización y conflicto armado: Magdalena medio santandereano*. Bogotá: CINEP.

Vargas, Mauricio. 1993. *Memorias secretas del revolcón*. Bogotá: TM Editors.

Vega, Renán. 2002. *Gente muy rebelde*. Vol. 1. *Enclaves, transportes y protestas obreras*. Bogotá: Ediciones Pensamiento Crítico.

Vega, Renán, Luz Ángela Núñez, and Alexander Pereira. 2009. *Petróleo y protesta obrera: La USO y los trabajadores petroleros en Colombia*. Vol. 1. *En tiempos de la Tropical*. Bogotá: Corporación Aury Sará Marrugo.

Verdad Abierta. 2008. "Justicia y Paz." Accessed May 2009. http://www.verda dabierta.com/web3/nunca-mas/80-versiones-seccion/647-la-lista-negra -de-las-auc-en-barrancabermeja.

———. 2009. "Julián Bolívar reconoce que AUC cometieron 20 masacres en Santander." Accessed May 2009. http://www.verdadabierta.com/justicia -y-paz/versiones/514-bloque-central-bolivar/959-julian-bolivar-reconoce -que-auc-cometieron-20-masacres-en-santander.

Whitehead, Judith. 2012. "Global Connections and Disconnections: Space and Labor in Mumbai's Slums." In *Confronting Capital: Critique and Engagement in Anthropology*, ed. Pauline Barber, Belinda Leach, and Winnie Lem, 163–86. New York: Routledge.

Williams, Raymond. 1973. *The Country and the City*. New York: Oxford University Press.

———. 1989. *Resources of Hope*. London: Verso.

Winn, Peter, ed. 2004. *Victims of the Chilean Miracle: Workers and Neoliberalism in the Pinochet Era, 1973–2002*. Durham, NC: Duke University Press.

Zamosc, Leon. 1986. *The Agrarian Question and the Peasant Movement in Colombia, 1967–1981*. New York: Cambridge University Press.

Note: Page numbers in *italics* indicate figures.

Defensoría del Pueblo, 183, 188, 192
Delgado, Álvaro, 93
demobilization (of paramilitaries), 181–82, 217–18, 225, 233–36
Denning, Michael, 10
denuncias, 185, 192–93, 196–97, 207, 224, 230, 234–35
de Soto, Hernando, 9
development discourses. *See* modernization theory
Díaz, Eduardo, 79, 81
dirty war, 6, 12–13, 18, 28, 86–99, 104–5, 121, 183, 185, 196, 217–18, 221–24, 242
disappearances, 6, 21–23, 86, 95–99, 176–77, 227
disorganization: of family relationships, 112–13, 228–29, 243–44; of labor, 113, 121, 124–26, 233–36, 241–43; of social life, 86–90, 93–99, 115, 117, 130, 134–36, 141–42, 145–51, 186, 217–18, 228–36, 239–40. *See also* betrayal; fear; neoliberalism; unions; violence
displacement, 6–13, 21–27, 38–42, 66–74, 86–93, 101, 113–14, 183, 219–28, 237–38, 250n10, 253n1. *See also* immigrants; violence
drip by drip, 166–67
drug trafficking: dirty war and, 12, 18–21, 87–93; guerrillas and, 26, 87–93, 102, 254n13; paramilitary violence and, 100, 107–8, 111–12, 156–58, 160–62, 165, 169, 179, 228, 241, 244, 256n5; right-wing coalitions and, 21, 88–90, 98–99, 104, 244; U.S. responses to, 89–90, 100–101, 155–56, 243, 261n2
Drummond Corporation, 134
Dudley, Steven, 127
Duque Gaviria, Iván Roberto, 159, 162–63, 180, 257n9

earning a living, 10, 30, 38–39, 113, 167, 226, 239
ECOPETROL (Empresa Colombiana de Petróleos): Coca-Cola's employment and, 136; guerrilla attacks against, 92; human rights commissions and, 191; outsourcing and, 4; paramilitaries and, 159–60, 174; peasant immigrants and, 69–70, 72; photos of, 70; privatization of, 102, 127; state control of, 16, 59–60; strikes against, 2, 61–65, 74, 242; temporary employment policies of, 70–71, 167, 231; USO's agreements with, 81–82, 85
Ecuador, 15, 60
education, 64, 66–67, 83, 89, 124, 127
Ejército Anti-Restitución del Magdalena Medio, 221
El Centro, 42–43, 45
ELN (Ejército Nacional de Liberación): delegitimation of, 93, 109–11; emergence of, 76–77, 252n15; goals of, 17, 78; human rights movements and, 192, 200; paramilitary responses to, 102–3, 223; state responses to, 86, 90, 99–100, 132–33, 225, 234, 257n6; territorial control by, 20; urban spaces and, 91–92, 163; USO's relationship to, 82, 103–4. *See also* counterinsurgent war; guerrillas; paramilitaries
El Parnaso, 69
El Salvador, 127, 155–56, 190
El Sindicato, 161
El Tiempo, 133
emblematic memory, 219
EPL (Ejército Popular de Liberación), 90, 108, 147, 163, 234, 253n6
Escobar, Pablo, 256n5
Espacio de Trabajadores y Trabaja-

Jaraba, Enrique, 203–10, 220, 246
Jiménez, Carlos Mario, 158–59, 180
Jiménez, Osvaldo, 230
job agencies, 162, 164–66
Justice and Peace Law, 179, 223, 233

Kalb, Don, 159
Kasmir, Sharryn, 8, 10
Kennedy, John F., 17, 66
kidnapping, 78, 87–88, 92–93, 95–99,
　110, 114, 139, 166, 183–84, 197–98,
　253n1. *See also* disappearances;
　fear; violence
Korean War, 252n14
Kramer, Paul, 15
Krupa, Christopher, 20, 256n3

labor. *See* unions
La Esperanza, 79, 105–15
Lancaster, Roger, 201
landlord violence, 16, 20–21, 65–67,
　72–73, 84, 127, 237
land tenure, 38–39
Land Tenure Center (UW), 72, 74
Lara Parada, Ricardo, 77, 131
La Violencia, 12, 56–60, 62, 65–66,
　70–71, 76–77, 89, 238
Law 45, 101
Law 49, 101
Law 50, 101
Law 83, 54
Law 100, 101, 164
Levenson-Estrada, Deborah, 23
LGBT rights and, 200–210
Li, Tania, 254n19
Liberal Party, 34–39, 48, 52, 62, 74,
　76–77, 83, 88, 159–61, 250n1
Liberal Republic, 52–56
liberation theology, 78–80, 186, 195
Life magazine, 45
Lleras Camargo, Alfonso, 55
López Michelsen, Alfonso, 74, 83

López Pumarejo, Alfonso, 52–53, 55
Los Rastrojos, 180, 221
Los Urabeños, 221
Lozada, Alirio, 240
Lozada, Pedro, 41, 56, 66–67, 87, 114,
　237–39, 239, 246
Lucerna, Pablo, 228–29

M-19, 90
Macaco, 158, 227
Mahécha, Raúl Eduardo, 49–51, 58,
　224
making a living, 10, 30, 38–39, 113,
　167, 226, 239
Mancuso, Salvatore, 161
maps, *32–33*
Marín, Evangelina, 91
Marx, Karl, 1, 9, 80
masculinity, 139
massacres, 21–23, 86, 93, 96, 104–5,
　157, 199. *See also* dirty war; vio-
　lence
Medellín, 45, 156–57, 201, 254n13,
　256n1, 256n5
memory, 28, 217–28, 237–39
memory knots, 224
Menacho, Mariana, 200
Mendoza, William, 3, 79–80, 106–7,
　118–19, 137–50, *146*, 190, 192, 216–
　18, 234–36
Meta, 243
Mexico, 15, 30, 41, 50, 59
microentrepreneurs, 9, 138–40, 231–
　32, 242. *See also* independent con-
　tractors; temporary employment
migrants. *See* immigrants
Ministry of Social Protection, 137
Miraflores neighborhood, 79, 103,
　120
modernization theory, 16–17, 63,
　71–72, 74, 83, 250n1
Molina, Luz, 221

money laundering, 87, 102–3, 108, 155, 166

Morantes, Camilo, 158

MORENA (Movimiento de Reconstrucción Nacional), 89

Morón, Julio, 54

Mosquera, Andrés, 119

mototaxistas, 231–32

Movimiento Alianza Social Inígena, 227

Moyn, Samuel, 186

MRL (Movimiento Revolucionario Liberal), 74, 77

Muerte a Secuestradores, 88, 157

Muñoz, Ruben, 138

Narotzky, Susana, 118

National Front, 16–17, 61–76, 82, 163

nationalism, 6, 15–16, 26, 35–36, 46–47, 49–50, 53–54, 58, 83, 92, 141–42

nationalization, 59–60

National Security Doctrine (U.S.), 76

National Security Statute (Colombia), 86

neighborhood organizations, 17–18, 68–70, 79–80, 84, 91, 125–26, 170–75, 228–33, 258n21

neoliberalism: accumulation by dispossession and, 124–36, 217–18, 229–33, 237–38, 240–41, 244; definitions of, 8, 24, 241–42; foreign corporations and, 6, 227; geographies of power and, 13–21, 151–55, 255n7; guerrilla activities and, 132–33; human rights discourse and, 24–25, 27–28, 187, 189–93; individualism and, 113–15, 230–31, 241, 243–44, 259n10; legitimizing of, 182; paramilitaries and, 2–3, 10–11, 150–51, 160–68, 227–28; privatization and, 152–55; right-

wing politics and, 12; social order and, 5, 136–45, 191, 221–22; U.S. foreign policy and, 23; violence's lubrication of, 93–94, 97–103, 227–28; working class's destruction by, 4

neoparamilitary groups, 221, 225, 232, 241

Nestlé, 130

New Deal, 53

NGOs (nongovernmental organizations), 25, 105–6, 170, 176, 187, 191, 194–203, 206–15, 246

Nicaragua, 47, 86, 155–56, 190, 201–2

Nieto, Alejandro, 143–44

Ninth of April neighborhood, 174

Nixon, Richard, 261n2

Noguera, Jorge, 180

NSA (National Security Agency), 260n9

Nugent, David, 20, 256n3

Nuñez, Rafael, 43, 53

Obama, Barack, 19

Occidental Petroleum, 134

Occupy Wall Street, 9

OFP (Organización Feminina Popular), 80–81, 84, 183–85, 194–203, 195, 207, 212–14, 219–20, 234

oil industry: Coca-Cola and, 136–37; emergence of, 11–12, 34–39; environmental problems and, 81–82; hazardous working conditions of, 38–39; labor organization and, 81–87; La Violencia and, 57–60; nationalization of, 26, 31, 62–65; postwar peace and, 216–17; regional power and, 34–39; strikes and, 2–3, 49, 61–65; temporary employment and, 83

One Hundred Years of Solitude (García Márquez), 30

outsourcing, 8

unemployment, 54, 83, 102, 111, 144–45, 163–64, 172, 216, 229, 231. *See also* independent contractors; temporary employment

Unidad Dinamizadora, 79

unions: assaults on, 4–5, 8, 21–28, 30, 86–87; banana plantations and, 24, 30, 46, 49, 53, 157–58; betrayals and, 145–51; class formation and, 8–13, 29–34; Coca-Cola Company and, 123–26, 137–45; geographies of power and, 17–18, 34; guerrillas' relationship to, 82, 92–93, 103–4, 126–27, 132–34, 147–49, 177; human rights frameworks and, 187–203, 205, 208–10; insurgent individualism and, 86–87; job agencies and, 164–65; La Violencia and, 56–60; Liberal Republic period and, 52–56; memory and, 219–28; oil industry and, 11–12, 39–48; paramilitaries and, 115–22, 126–28, 157–60, 180–82; peasant solidarity and, 69–71, 77–78; state-controlled entities and, 16, 26, 34, 48–49, 62–65, 73; temporary employment policies and, 136–45; TROCO's relationship to, 14–16, 242. *See also* neighborhood organizations; neoliberalism; strikes; violence; *specific unions*

UNIR (Unión Izquierda Revolucionaria), 53

United Fruit Company, 30, 47, 53, 59

United States: cold war policies and, 23, 66, 76, 81, 89–90, 100, 155–56, 243; human rights discourses and, 175–76, 189–93, 211, 235–36, 246–47; imperialism and, 6, 14–15, 17, 19–20, 35–36, 38, 45–47, 53–54, 59–60, 76, 89–90, 141, 190, 252n14; war on drugs of, 19, 98–99, 155–56, 243, 254n13, 261n2

Universidad Industrial de Santander, 77

unwaged workers, 6, 10–11, 64–65, 73, 113, 136–37

UP (Unión Patriótica), 89, 99, 131, 192, 237, 253n30

Urabá region, 24, 59, 101, 123, 157, 258n21

urbanization, 38–39, 42, 61–72, 90–91, 163, 239–40, 242

Uríbe, Álvaro, 179–80

Uríbe, Tomás, 49

USO (Unión Sindical Obrero): formation of, 26, 54; guerrillas' relation to, 77–78, 82, 92–93, 103–4, 118–19; human rights discourses and, 190–91, 193–203, 208–10, 220; memory and, 220–21, 225; peasant immigrants and, 72, 81; SINALTRAINAL and, 125–26; solidarity and, 114; strikes of, 2–3, 74–75, 82, 96, 103–4; student organizations and, 77; violence against, 3–4

Valencia, León, 156

Vanguardia Obrera, 49

Vargas, Alego, 252n15

Vásquez, Fabio, 77

Vega, Renán, 50, 82

Vélez, Jorge, 51

venereal disease, 44–45

Venezuela, 15, 30, 40–41, 50, 132, 246

Vesalles neighborhood, 79

Villamizar, Carmen, 120

violence: corporate land grants and, 36–37, 47; definitions of, 22; guerrilla tactics and, 91–93, 132–33; homosexuality and, 203–6; impunity and, 103–15, 187; labor uprisings and, 56–60, 74–75, 84–85; memory and, 217–28; neoliberalism's entrenchment and, 93–94, 97–103, 227–28; paramilitaries and, 4, 18, 95–99, 126–28, 155–68, 175–78, 197–99, 238, 244–45, 253n1; political process and, 160–62; solidarity and, 26–27, 58–59; state and class formation and, 7–8, 20–28, 34–35, 50–51, 70–81, 84, 181–82. *See also* assassinations; displacement; guerrillas; kidnapping; massacres; paramilitaries; state, the

waiting, 143–44
war on drugs (U.S.), 19, 89–90, 98–99, 155–56, 243, 261n2

Washington consensus, 100
water, 81–84
welfare, 9
Whitehead, Judith, 11
Williams, Raymond, 131, 240
Witness for Peace, 187, 210
World Bank, 100, 188
WTO (World Trade Organization), 1

Yariguíes, 38
Yondó, 42
yumecas, 39–40, 43

Zurmay, Efraín, 137, 144